DATE DUE

DEMCO, INC. 38-2931

Human Factor Engineering and the Political Economy of African Development

Human Factor Engineering and the Political Economy of African Development

Edited by

Senyo B-S. K. Adjibolosoo

PRAEGER

Westport, Connecticut
London

Library of Congress Cataloging-in-Publication Data

Human factor engineering and the political economy of African
  development / edited by Senyo B-S. K. Adjibolosoo.
      p.   cm.
    Includes bibliographical references and index.
    ISBN 0–275–95491–9 (alk. paper)
    1. Human capital—Africa.   2. Manpower policy—Africa.   3. Africa—
  Economic policy.   I. Adjibolosoo, Senyo B-S. K.
  HD4904.7.H859   1996
  331.11'096—dc20   95–51429

British Library Cataloguing in Publication Data is available.

Library of Congress Catalog Card Number: 95–51429
ISBN: 0–275–95491–9

First published in 1996

Praeger Publishers, 88 Post Road West, Westport, CT 06881
An imprint of Greenwood Publishing Group, Inc.

Printed in the United States of America

The paper used in this book complies with the
Permanent Paper Standard issued by the National
Information Standards Organization (Z39.48–1984).

10   9   8   7   6   5   4   3   2   1

when the sun smiles
snow-clad trees
lose the burden of tears
and dance arm-in-arm
on the lively lullaby of the wind
with a glimmer of hopes
nested in their mind

Senyo Adjibolosoo

This book is dedicated to my mother,
Atsupui Blemewu Adjibolosoo,
and to my mother-in-law, Annie Tete,
for their invaluable contributions
to the world in general, and to
Africa in particular.

Contents

Figures and Tables   ix

Preface   xi

Acknowledgments   xiii

1. Rethinking Africa's Educational Strategy   1
   Senyo B-S. K. Adjibolosoo

2. Human Factor Engineering: The Primary Mission of Education
   and Training   19
   Senyo B-S. K. Adjibolosoo

3. Educating Sub-Saharan African Students to Participate in
   National Development Programs: The Role of Indigenous
   African Writers   37
   John A. Anonby

4. Preparing for Effective Constitutional Democracy in Africa:
   Political Education and Training   53
   Mike Oquaye

5. Entrepreneurship Development for Industrial Progress in Africa   71
   Francis Adu-Febiri

6. Education and Training for Effective Leadership Development
   and Productivity and Quality Management in Africa   83
   Senyo B-S. K. Adjibolosoo

 7. Human Factor Development and Labor Productivity Growth in
    the Agricultural Sector in Africa   99
    Harold J. Harder

 8. Human Factor Development and Technological Innovation in
    Africa   111
    Benjamin Ofori-Amoah

 9. Accounting Education for Economic Development Management
    in Anglophone Sub-Saharan Africa   125
    Moses Acquaah

10. The Human Factor in Marketing and Development in the LDCs   141
    Samuel K. Bonsu

11. Staying Educated and Maintaining Professional Competency   161
    Senyo B-S. K. Adjibolosoo

Selected Bibliography   179

Index   183

About the Editor and Contributors   185

Figures and Tables

FIGURES

7.1	Africa: Food Production and Population Trends	100
7.2	World: Food Production and Population Trends	101
10.1	Determinist Model for Marketing in Development	143
10.2	Activist Model for Marketing in Development	145
10.3	Mutual Relationship between Marketing and Development	147
10.4	Factor Mix for Development Ethos	149
10.5	The Human Factor, Marketing and Development	155

TABLES

2.1	The Composition of the Human Factor	22
3.1	African Writers and Their Concerns	39
6.1	Ranking of Human Qualities as They Affect Worker Effectiveness, Efficiency and Productivity	85
6.2	A Model for Grooming and Managing the HF	88
6.3	The HF: Embodiments, Grooming and Management Objectives	91

Preface

For many decades, most African countries have tried rather hard to develop. However, their continuing efforts have not yielded any significant results. A careful and detailed study and evaluation of the present African condition brings into one's mind many pertinent questions: What has gone wrong with Africa's development program? What has development and technical assistance failed to perceive in the past and at present? What happened to the millions of dollars of foreign aid in its many forms? If mainstream development theory is correct and its practice appropriate, why has it failed to help achieve significant positive results in Africa? Why have all the domestic and external resources that have been channeled into human resources development not produced the type of labor force required for Africa's development program? Are educational policies and programs in Africa being faced with any difficulties that they cannot as yet overcome? Can the actual problems be identified and dealt with appropriately? What has the international community glossed over in its attempt to help African countries develop? This list of questions can be extended *ad infinitum*. The authors in this book believe that in the past, most programs designed to help African countries develop failed to correctly identify Africa's pertinent problem—human factor (HF) decay and/or underdevelopment.

In view of this observation, it can be argued that until the HF is developed in African countries, no plans, policies, programs, projects, institutions, institutional structures or technology will successfully achieve their intended goals of development. If African countries want to develop, they must first invest intensively in HF development by creating relevant and effective educational and training programs. This is because progress in every society requires improvements in the simultaneous preformance and functioning of its people and institutions in relation to the social, economic, political, cultural and intellectual aspects of human life and activities. To be successful, therefore, economic development plans, policies, programs and projects require the caliber of people who possess the HF necessary for their effective and efficient execution.

Yet for many years, African countries pursued education and training policies and programs that have failed to prepare Africans for the task of development. As such, Africans have not been fully equipped to solve pertinent problems of underdevelopment that are prevalent on the continent today. This dismal result is indicative of the fact that the African educational and training philosophy and its accompanying strategies and programs need to be altered to produce the required labor force that can lead to social, economic and political emancipation. It is the authors' view that an integrated multidisciplinary approach to an all-purpose (liberal arts) education and training is the key to preparing Africans for the task of development. It is, therefore, the primary objective of this book to outline how the HF can be developed in African countries through multidisciplinary studies.

This book takes a multidisciplinary approach to HF engineering. It draws on the expertise of scholars who have articulately shown that the best way to develop the HF in the African labor force is through integrated multidisciplinary education and training policies and programs. The types of HF engineering programs presented recognize and acknowledge the shortcomings of the existing traditional educational and training approaches to human resources development and problem-solving in Africa. The chapters also explain how the HF can be developed successfully in African countries. Although the contents of the book do not cover all subject areas, the issues presented and discussed can be easily extended to other disciplines.

The book proposes alternative procedures for training and educating the African peoples to acquire the necessary HF. Together, the chapters map out effective ways to successfully develop and implement HF policies and programs for all countries, especially those in Africa.

This book is aimed at the development community. It is relevant to professors and students of economic development theory, development planning and administration and all practitioners of development theory and policy. Nongovernmental organizations, government policy planners and program directors, international organizations and many other international agencies will also find it a useful planning tool. Its multidisciplinary approach will make it helpful to scholars of every discipline. Above all, it will be a tremendous help to those who plan educational, training and other related human resources development programs for developing countries.

Acknowledgments

As is always the case, my wife, Sabina, is the individual who deserves the lion's share of my gratitude. As such, I sincerely acknowledge her immeasurable contributions to the preparation of this book. Similarly, I am also extremely thankful to my daughters, Selassie and Selorm, for their support and willingness to assist me in their own ways to write the book.

I am heavily indebted to all my colleagues who have contributed the various chapters that make up this book. This book would not have become a reality without their willingness to prepare the required materials. May I take this opportunity to offer a special thank you to my colleagues, Dr. Benjamin Ofori-Amoah and Mr. Salomon Agbenya, for their continuing support and encouragement.

I also wish to offer my sincere thanks to my acquisitions editor, Dr. James R. Ice, and the Greenwood Publishing Group for their unfailing commitment in advising, guiding and, above all, providing the necessary assistance for the preparation of the book. This acknowledgment would be incomplete if I failed to give my appreciation to the International Institute for Human Factor Development (IIHFD) and the Board of Directors for their help and encouragement. I am very grateful for their invaluable contributions to the preparation of this book. Finally, I am grateful to my faculty secretary, Mrs. Brenda Sawatzky, for her invaluable secretarial assistance.

Human Factor Engineering and the Political Economy of African Development

1

Rethinking Africa's Educational Strategy

Senyo B-S. K. Adjibolosoo

INTRODUCTION

The role and relevance of education and training in human progress cannot be denied. It is with this view that every society strives to educate its young people to prepare them not only for the future, but also to equip them with what is required for continuing the civilization. Any society that neglects to perform this vital function will fail in developing the human factor (HF)[1] in its future labor force (Adjibolosoo, 1993, 1994). Aristotle once said that "all who have meditated on the art of governing mankind have been convinced that the fate of empires depends on the education of youth" (quoted in Peter, 1977, p. 161). Truly, Aristotle could not have been any more accurate. While Erich Fromm believed that "education is helping the child to realize his potentialities," Tryon Edwards noted that "the great end of education is to discipline rather than to furnish the mind; to train it to the use of its own powers, rather than fill it with the accumulation of others" (quoted in Peter, 1977, p. 160).

Education has the critical role of instructing the human intellect in nature's laws and principles (see Thomas Henry Huxley, quoted in Peter, 1977, p. 160). As such, the creation of institutions for the attainment of social, economic, political and intellectual goals of a society will not happen without proper HF development in the youth (Adjibolosoo, 1993, 1994). It is, therefore, evident that lack of appropriate education and training may lead to total HF decay and/ or underdevelopment. As the quotes of experts reveal, education is a *sine qua non* to human development and progress. This kind of education being talked about is not just for the acquisition of the "three Rs." Baldwin and Brucher (1959, p. 118) pointed out that:

There is a great difference between education and training. Education is a long-term process of developing individuals. . . . and is concerned with giving them general values, general skills and general knowledge. Training, on the other hand, begins not with people but with jobs; it is primarily interested in qualifying people with the skill necessary to perform a job effectively. This kind of instruction normally takes much less time than general education. Where training takes a long time (as in medicine, law and engineering) it is always called "education." . . . As a general rule, the more specific and specialized the skills required and the shorter the training period, the more should such training be kept out of the educational system and be made a responsibility of the production branch requiring the skill. (quoted in Harbinson and Myers, 1965, p. 146)

Before colonization, Africans had their own educational systems that served their purposes. During colonization, Africans were ruled, directed and supervised by the colonial administrators and their expatriate representatives. Africans were, therefore, educated and trained to meet the needs of the colonizers. During the colonial era, most of the indigenous education, training and mentoring programs were lost. The colonial educational legacy instituted education, training and mentoring programs that have done little to develop the necessary human qualities in the African labor force. Although these programs have been pursued rigorously, they have not achieved much success in preparing Africans for the task of economic development. This failure is indicative of the fact that African leaders need to reconsider existing methods of education, training and mentoring inherited from the colonial administration. It is my belief that this has to be done immediately if Africans truly desire the fruits of economic development.

It is, therefore, the objective of this chapter to review existing education, training and mentoring programs and their goals, point out their weaknesses and then to propose an alternative strategy for achieving better results than in the past. In what follows, there is a presentation on the existing education, training and mentoring programs in sub-Saharan Africa and their objectives. The major weaknesses of these programs are then enumerated and discussed. The subsequent section is devoted mainly to suggestions regarding how the existing programs can be reformed and/or redesigned to achieve the intended goals. The conclusions and recommendations are presented in the final section.

PAST AND PRESENT ATTEMPTS AT HUMAN RESOURCE DEVELOPMENT IN AFRICA

Technical assistance has come to African countries (ACs) from almost all over the world since the 1940s. The main areas of focus of the United Nations' regular technical assistance programs were development plans, public administration training facilities and social-welfare services programs. These were pursued to develop the required human resources for economic development in Africa south of the Sahara.

The United Nations initiated its Expanded Program of Technical Assistance

(EPTA) on July 1, 1950. Through its various functionaries, the program reviewed requests, established policies and coordinated technical assistance activities of all participating organizations. In the same year, the United Nations Commission for Technical Assistance in Africa was established. It was charged with the mandate to review and coordinate technical cooperation between ACs and the participating European powers. The attention of this program was directed to such vital areas as health, transportation and rural economic development. In 1956, the International Bank for Reconstruction and Development (IBRD) established the Economic Development Institute, whose headquarters was in Washington, D.C. This institute focused on (1) economic policy formulation; (2) economic development planning; and (3) the administration of economic development programs. Its objective was to assist African countries in economic policy making and development planning.

The International Development Association (IDA) was created in 1960. Its primary concerns were to (1) promote economic development; (2) help increase the level of productivity; and (3) raise the standards of living in the developing countries.

When the United Nations Special Fund was created in 1958, it was to (1) undertake feasibility studies; (2) survey natural resources; and (3) train human resources for economic development. The Fund was to provide education and training programs to develop and improve the skills necessary for human performance.

In 1959, the United Nations Operational and Executive Personnel Program was developed. Its main objective was to provide temporary help in overseeing civil service programs in developing countries. As is obvious from its mandate, activities were not necessarily designed to focus on the development of human resources in ACs. The program was more concerned about finding the necessary personnel to oversee the civil service, even if it meant the use of expatriates.

Many developed countries, probably in final attempts to improve their colonial records and/or images, have for many years helped design and operate bilateral educational and training programs for Africa. In sum, many of these programs were to (1) develop and operate teacher training programs; (2) create public administration and agricultural training programs; (3) make scholarships available for overseas studies and training in medicine, law, public health, engineering and many other important areas; (4) institute mining and university extension programs; and (5) develop and implement mass education programs.

The United States International and Educational Exchange Acts (also known as the Smith-Mundt Act) were promulgated in 1948. The main objectives were to (1) facilitate the exchange of people, ideas, knowledge and skills; (2) provide technical and other relevant development-related services; and (3) exchange ideas in education, the arts and the sciences.

Many non-governmental organizations also participated in technical skills development programs for Africa. For example, the communist-dominated World Federation of Trade Unions (WFTU) established a school in Budapest in 1959 for the training of trade union leaders from Africa. A similar school was also established in Conakry, Guinea. The International Confederation of Free Trade Unions (ICFTU), a 1949 breakaway group from the WFTU, established the African Labor College in Kampala in 1958. All these organizations also contributed their respective quotas to humanpower development needs of ACs. In many ACs, some of these trade union leaders became political activists and/or figures.

The colonial administrators tried their best to help meet Africa's humanpower requirements, and both Catholic and Protestant missions participated in development programs. Israel also provided technical assistance and education and training programs for African industrialists and agriculturalists. The Soviet Union and other communist-bloc countries were not excluded from the race to provide technical and economic assistance to ACs.

Each of these countries and organizations did what it deemed appropriate in its sight and estimation. Whether or not these programs actually addressed Africa's humanpower needs was not a crucial issue then. Zack (1966) pointed out that many African scholars were sent abroad to study in both Western and Eastern European countries. Hundreds of other students went to Canada, China, Cuba and the United States. In many cases, these students came back home more steeped in ideologies than in the HF necessary for Africa's development.

THE SHORTCOMINGS OF EXISTING EDUCATIONAL AND TRAINING PROGRAMS

Over the years, ACs have participated in extensive education and training assistance programs, with the main goal of helping Africans develop their human resources. Regardless of these attempts, however, little has been accomplished by way of equipping Africans to successfully apply these educational developments to initiate, implement and manage their economic development planning, policies and programs. This failure raises a basic question: "What went wrong with the countless number of education and training programs designed for Africa?"

A careful study of the programs reviewed earlier in this chapter reveals that the various agencies involved in developing education and training programs for ACs had their own agenda to pursue. It seems, therefore, that each of these missions, governments, non-governmental organizations, the United Nations and many others had a conceptualization of what kinds of humanpower training programs should be instituted in each African country and did as they thought fit. There was little coordination among participants. Varying degrees of emphasis were placed on different levels of education—primary, secondary and university. Yet mere emphasis on each of these areas in relation to increasing total enrollment is not only meaningless, but also wasteful. Many of the programs failed to focus on the long-term needs of African economies. That is, initial education and training programs did not pursue target or goal-oriented education. Coordination and balance, however, are critical to the success of any education and training program. Such programs developed for many ACs failed to take these issues into account. Shaplin (1966, pp. 116–117), writing about education in the British Commonwealth of nations, observed:

[T]here is [a] totally different lack of balance in the educational system. It can be broadly described as quantitatively overbalanced toward primary education and qualitatively over-balanced toward the classic secondary grammar school and elite university, but under-balanced toward post-primary, higher technical education and teacher education. The result, of course, is a rigorously selective educational system, with fewer and fewer students surviving the competitive examinations at each level. Since the secondary and university parts of the system have developed primarily to provide an educated civil service, survival depends heavily upon the possession of literacy, rather than personal, intuitive, and practical, skills.

Shaplin (1966) noted that oversupply of humanpower exists at two different levels. First, there is an oversupply of educated people in the arts. Most of these individuals have been trained for the existing civil service. Second, many primary school leavers, although functionally literate, are strongly unskilled in many regards. Even though the secondary schools and the existing universities have also produced many graduates, most have been prepared for civil service jobs that are usually nonexistent. In this regard, there exist huge shortages of skilled technicians required for industry, agriculture and other relevant areas of the African economy. Shaplin (1966) pointed out that by the year 1956, Congolese educational programs focused mainly on technical training to the neglect of both grammar school and university education. The failures of this system became obvious in 1961 when there were only fifteen university graduates— insufficient to meet the human resources needs of a newly independent country.

Zack (1966) observed that colonial educational programs for sub-Saharan ACs most frequently brushed aside technical and vocational education. The focus was on how to meet the demand for simple literacy skills. Africans were therefore trained to acquire these skills to the neglect of long-term productive and creative skills. Zack argued that in accordance with the colonial skill needs, especially in the British colonies, Africans were offered courses and/or programs that prepared them to write and pass European academic examinations. Course content was of little relevance to Africans and their economies.

Thut and Adams (1964) pointed out that the pattern of colonial education was based on economics, and the chief concern was how the colonial educational program would maximize net benefits to the mother country. The education, training and mentoring of Africans was only relevant as long as it promoted the economic enterprise of the colonial administration, foreign traders and merchants. The Christian missions were, however, more concerned with personal development. Thut and Adams (1964, p. 436) noted that, ''because of lack of sufficient funds, and possibly, reluctance to face an 'educated unemployed,' the

French limited their courses in both secondary and higher education to those which would train students for positions in which a particular need existed.''

The four fields of specialization in the three-year upper secondary curriculum in the Belgian Congo included (1) administration and commercial; (2) survey; and (3) science, or the preparation for agriculture, veterinary work and medicine. Teacher training was also included in these programs. Other related secondary schools provided the more traditional academic programs in the arts and sciences. As observed by Thut and Adams (1964), the Belgian education and training programs were aimed more at the certification needed to receive diplomas that could be used by Africans to earn a living. The relevant fields of financial administration and the general art of administration were not taught. These colonial education and training programs failed to teach and promote the concept of national identity and unity.

Regarding the Belgian educational policy in the Congo during the 1950s and 1960s, Kimble (1960) noted that paternalism and religion played critical roles. He pointed out that the Belgian administration believed it would be more effective to help, for example, 90 percent of the Congolese comprehend what the government was doing for them and what role the indigenous Congolese could competently play, rather than to educate the top 10 percent, who would spend most of their time and energy instructing the government on what to do. That is, the Belgians viewed educated Africans as troublemakers rather than contributors to the attainment of colonial goals. True education, training and mentoring for successful long-term HF development was, therefore, not the main goal, but was in fact deliberately impeded in the Congo at the time.

Today, existing education systems and training programs in ACs continue to be inadequate in meeting the needs of the African peoples. They seem to have failed in attaining desired goals. The systems and programs lack procedures necessary for encouraging creativity and productivity; in their existing form, education and training programs in ACs hardly provide the environment and the opportunities for African students to either question theories and/or principles being taught or enter into productive dialogues with their teachers and instructors. Students are made to believe that everything the teacher teaches in the classroom is the truth and, therefore, need not be either challenged or altered. They have been made to accept and memorize materials culled from books, without the opportunity to evaluate and/or analyze underlying assumptions, presuppositions and ideologies. This attitude forces students to think that there is no room for any creativity and innovations, since everything they are being taught is deemed to be true wisdom from abroad that will redeem them.

Book Knowledge, Cultural Stagnation, Power and Authority Structure

Another serious limitation of existing education and training programs in Africa is how both teachers and students have come to equate memorization and the recall of facts and theories learned in the classroom with intelligence. If a student can commit into rote memory and reproduce the same to his or her professor in all required examinations, he or she is deemed to be an excellent student. This is evident in the fact that many African universities have produced tens of thousands of graduates who have passed their final degree examinations with flying colors. Yet, after their graduation, most of these students have little to contribute to the economic development of their nations, because the university programs they went through failed to properly educate, train and equip them to deal with the day-to-day social, economic and political problems of African societies. Truly, it must be realized that continuing success in mere memorization of information is not really equivalent to the possession of the required abilities for solving problems.

In Ghana, for instance, since many graduates usually fail to read, write and do critical thinking, regardless of the number of years spent in school, their diplomas have been referred to as *Gye ko didi,* which literally means "get [this diploma or certificate] and use it to earn a living." These diplomas are no more than mere certification of having passed formal examinations in specific subject areas within which the diploma holder has taken a series of courses or apprenticeship. Those who receive these certificates are, therefore, wrongly deemed to have been fully prepared to assume responsibilities in the civil service. As such, many African scholars are in the habit of chasing one degree after another, and the process continues *ad infinitum.* Yet on the job, many intelligent graduates, who previously received first-class diplomas from prestigious institutions (either at home or abroad), fail to successfully accomplish expected tasks because they are unable to apply their acquired book knowledge to decipher and solve everyday social, economic and political problems. They lack the intuition and practical skills necessary for effectiveness on the job. This phenomenon reveals the weaknesses of the education and training programs that have been mainly concerned with mere acquisition of rudimentary knowledge. The inability to do more than basic rote learning has denied many African graduates the ability to develop critical thinking skills.[2]

Above all, the colonial educational legacy has failed to provide education and training programs that can create fertile academic environments that encourage African students to take a closer look at existing cultural standards and critically evaluate and challenge their validity and usefulness for solving current social, economic and political problems. Although some scholars may argue that culture should neither be altered nor destroyed, the truth is that culture must never be viewed as stagnant. A people's culture must be displayed for extensive analysis and/or comparison with others in relation to its effectiveness in dealing with complex problems in modern society. By so doing, students can compare and analyze the state of their culture and then make conclusions regarding whether their culture needs any alterations. Any changes that have occurred must be studied to discover whether they have either enhanced or diminished human welfare in that society. When a people's culture stagnates, that society will never experience progress, because it will continue to do things in the same way as past generations have done. This is not proper, because as the needs of African societies change, along with the global political economy, so also must the means for attaining objectives change.

African societies need to devise relevant educational programs that have the capacity to meet their changing needs and also stand up to the dictates of the global economy. This implies that the educational environment must encourage relevant knowledge, skill and human qualities acquisition that will lead to the dismantling of the shackles of unproductive cultural practices in every African country. Otherwise, the continuing cultural stagnation will perpetrate development inertia, a problem evidenced in lack of improvement in existing indigenous technology in Africa. This is a powerful way to deal with current unproductive cultural mind-sets and narrow-minded intellectualism.

The existing African power and authority structure also militates against the necessary rapport between professors and students. In many cases, since the power and authority structures do not allow for inquisitive minds, students find it too difficult to approach professors (whether inside or outside the classroom) to ask questions. Therefore, the students are more than satisfied with lecture notes, which their professors often took while studying in the United Kingdom, the United States, Canada and many other places. These notes are used by professors as standards that must be met by their students. Either directly or indirectly, students are forced to memorize this stagnant and questionable material in order to pass their required examinations. African students are forced to read foreign textbooks presenting illustrative examples that mean little to them. This practice usually clouds the meaning of simple concepts and theories. Information is memorized solely to pass examinations and gain diplomas, which also have little meaning and practical value. All this needs to change if Africa is to make gains in development planning, policy and programming.

The Lack of Ongoing Evaluation Systems

Another area of failure in relation to professors and trainers is the lack of effective and efficient evaluation systems to serve as checks and balances on their performance and professional conduct. In most advanced countries, there is continuing assessment of the performance of professors in their scholarship by their peers and of their teaching effectiveness and competency by their students. Since information from these peer reviews and student evaluations is seriously taken into account for tenure and promotion considerations, most faculty members are usually on guard and do their jobs to the best of their abilities. This is, however, not always the case in Africa's institutions of higher learning, where the absence of evaluation systems discourages enhanced productivity in teaching and scholarship in faculty research.

The Natural–Social Sciences Dichotomy, Educational Base and Entrepreneurship

The existing African educational system fails to provide a solid, broad-based multidisciplinary foundation on which to build further knowledge acquisition and development. As a result of this handicap, the educational system has not produced an effective and conducive intellectual climate for the efficient cross-fertilization of ideas and/or knowledge. For example, in the universities, natural science students are not given the opportunity to take courses in philosophy and the social sciences (i.e., psychology, economics, sociology, history, music, fine arts, the humanities, physical education, and so on). Similarly, social science students also miss the same opportunity to take some classes in the natural sciences (i.e., chemistry, physics, biology, health science, agricultural science and many others). African university students and scholars are, therefore, denied the opportunity to acquire the relevant education to make them well-informed scholars.

In spite of the validity of this observation, Africans still continue to provide their youth with education and training programs that hinder rather than promote true scholarship. At the time of graduation, for example, many students become severely handicapped in that their academic programs have led them to become intellectual experts, who have narrow specializations and, therefore, tunnel vision. African scholars become intellectually knowledgeable in their chosen fields, without necessarily developing problem-solving abilities and insights for unraveling the problems of their societies. This natural–social sciences dichotomy created by existing African education and training systems must be removed to provide students with the opportunity to broaden their educational base, especially at the lower levels of their educational pilgrimage. By so doing, African students will be provided with a much stronger knowledge base with which more extended and further intensive analysis and critical thinking could proceed.

Little help is available for students who greatly need subject selection and career choice. In most cases, students either go by what their intuition suggests or do as their colleagues do. In certain cases, their choices of subjects and careers are based on the value of expected returns and/or prestige or power gained by entering that field.[3] Professions such as medicine, law, engineering and a few others become more appealing in this regard. Existing national remuneration structures do not encourage students to enter certain vital subject areas, vocational and other practically oriented subjects and professional studies are usually perceived as areas for either academic failures or the ne'er-do-wells (i.e., dropouts).

Furthermore, the education and training system does not have programs for school dropouts. Some dropouts turn to agriculture, fishing and street vending (i.e., trading) at the most basic level, and others find their way into traditional informal apprenticeship agreements where they learn sewing, carpentry, bricklaying and many other trades. Little respect is accorded to people who learn through these channels, since many in society do not view them as part of the formal education and training system. Technical schools have also been viewed in this light. The general perception is that the most brilliant students must go to a university to earn degrees, while average or failing students go to technical, commercial and vocational schools to earn diplomas and trade certificates for earning a living.

An International Labour Office report completed in 1979 noted that the dropout rate was exceptionally high in Lesotho, varying from 9 to 10 percent. Repeaters numbered about 15 percent of total enrollment in 1977. Worst of all, the teacher/pupil ratio was about 1:53, and about 31 percent of the teachers were not qualified. The report also revealed that primary education has failed to prepare pupils for a worklife, since it is more academic than vocational, technical or agricultural. The primary program is designed for those who will continue to higher academic education levels (i.e., a university). There is neither any place where dropouts can go nor any readily available employment opportunities on which to capitalize.

These views and perceptions strongly influence both career choice and subject selection, with students often making these decisions with insufficient counseling. A devastating result of this is the lack of encouragement for students to consider careers in useful subject areas and/or careers.

Existing education and training systems have therefore failed to produce astute entrepreneurs who are necessary requirements for human progress. However, many indigenous African entrepreneurs have been produced through the informal traditional apprenticeship system. These are individuals, mostly women, who have become extremely successful and well-known in their market (retail trade) activities. A notable class among these, often referred to as *Makola* women, operate in Accra, Ghana. They have their counterparts in many other cities all across Africa. Their economic knowledge, gained through experience rather than formal schooling, makes them more knowledgeable in the functioning of the Ghanaian economy than those African scholars who have earned their Ph.D. degrees in economics from such schools as the University of Chicago, Harvard, Yale, London School of Economics, and the University of British Columbia—and even from universities in Africa. Because this class of traders has not been studied extensively by African economists and other social scientists, little is known about their true contributions to national economies in ACs.

The Colonial Legacy

When ACs attained political independence, many legacies were left for the first generation African leaders who had no other systems apart from what they inherited. Worst of all, these leaders were intellectually trained abroad and returned home with little regard for the traditional social, economic and political structures. These scholars and leaders preferred to borrow from abroad to the total exclusion of their own indigenous systems. African ethos, ethical systems and principles have since run the danger of becoming extinct. Since principles and presuppositions of African cultures were not critically studied and thoroughly examined at the existing education and training institutions, much has been lost (either good or bad).

In view of this, how can Africans learn to rule themselves by creating the vital environment within which success can be achieved? Can Africans learn to lead, experience economic freedom and increase labor productivity? Is it possible that Africans can shake and take off the colonial cloak of institutions and structures that have failed to produce the necessary HF? Can the colonial mentality that has been perpetrated for several decades be erased to change people's thinking processes and expectations in Africa? If these cannot be achieved, the future of Africa will be bleak indeed. History shows that when imminent failure stares people in the face, the fear of continuing poverty, hunger and death forces vocal individuals or groups of individuals who lack the HF to champion a cause that supports no change in the existing culture and its perpetrated mind-set. They call for a return to the old goddess, culture. This action, based on the view that "the devil you know is better than the angel you don't know" can, and has, destroyed the winds of change. To succeed, the African education and training system must instead focus on finding workable solutions to these intricately complicated problems.

Commenting on the colonial and the United Nations education and training programs, Zack (1966, p. 141) noted,

the programs of Western governments, particularly the former colonial ones, are uncertain of success because they appear to the African as further imperialist activities. Such programs are, perforce, limited to surveys, legislative consulting functions, and other advisory roles. Thus we find that all the multilateral programs, while seemingly ideal in terms of community participation, are watered down in terms of their impact, and have, therefore, little likelihood of meeting the vast needs of the underdeveloped countries, except on a piecemeal, overlapping, uncoordinated basis.

Sir Eric Ashby (1964) drew a relevant parallel between African universities and foreign automobiles. He observed:

[T]hose founded by the British displayed at independence the three attributes of British universities. In constitution, they were autonomous, deliberately detached from the state. In standards and curriculum, they emphasized the thin stream of excellence and the narrow specialism. In social function, they regarded themselves as restricted to an elite. (quoted in Adedeji, 1989, p. 618)

This description is typical of the African education scene. Unless the real needs are identified, any calls for reform may miss the point once again. This is what is addressed in the next section for analysis and evaluation.

THE NATURE OF THE REQUIRED PEOPLE

Educational reform in ACs must begin with a meaningful vision and selected goals and objectives. In addition, ACs must decipher the human qualities and skills they wish to develop to enhance their future planning, policy formulation and programming capacities. At the most basic level, the reformed educational system and training programs must develop the HF. The developed human resources must be:

1. People who will commit to the principles on which the society's work ethics are based.

2. People who are ready to seek economic resources (machines, tools, technology, etc.) and be willing to work hard around the clock to solve pertinent problems.

3. People who are perceptive regarding the value of their produce and personal worth.

4. People who think continuously and practice problem-solving.

5. People who are prepared and ready to give a helping hand to others when they have the required ability to do so. This must be done strictly according to the law, rules and universal principles.

6. People who are honorable, knowledgeable and have both understanding and wisdom. They must be committed to exploring possible opportunities and diligently seek solutions for everyday social, economic and political problems.

7. People who are not only perceptive, highly motivated and action oriented, but are also rewarded fully for their hard work (see Adjibolosoo, 1995, pp. 84–85).

HUMAN FACTOR ENGINEERING PROGRAMS

To revamp the African educational system, it is important to ask certain questions for which answers must be sought with commitment and diligence. In line with this view, Adedeji (1989, p. 627) asked the following insightful questions:

[T]o what extent have our education systems produced the categories of specialists required to enable us to face the challenge posed by the rapidly deteriorating economic and social conditions? To what extent, and with what success, have our institutions of higher learning stimulated ingenuity and inventiveness in their products, to the extent that Africa requires today for survival and for self renewal? How successfully have these institutions developed, in our people, self-confidence and the capability and determination to stand on our own feet? Have they produced the genuinely learning and/or genuinely thinking student? And how far have they prepared our countries, our people, and our governments, for the days of turbulence and the discontinuity of the unforseen that lies ahead?

As is obvious from the panorama of questions, Adedeji's concern and emphasis are on the quality of the African human resources rather than their quantities.

These questions are asking about the characteristics of Africa's educated class. If the answers to these questions are negative, they will clearly imply that the existing education and training programs have failed to achieve their intended goals. As is obvious from the material presented so far, I am convinced that sincere answers to these questions are indeed negative. ACs need to rethink and reform their inherited educational systems and make sure that the new system will help provide affirmative answers to these questions in the not-too-distant future. As such, the next question is: "Where do ACs go from here and what must they be doing to effect the necessary changes?"

Tyler (1972) noted that it is important for every professional education institution to thoroughly study the needs of their professions in terms of skills, abilities and other relevant human qualities and then develop education and training programs to help their trainees acquire them. When this is done in the most efficient and effective manner, newly graduated members of these professional institutions will be fully prepared to play their roles in these professions. At the commencement of the program, it is necesary to identify those students who show great promise of becoming contributors to the success of the profession and to provide them with the necessary requirements to develop their talents. Whatever is required for improving productivity in the profession must be both taught and modeled to the students in training.

For the professions, emphasis must be placed on continuing practice and/or apprenticeship during the school years (Tyler, 1972). Every education and training program must be aimed at HF development. Principles of behavior and relevant theories of the profession must be made the foundation stone on which the whole education and training program must stand.

EDUCATION AND TRAINING

The 1962 conference, "The Development of Higher Education in Africa," held in Tananarive, Madagascar, gave critical consideration to Africa's education and training needs. The conference report suggested that the goals of higher education in Africa must necessarily include:

1. The maintenance of academic standards equivalent to those found elsewhere.

2. The achievement of African unity.

3. Appreciation for the African culture. Scholarly research and African studies courses are to be used as the main basis for debunking misconceptions about Africa.

4. Human resources development to meet the acute humanpower needs.

5. *Whole person* training (see Chapter 2) for national development.

6. The development of patterns of African learning at higher levels; not disregarding what is happening in the rest of the world.

Although these goals are very illuminating, one wonders how much has happened in the last 34 years since the Tananarive conference. The goals are reasonable and can easily be attained had African governments, themselves, adopted them and put structures and programs in place to pursue them. These goals, although still relevant, need some modifications for today's African environment. One of the most primary goals of an effective educational program is, however, missing from the list made at the 1962 Tananarive conference. That is, the conference glossed over HF development. With a complete set of objectives in place, ACs can proceed to discuss what kinds of people they need for their development programs and how each country can proceed to prepare them. The basic question, therefore, is: "How can Africans pursue relevant goals and what is required for success?"

DIMENSIONS OF THE EDUCATIONAL PROGRAM

It is necessary that ACs become aware and convinced about what they want their education, training and mentoring policies and programs to achieve. When this is known, it is much more likely that effective education and training programs will be designed and implemented towards the preparation of the future labor force. The reformulated programs must deal effectively with the weaknesses noted in this chapter and Adedeji's pathfinding questions. This implies that sub-Saharan African education, training and mentoring programs must be designed with specific principles and/or objectives in mind—that is, HF development. The new education, training and mentoring programs at all levels (i.e., primary, secondary and university) must focus on:

1. The development of communications, comprehension, critical thinking and writing skills.
2. The critical study and analysis of the philosophy underlying the African mind-set and way of life as evidenced in African proverbs, stories, puzzles, riddles, etc.
3. The study and evaluation of existing indigenous and foreign technological developments.
4. The teaching and studying of African history and its relevance to the future of the continent.
5. The study and continuing evaluation of traditional engineering processes and procedures.
6. The critical review, analysis and continuing study of administrative science and management.
7. The teaching and study of the natural sciences and agriculture.
8. The teaching and study of vocational and technical subjects.

As I have noted elsewhere in this chapter, the primary objective of the reformed education, training and mentoring programs is HF development. Those

ACs who are not sure about how to begin educational reform may consult Katz (1971), Spring (1976) or Bowles and Gintis (1976) for some relevant ideas with which to begin. I am convinced that when educational changes are not properly designed and aimed at specific targets, the end results will be disastrous. Relevant areas of concern must include (1) intellectual development; (2) political emancipation; (3) social development and progress; and (4) economic development[4] in sub-Saharan ACs. To successfully achieve these goals, the education, training and mentoring programs must integrate the following programs into the system. That is, at the primary, secondary and university levels, the spotlight must focus on:

1. Continuing education: Always staying educated and maintaining professional competence (see Chapter 11 for a detailed discussion of this issue).
2. Cooperative education: Creating the environment for students to gain the hands-on experience for the life of work (see Adjibolosoo, 1995).
3. Personal development programs: Continuing to keep one's knowledge base broad and always well-informed (see Adjibolosoo, 1995).

At every level, programs must focus on critical analysis, intensive discussions and creative explorations rather than rote memory. It is important to define and design an integrating core made up of relevant subject areas from which every student must take a required minimum number of credit courses. Examples of core courses for the new education, training and mentoring programs include philosophy, ethical studies, the natural sciences, religious studies, education, political economy, language and culture and other social sciences deemed critical by those who plan and develop the program. When all these have been put in place, the implementation of the reformed system must be as suggested. When successfully accomplished, the required HF will be developed and ACs will rise above the pertinent problems of continuing underdevelopment.

CONCLUSION

When Africans begin to rethink the redesign of their existing education policies and training programs, there must be a detailed review and analysis of Africa's needs. It is important to review the successes and failures of the past and current educational systems and training programs. Problems are better solved when one knows what they are and the reasons why they could not be previously solved. The questions then become: "Can they be solved? If not, what must be done to get them solved with the available tools?" Existing African education and training programs have failed because they pursued policies and programs designed by the colonial administration to meet their needs. Since the colonial rulers were not necessarily interested in developing the African HF, the educational legacy they bequeathed to the first generation of African leaders could not produce the caliber of people Africa needs for development.

There is, however, hope for Africa's economic development, political emancipation, social progress and intellectual redirection if Africans restructure existing educational policies and programs to develop the HF necessary for progress. As discussed in this chapter, a critical and detailed rethinking, reformulation and reformation of the current African educational system and training programs will lead to positive gains. Existing educational policies, programs and international assistance have focused their efforts on issues that have made few contributions toward true and lasting development in Africa. The race into the twenty-first century calls for rethinking and serious reorganization of Africa's educational systems and programs to meet pressing human needs.

NOTES

1. See a detailed definition to the HF in Chapter 2.
2. I must point out, however, that this has nothing to do with genetics. If a country's education and training programs are poorly designed, they will produce men and women who will lack the necessary requirements for critical thinking and the acquisition of the ability to critically analyze and solve pertinent social, economic and political problems.
3. It is not wrong to enter a specific field based on the expected future income returns on one's investment. Rather, the basic argument here is that while the individual specializes in that area, he or she must be given the opportunity to experiment with other disciplines. This will help in his or her HF development. Every student must be educated to learn and know that there is more to education than mere private financial returns.
4. The new education, training and mentoring program for sub-Saharan Africa must be aimed at HF development and the dismantling of the shackles of unproductive cultural practices (see Adjibolosoo, 1993, 1994). The education, training and mentoring policy must lead to the creation of a fertile academic environment in which African students and scholars alike can explore ideas, philosophies, principles and patterns that could lead to the carving of solutions to problems of economic underdevelopment. This environment must also foster the continuing application of principles and theories to problem-solving. The whole education, training and mentoring program must not lead to enslavement of the sub-Saharan African culture to ideologies and/or institutional structures from non-African societies. Knowledge of foreign techniques, procedures and ideologies must provide opportunities for further exploration and the willingness to search for better procedures for solving problems and accomplishing relevant tasks. The properly educated and effectively trained African peoples must be well-informed, curious, creative, discerning, articulate, responsible, accountable and highly principled.

REFERENCES

Adedeji, A. 1989. *Towards a Dynamic African Economy: Selected Speeches and Lectures (1975–1986),* compiled and arranged by J. C. Senghor. London: Frank Cass.

Adjibolosoo, S. 1993. "The Human Factor in Development." *The Scandinavian Journal of Development Alternatives* 12 (4): 139–149.

Adjibolosoo, S. 1994. "The Human Factor and the Failure of Economic Development and Policies in Africa." In F. Ezeala-Harrison and S. Adjibolosoo, eds., *Per-*

spectives on Economic Development in Africa. Westport, Conn.: Praeger, pp. 25–37.

Adjibolosoo, S. 1995. *The Human Factor in Developing Africa.* Westport, Conn.: Praeger.

Ashby, E. Sir. 1964. *African Universities and Western Tradition.* Cambridge, Mass.: Harvard University Press.

Bowles, S. and Gintis, H. 1976. *Schools in Capitalist America: Educational Reform and the Contradictions of Economic Life.* New York: Basic Books.

Harbinson, F. and Myers, C. A., eds. 1965. *Manpower and Education: Country Studies in Economic Development.* New York: McGraw-Hill Book Company.

International Labor Office (ILO). 1979. *Options for a Dependent Economy: Development, Employment and Equity Problems in Lesotho.* Addis Ababa: Saint George Printing Press.

Katz, M. B. 1971. *Class, Bureaucracy, and Schools: The Illusion of Educational Changes in America.* New York: Praeger.

Kimble, G. H. T. 1960. *Tropical Africa. Vol. I.* New York: Twentieth Century Fund.

Peter, L. J. 1977. *Peter's Quotations: Ideas for Our Time.* New York: Bantam Books.

Shaplin, J. T. 1966. "A Sea of Faces: Teacher Training for Nigeria and the Ashby Report." In W. Y. Elliott, ed., *Education and Training in the Developing Countries: The Role of U.S. Foreign Aid.* New York: Praeger.

Spring, J. 1976. *The Sorting Machine: National Educational Policy Since 1945.* New York: Longman.

Thut, I. N. and Adams, D. 1964. *Educational Patterns in Contemporary Societies.* New York: McGraw-Hill Book Company.

Tyler, R. W. 1972. "More Effective Education for the Professions." In I. Berg, ed., *Human Resources and Economic Welfare: Essays in Honor of Eli Ginzberg.* New York: Columbia University Press.

UNESCO. 1963. "The Development of Higher Education in Africa: A Report of the Conference on the Development of Higher Education in Africa" (Tananarive, Madagascar, September 3–12, 1962). Paris: UNESCO.

Zack, A. M. 1966. "Developing Human Resources: A New Approach to Educational Assistance in Africa." In W. Y. Elliott, ed., *Education and Training in Developing Countries: The Role of U.S. Foreign Aid.* New York: Praeger.

2

Human Factor Engineering: The Primary Mission of Education and Training

Senyo B-S. K. Adjibolosoo

INTRODUCTION

Throughout the centuries, men and women have looked for and fashioned tools and sophisticated machines to help them deal with problems they encounter on a continuing basis. While some societies frequently maintain their machines and the available infrastructure they have developed, others fail to. The primary objective of existing preventive maintenance management programs is to sustain effectiveness and efficiency in performance (Adjibolosoo, 1995a, chapter 8). Even today, the great explosion of the technological revolution is aimed at facing and containing the pertinent problems of humanity. Although humanity has made much progress, it is still faced with primary social, economic, political, cultural and intellectual problems. The difficulty is that the great advances made at all fronts have not been successful in improving the well-being of all humanity. This dilemma raises the question: "What has gone wrong, and how can it be fixed?" Even though much attention is paid to technological advancement and its improvement, very little attention is paid to the total development of the whole person. This neglect of duty to humanity has compounded the pertinent problems of humanity throughout the centuries (Adjibolosoo, 1995b).

For centuries, humanity has been troubled by the continuing problem of scarcity. As such, men and women have struggled throughout the years to overcome this problem. The pursuit of meaningful solutions has created other accompanying problems. The social, economic and political institutions developed by humanity to deal with its problems seem to be rapidly failing to accomplish their intended goals (Adjibolosoo, 1995b). Both private and public plans, policies and programs are facing problems of immeasurable proportions in the modern world.

Diversity of ideologies[1] has prevented a consensus on the real causes of social, economic and political problems in society. In fact, the diversity of perceptions and ideas has increased the dissension among various factions and their proposed solutions to the problems at hand. Yet, until society discovers what the real causes of its problems are, it cannot hope to solve them successfully. In the midst of all these competing ideologies, humanity is still struggling to reach concrete agreements on the actual sources of existing problems. Hence its failure to develop effective and workable solutions to them. Problems arising from criminal activities, business fraud, political scandals, progressive social decay, economic stagnation and political ineffectiveness are escalating. In view of this, it is reasonable for all humanity to pause for a moment and begin to reevaluate the present state of the human condition.

The search for solutions to social, economic, political, cultural, and intellectual problems seems to continually ignore the relevance of the human factor (HF) to existing problems and human well-being. Every society needs to correct this oversight. Every individual requires thorough and continuing development to perform as expected. It seems to me that society is failing to develop and maintain all levels and/or components of the HF (see Table 2.1). In view of this, the primary objective of this chapter is to present and discuss the current state of the HF, its role in the human enterprise and how HF development must be viewed as the primary mission of education and training. The chapter, therefore, points out that improper development of the HF is the primary cause of existing problems in all developing countries, including Africa, and will continue to create more problems for society in the future if not dealt with as soon as possible. In short, the continuing disregard for HF development will stall human progress in the long run.

Specifically, the chapter discusses and analyzes the state of the HF and its relevance to society. It stresses that institutions of higher learning must create and implement relevant programs to facilitate HF development and hence contribute positively to the quest for answers to the problems of humanity.

THE STATE OF THE HF AND ITS RELEVANCE

The concept *the development of the whole person*, used in this chapter, is viewed as the integrated education and training of the individual to acquire the necessary human qualities for effective performance. The total development of a person makes him or her capable of living a stable and productive life, functioning together with other people in an interrelated and integrated manner to successfully accomplish relevant tasks. The many intertwining elements of the whole person, the HF, must of necessity be continually developed in order for the individual to perform effectively and efficiently. Any suboptimal performance of an individual is therefore a direct result of HF decay and/or underdevelopment, *ceteris paribus*.[2] The HF is the spectrum of personality characteristics and other dimensions of human performance that enable social, economic and political institutions to function and remain functional, over time. Such dimensions sustain the workings and application of the rule of law, political harmony, a disciplined labor force, just legal systems, respect for human dignity and the sanctity of life, social welfare, and so on. As is often the case, no social, economic or political institutions can function effectively without being upheld by a network of committed persons who stand firmly by them. Such persons must strongly believe in and continually affirm the ideals of society. (Adjibolosoo, 1993, p. 142; 1994, p. 26)

Viewed from the HF perspective, the total development of the human being is the most neglected and the least emphasized among all known agents of civilization and wealth-creation. Even in cases where human performance and contributions are discussed, it is often difficult for leaders, planners, scholars, interest groups, academicians and many others to agree on what constitutes the best procedure for successful human development. Smyth (1969, p. 311), for example, observed:

[I]n human life, there should be a close relationship between our formal education, our character, our conduct and the resultant conditions of our individual collective life. Unfortunately, however, too often when we discuss the present impact and desirable directions for the reform of systems of learning we are concerned neither with the character, conduct and conditions of individual life, nor with our community life. Rather we are concerned too exclusively with improvement of techniques or the development of some particular or desirable skill.

Contrary to popular opinion, the achievement of true justice, peace, harmony and judgment in the operation and/or performance of the social, economic and political institutions in society seems elusive because the necessary human qualities that are required for the attainment of these cherished human goals and ideals are lacking. In the continuing absence of required human qualities (i.e., the HF), these primary objectives will be as slippery to achieve as maintaining balance and stability on the surface of an icy winter highway. Plan, policy, program and project failures in many societies are primarily problems of HF decay and/or underdevelopment. The rush to scrap existing plans, policies, programs and projects in order to replace them with others will not lead to a quick and easy attainment of better results as long as the necessary HF is non-existent (see Table 2.1). To always terminate plans, policies, programs and projects that are failing and replace them with other irrelevant ones is like treating a successive series of symptoms but never diagnosing and dealing effectively with the actual cause of the disease. The attainment of true and lasting progress requires people who have acquired the HF (Adjibolosoo, 1995a). Attempts to find solutions to social, economic, political, cultural and intellectual problems need to address HF decay and/or underdevelopment in society.

Many human efforts made to achieve human comfort and the good life fail to acknowledge and address the existing primary root causes of human failure

Table 2.1
The Composition of the Human Factor

HF (Type of capital)	Description
Spiritual Capital	It is the aspect of the human personality that is usually in tune with the universal laws and principles of human life. It equips the individual to see beyond what the five senses are able to grasp and also furnishes him or her with deeper insights into the non-material world.
Moral Capital	It represents habits and attitudes of the human heart that are based on universal principles regarding right or wrong. It refers to the qualities individuals possess that lead them to conform or not to conform to universal principles of life. Its constituents include integrity, humility, justice, charity, patience, honesty, sensitivity, fairness, etc.
Aesthetic Capital	A deep sense of and love for beauty. It includes a strong passion for music, art, drama, dance and other artistic capacities (imagination and creativity are strong components).

Human Capital	The know-how and acquired skills (i.e., technical, conceptual, intellectual, analytic and communications); human experiences, knowledge, intelligence, physical well-being, emotional health, etc.
Human Abilities	These constitute the power or capacity of an individual to competently undertake projects or effectively perform tasks requiring mental and physical effort. They are required for the effective use of human capital. Examples include wisdom, vision, commitment, determination, diligence, courage, accountability, judgment, responsibility, competence, motivation, human energy, optimism, endurance, self-control, objectivity, reliability, adaptability, alertness, etc.
Human Potentials	These are the human talents that may or may not be harnessed and employed for human utilization. They may be referred to as the yet undeveloped and unused dimensions of the HF.

Source: Adjibolosoo (1995a), pp. 33–38.

in many areas of human endeavor. The human search for workable solutions to problems has yielded negligible results. Throughout history, society has tried some[3] of every known policy, program and scheme that was thought to have had the ability to deal with the human predicament. All things considered, humanity is like the legendary man, Humpty Dumpty, illustrated in one nursery rhyme. This rhyme goes:

> Humpty Dumpty sat on the wall,
> Humpty Dumpty had a great fall,
> All the King's horses and all the King's men
> Couldn't put Humpty Dumpty together again.[4]

When Humpty Dumpty had that great fall, all the King's chamberlains, tools, instruments, resources, etc. were unable to restore him to his original condition and/or position. From this nursery rhyme, many observations can be made. For example, one wonders what actually happened to Humpty Dumpty. Did he just fall out of the King's pleasure and, therefore, was no longer needed for his usual duties in the palace? Were the injuries he sustained so severe that he could not be cured and restored to his former position of service? Did he fall into the trap of apostasy? Did the people who tried to restore him use the wrong procedures and therefore fail in the attempt? Did everybody, like the proverbial ostrich, bury his or her head in the sand and pretend not to have seen that Humpty Dumpty had fallen and might have been severely injured? Why did they not appeal to the rest of their country people (both commoners and the intelligentsia), and even the King himself, to help find ways and means to restore Humpty Dumpty? Whatever the case was, one is puzzled about why those who were there to help Humpty Dumpty failed to achieve their intended goal. They either lacked the necessary knowledge to have the job done or were so confused and caught up in their individual views that they could neither listen to each other nor agree on a detailed rescue plan and, therefore, left the restoration process unaccomplished.

Relating Humpty Dumpty's experience and/or plight to that of humanity, it is obvious that the problems of society today are significant and will not go away by themselves.[5] Humanity has made great inventions, innovations, technological advancements, etc. The presence and the elegance of the wonders[6] of the world attest to the achievements of humanity throughout the centuries. Yet, as is the case today, it is becoming increasingly difficult to get social, economic and political institutions working effectively and efficiently in societies. As such, scholars, sages, religious leaders, cultural gurus, masters, leaders of varying persuasions and many others have immersed themselves in the continuing search for answers to the problems that have beset humanity throughout the centuries. As time rolls by, new problems that surface seem to be more difficult to solve than preceeding ones and too devastating to contain. Humanity has successfully set foot on the moon and has also acquired an incredible wealth of knowledge and understanding of the galaxy and many other phenomena. Yet, society seems to be failing to find true solutions to the problems and hindrances that are denying it the ability to live in love, peace and harmony and also to comprehend the supernatural—the true essence of human life.

In view of these observations, one may ask the following questions: How different is the experience of humanity from that of Humpty Dumpty? Did the sages, cultural gurus, scholars, researchers, religious leaders, etc. discover the true answers to the human dilemma? If they did, what has society done with these answers? If they did not, why did they fail to arrive at the necessary solutions? Can present and subsequent generations discover permanent solutions to the human predicament? In view of these queries, this chapter argues that as long as the ongoing search for answers to the human predicament continues to ignore the required and necessary rehabilitation of a severely damaged and handicapped human person, humanity will permanently remain like Humpty Dumpty—with a fallen and/or distorted nature—and may not be put back together again by its own ingenuity and creativity. Weaknesses observed in the human personality have usually led to inefficient human performance. Just as a malfunctioning clutch, accelerator and brakes of a standard automobile lead to inefficient vehicle performance, so will an individual with a poorly developed HF continue to function inefficiently. Like a puppet,[7] unless humanity's "joints and strings" are restored to their original functioning state, its theatrical performances will be mediocre and unentertaining in the global stage of life.

In many societies today, it is the habit of people to shout angrily at those who commit heinous crimes. A kidnapping, violent act of rape, drive-by shooting, armed robbery involving a death or life-threatening injuries, and many other acts of a similar nature often raise hue and cry.[8] Intentional and/or premeditated acts of violence committed by youth lead many adults to gasp spasmodically for breath. People, therefore, call for tougher laws to either regulate unacceptable behavior or incarcerate criminals, young offenders or both. Gun control laws and crime bills have mushroomed and are ubiquitous in many nations. Yet this band-aid approach for dealing with the continuing problems of humanity seems to be failing primarily from either the severe neglect or poor development of the HF. The results of this failure include all kinds of human inefficiencies and lack of success in the quest for true justice and right judgment, protection of inalienable human rights and continuing respect for the rule of law, equity, fairness and true and long-lasting human belongingness.

Through the use of its many makeshift programs, society continues to ignore Alexis de Tocqueville's view that "the health of a democratic society may be measured by the quality of functions performed by private citizens" (quoted in Peter, 1977, p. 89). John Stuart Mill shared this view when he noted that "the worth of a state, in the long run, is the worth of the individuals composing it" (quoted in Peter, 1977, p. 90). Society does not only neglect these views when it develops its plans, policies and programs, but also lavishes its resources on developing and setting up quick-fix procedures. When these fail, other programs of similar characteristics and/or magnitude are quickly designed to replace their unsuccessful predecessors. As such, fads come and go. Programs are developed and implemented and then fail or are abandoned. Eloquent speakers and renowned experts are called on to demonstrate and/or prove the wonders and promises of new ideas, programs, activities, techniques and methodologies. Yet, from the rising till the setting of the sun, these evasive plans, policies and programs hardly ever exert any significant positive impact on the problems confronting humanity. Rather, society always looks for the easier solutions that are based on throwing more financial resources at pertinent problems and thereby begging their required and lasting solutions (Adjibolosoo, 1995b). Moyers (1989, p. vii) could not have been more accurate when he noted that "sometimes during the 1988 [U. S.] election season, it had seemed to me that we were all 'institutionalized' in one form or another, locked away in our separate realities, our parochial loyalties, our fixed ways of seeing ourselves and strangers." By placing themselves in boxes that are much narrower than pigeonholes, people are unable to interact with each other and therefore fail to solve their common problems. Sadly, they may even fight and kill each other for no reason.[9]

When programs and projects fail, the authorities in charge are blamed. These authorities, in turn, blame the failure on their subordinates, who finally dump the blame on the lack of appropriate tools and/or resources. This blame-shifting attitude is what I refer to as *the systems fallacy syndrome* or *the denial and projection syndrome* (Adjibolosoo, 1995c, pp. 412–426). At best, it is an excellent, but temporal, hideout for concealing the weaknesses and inefficiencies inherent in the human personality. At worst, it leaves pertinent problems of society unresolved. If humanity is truly bent on dealing successfully with its problems, it must focus on long-term plans, policies, programs and projects whose primary purpose must be human quality (i.e., the HF) development. The caliber of people every society needs for its survival in a competitive global marketplace are individuals who have acquired the relevant HF. This is what society must be fully committed to.

DEVELOPING THE HF TO ENRICH THE WHOLE PERSON

The effective and efficient development of the HF requires unflinching efforts to develop and sustain every dimension of the HF. This process of *whole person* development can be loosely likened to tuning up an automobile.[10] At the garage, the mechanic uses the appropriate tools to observe different parts of the vehicle and checks out whether or not they are in good shape. The brakes, transmission, muffler, spark plugs and many other parts are frequently evaluated. When any faults are detected, they are corrected. Frequent tune-ups are critical to vehicle efficiency. Vehicles that are poorly maintained run the risk of frequently breaking down, causing accidents or both. Similarly, for more effective and efficient performance, a person requires an extensive and ongoing "automobile garage experience."[11] With the education and training that can enhance the six major dimensions of the HF—spiritual, moral, aesthetic, human capital, human abilities and human potential (Table 2.1, Adjibolosoo, 1995a). Each of these complex, integrated and intertwined components of the HF must be developed and maintained on an ongoing basis. Continuing neglect of any of these will create problems and untold hardships for society in the long run.

The development and maintenance of each of these component parts of the human being not only requires hard work, but also takes considerable length of time to achieve. Thus, people who are fond of quick-fixes and ad hoc programs will find these tasks too difficult to complete. Also, *all* six aspects of the HF listed in Table 2.1 need to be developed and maintained on an ongoing basis to guarantee the best performance of every human being. For example, it is a great mistake to focus on only the development of the human intellect, physique and health of the physical body to the glaring neglect of worthwhile investment in the development of both the spiritual and moral capital. Sad to say, however, that this is the plight of humanity today. The development of both the spiritual and moral capital has been severely neglected in many societies. In certain circles, it is even a taboo to mention or discuss such topics, and students in many classrooms are not led to discover these areas for themselves. They are only taught knowledge and expected to be wise. Yet, these dimensions of the HF are so critical to the effectiveness of the individual and his or her performance that their decay and/or underdevelopment will without any doubt create social, economic, cultural, intellectual and political problems of unbearable proportions in society. Plans, policies and programs will fail. Social institutions will not achieve their intended goals. Any society that finds itself in these situations has either experienced HF decay and/or underdevelopment or is currently going through it.

From the HF perspective, therefore, the state of the human heart requires that both moral and spiritual surgery be conducted on the heart in the theater of purposeful education systems and training institutions on the operating tables of universal principles of life. This will, somehow, facilitate the development and continuing expansion of both the moral and spiritual capital stock of humanity. As is the case at present, it is the continuing depreciation and/or running down of these elements of the HF that is leading to social decay, economic stagnation, political naivity, corruption, bankruptcy and all forms of business scandals. For example, imagine a person who is completely paralyzed and lives without the sense of feeling and/or touch. Can such a person experience the reality of the physical world around him or her? What about the intellectual reality? Whatever one's answers to these questions may be, it is the case that people who suffer from such difficulties will live in a secluded world where their own intellect will have fashioned an understanding of human life and existence. The knowledge and/or wisdom developed in this kind of seclusion will rule and direct their lives and activities in this world. Yet, because their knowledge may not be complete, they may not be freed from their existing imprisonment. Only when they receive new knowledge and gain enlightenment about how to be healed of their severe handicaps will true freedom come and life change for the better. Human ignorance about the existence and relevance of the universal laws and/ or principles of life traps humanity in a similar bondage. Unfortunately, this is one of the greatest mishaps that can befall an individual or society in general. This lack of knowledge and/or learning can, however, be ameliorated through well-crafted education, training and mentoring programs based on universal principles. The quest for effective ways for dealing with social, economic, cultural, intellectual and political decadence must be genuine, precise and continuous. Open-mindedness and continuous learning to improve human welfare, longevity and dignity must never cease to be.

Since adherence to habits, customs and/or culture drawn from human traditions has the power to either build or destroy societies, it is critical for progressive societies to initiate viable programs whose permanent objectives must be to uproot, pull down, destroy and throw away inefficient practices and then construct new ones that will promote social, economic and political progress.[12] Societies that fail to achieve these goals will neither fully perceive nor comprehend the real causes of policy failure, but rather will see obliquely through the contaminated cultural and/or intellectual lenses and lopsided knowledge acquired by their intellectuals, scholars and leaders. They will develop tunnel vision about what makes social, economic and political plans, policies, programs and projects either work or fail (Adjibolosoo, 1994, pp. 25–37). Leading men and women who are in charge of running the society may often be severely devoid of the knowledge about the relevance of universal principles and/or natural laws that form the unshakable foundation of human life and true progress. It is also possible that many others who make, interpret and/or enforce the laws in society will be ignorant as well. As such, they will all pursue the quest for justice in society in various directions. In the long run, innocent and law-abiding citizens will fall victim to the continuing human failure in their legal systems.

Any positive successes achieved in developing and enhancing the HF will significantly alter society's views and/or perception of the reasons for the development of legal precepts, institutions and law enforcement agencies. That is, individuals in society will begin to perceive and treat the rate of growth of punitive laws as approximate measures of the magnitude of HF decay and/or underdevelopment rather than good procedures for dealing with problems in society (Adjibolosoo, 1995b).

HUMAN FACTOR DEVELOPMENT: THE PRIMARY MISSION OF ALL AGENCIES OF EDUCATION AND TRAINING

In view of the earlier discussions, universities, other institutions of higher learning and all agencies of education, training and mentoring in every society have the mandate to equip their students with the necessary skills, knowledge, principles and human qualities with which to lead their countries to successfully accomplish the tasks of sustainable human-centered development. The quest for knowledge in these institutions must be an unrelenting search for the truth that will redeem all humanity from its present predicament.

According to a Chinese proverb, "if you want one year of prosperity, grow grain. If you want ten years of prosperity, grow trees. If you want one hundred years of prosperity, grow people" (Kouzes and Posner, 1991, p. 161). The wisdom revealed in this proverb transcends any plans, policies, programs and legislations aimed at improving human performance and well-being through technical improvements. It also refutes the view that continuing technological advancement will solve every human problem in time—maybe when every human being is transformed into a well-behaved robot! Society needs to focus on how to educate, train and mentor people to serve successfully in all marketplaces. The foundation of these programs must be the universal principles and/or laws of life.

Posted in the Abbotsford School District Board Room (British Columbia, Canada) is the following mission statement: "The mission of School District No. 34 (Abbotsford), in partnership with parents and community, is to awaken and nurture in each of its students a drive for life-long learning and excellence through the provision of relevant educational programs which ensure competence, creativity, self-esteem, integrity and social responsibility." Great as this may sound, it cannot be accomplished through temporary ad hoc and/or makeshift education and training programs. The object of this mission statement must be viewed as transcending the short run. Its attainment requires long-term plans, policies and programs devoted to HF development (Adjibolosoo, 1993, 1994, 1995a) rather than the continuing promotion of mere invention, innovation and/or the crafting of technology and its advancement to improve the teaching and learning processes. Likewise, neither could any lasting changes be effected by throwing money at the difficult problems facing all of humanity today. Although technological advancement has been on the increase, humanity needs to understand that it will not solve all its problems.[13] Even in a state of total HF decay and/or underdevelopment, any technological invention and/or innovation may instead increase human suffering, uncertainties and the risk of total annihilation.[14]

The recent financial difficulties besetting the educational sector in the developed countries (DCs) and the national debt situation in developing countries (LDCs) have already dealt severe blows to development programs in each country grouping. These problems must be dealt with as soon as possible. The social, economic, political and cultural difficulties being experienced by both the DCs and LDCs are due primarily to the lack of people who are rich in the necessary HF, not necessarily to lack of technology and abundant capital. To develop the required HF to help overcome these problems, every society needs to pay continuing attention to its existing education systems and training programs to uncover their teething problems. If the education system and training and mentoring programs have failed to produce men and women of dedication, commitment, responsibility, accountability, integrity, trustworthiness, etc., then there is need to make them better equipped to achieve the intended HF development goals. Any quest for knowledge that is not aimed at the improvement of the quality of human life in the long run is a misplaced and wasted effort. Yet, the quality of life cannot improve without HF development.

A restructuring program must, without fail, call for the development of benchmarking standards to be used as performance measurements for the educational system and training programs. All agencies of education in every country must either create new, or revise existing, mission statements to reflect the primary intended national goal—HF development.

The effective and efficient running of business organizations, political machinery, the economy and social institutions requires well-educated, knowledgeable, responsible, trustworthy and accountable citizens. The planning, organization and operation of these institutions require appropriate human qualities and/or characteristics (i.e., the HF) if they are to function as expected in society.

Contrary to popularly held opinion, "the development of human qualities and/or characteristics does not necessarily refer to mere human resource development and human capital acquisition through education and training" (Adjibolosoo, 1993, p. 143). To be effective and efficient in the production process, the people of a nation must also acquire unique human qualities and/or characteristics that will encourage and promote economic progress (i.e., discipline, dedication, responsibility, accountability, integrity and the like). It is these attributes and similar ones that contribute to a successful or unsuccessful utilization of acquired knowledge and skills (Adjibolosoo, 1994, p. 26). Human capital is, therefore, a small segment of the HF (see Table 2.1). Yet, unfortunately, most institutions of higher learning and other agencies of education and training focus solely on knowledge and skill acquisition to the total neglect of whole HF development. This neglect of duty to develop the HF has led to continuing social, economic and political problems in all societies. The LDCs have suffered more severely than the DCs in this regard in the past. At present, the DCs are, unfortunately, depreciating their HF stock.

If all universities and other institutions of learning desire to regain their integrity, it is crucial for them to not only focus on knowledge and skill acquisition, but also to link their academic programs to ongoing HF enhancement. That is, every academic program in each university and other institutions of learning must be tied to the development of human qualities and/or characteristics in order to restore the credibility and effectiveness of education and training in all nations. The acquisition of these unique human characteristics will prepare the labor force to use and/or apply acquired knowledge and information to identify and solve those problems posed by the lack of the HF and economic underdevelopment.

It is definitely the absence of the relevant HF that makes it extremely difficult for graduates from most institutions of learning to enter into their first jobs, ready to perform effectively and efficiently. As universities and colleges look for better ways of accomplishing their duties, attention must be paid to the fact that the integrating core of the education and training programs, the HF, must be made a primary target. Otherwise, these institutions of higher learning will fail continuously to achieve their desired goals.

University mission statements must, therefore, reflect their total commitment to the whole HF development. Institutions that are successful in developing the HF will truly attract huge sums of money for research and continuing HF development programs. However, those universities that continue to focus elsewhere must instead prepare for the day when they will outlive their usefulness and subsequently suffer a similar plight to the dinosaurs. If this happens, the development programs will be faced with severe difficulties of finding the right people to spearhead future recovery initiatives. Husain (1969, p. 365) observed:

[T]he development of the individual enriches and improves society, and a well-organized, free, and just society provides wider opportunities for the individual to grow. In certain situations, however, a greater emphasis deliberately has to be placed on the social purposes of education, and education has to be used as an instrument of social change. . . . We want to raise our standard of living substantially, and to assure a minimum income for each family, or at least, to each planned family. We want to create a new social order based on justice, equality, freedom, and the dignity of the individual. We want to adopt modern science and technology, and, side by side, develop a sense of social responsibility; to generate moral and spiritual values [capital] based on our great traditions.

Truly, education and training must erase previously ineffective cultural practices, attitudes and norms and grow in their place new ones that will meet the challenges and growing needs of specific societies and humanity in general. The role of universities and colleges, again, becomes critical. Pandit Jawaharlal Nehru, speaking at one of the many convocations of the University of Allahabad several years ago said, ''a university stands for tolerance, for reason, for the adventure of ideas and for the search of truth. If it stands for the onward march of the human race toward ever higher goals then it is well with the people'' (quoted in Husain, 1969, p. 367). Likewise, Korolev (1969) once argued that well-rounded educational development implies shaping individuals to successfully undertake both physical and mental work and to acquire and exude spiritual values. Such individuals must contribute to the material well-being of society and participate actively in it.

Drawing from Moyers (1989), it can be suggested that the human search for workable and effective procedures for HF development requires that educational planners and developers walk into the laboratory of the scientist, delve into the vision of the poet, excavate the memory of the historian, dig deeper into the imagination of scholars and writers and thoroughly equip the teacher who will have to employ his or her skills and passion for the continuing well-being of students in particular and humanity in general. The future of both the natural and social sciences in shaping the future of humanity lies in HF development through continuing knowledge acquisition, revision and total integration. The pigeonholing of ideas by higher learning must be dethroned because it hinders true human development and progress. From the HF perspective, people must acquire an understanding of the universal principles of life, live by them, and utilize the six critical dimensions of the HF (see Table 2.1). Any successes achieved in this area will provide every society with the hope and expectation that it discovers lasting solutions to its problems.

At this point, one may ask: ''What do all these observations about the HF mean for African countries?'' To answer, it may be argued that in reality, it means a great deal to them. African countries need to focus on HF development. Failure to do so will keep them in a permanent state of underdevelopment.

CONCLUSION

Modern educational systems and training programs are often simply adhering to techniques rather than attempting to instill in students the central factors of truly valuable education—HF development. Truly, without dedicated, committed, responsible, trustworthy and accountable people, no nation will be able to maintain its status quo, let alone be in a position to achieve meaningful progress. Many LDCs ignored this fact in the past and have, therefore, failed to achieve development. This failure can be turned around when the educational system and training programs are reformulated to produce men and women with an unqualified reservoir of integrity, accountability, responsibility and commitment. For the LDCs, there is no other better way to achieve economic development than a continuing pursuit of HF development. Truly, economically advanced countries that are currently depreciating their existing HF stock will one day face the music of economic underdevelopment, increasing social and political problems, industrial deterioration, and above all, the decline of their civilization. By that time, Africa might have already received the message regarding the significance of the HF to its development program.

It is people who have acquired the HF that will turn the human quest for the ''good life'' into reality. They are a permanent blessing to societies. In their absence, society suffers decay, degradation and permanent decline. It happened to flourishing ancient civilizations in the past; it can happen to modern civilizations, too. Technological development cannot replace HF development programs. These two are more aptly thought of as complements than substitutes. If continuing progress and the ''good life'' are desired by any societies, HF development cannot be a choice—it is a must.

NOTES

1. Professor Harro Van Brummelin's comments on an earlier draft of this chapter are insightful: An obvious conclusion is that you cannot provide meaningful education

unless you have a community that agrees on some basic spiritual, moral and aesthetic value factors. And, in a pluralistic society, that implies the necessity of choice in education—school-based management, charter schools, educational vouchers, funded independent schools, and so on. If there is one conclusion we can draw from research on effective schools, it is that they have a united mission and vision usually based on spiritual, moral and educational approaches.

2. This is assuming that the individual is neither sick nor mentally ill. Individuals who have any other forms of physical disability are capable of developing and/or acquiring the HF. Those with very severe physical disabilities may, however, not be in a position to engage in certain activities, programs, jobs, etc. that require the exertion of continuing physical energy and/or skills. Some of these individuals, depending on the extent of their HF development, may be able to act as excellent leaders for many programs and activities. Suboptimal performance may also result from lack of proper knowledge regarding the stipulations of the laws of nature concerning every sphere of human life and endeavor.

3. In reality, and in general, some leaders often do act like the proverbial ostrich. That is, when problems arise in their societies, they bury their head in the sand after unsuccessfully trying a few ideas that conform to their own ideologies. They then avoid other probable solutions that do not seem to endorse their personal worldview. By so doing, they not only cause more pain and suffering for others in their societies, but also deny them a life of tranquility and comfort.

4. See *My First Nursery Rhymes*, pp. 14–15.

5. Recall that when the proverbial ostrich buried its head in the sand, its assailant was still relentlessly on the chase. As such, the problems being faced by the ostrich did not go away when it buried its head. Although it could no longer see the pursuer, its time of doom was imminent. Truly, certain problems do not go away by merely ignoring or leaving them to chance.

6. Read about the Seven Wonders of the World from any historical source to discover what a well-developed HF can accomplish. In addition, new developments in technology have opened a whole new dimension of knowledge to humanity, and we are now able to accomplish tasks that were only thought to be science fiction a few decades ago.

7. The case of the puppet, Pinnochio, is an illustrative example. Up until the fairy mother came to give it life, Pinnochio was still a lifeless wooden puppet. Even after being blessed with the ability to act and live like a real boy, his conscience rested with a tiny grasshopper who lived in his outside world. Because he hardly ever listened to this external conscience, Pinnochio often got into trouble. In fact, even at times of trouble he would still not listen to sound advice from his conscience.

8. Cases in point include the recent abduction, rape and murder of Melanie Carpenter of Surrey, British Columbia, Canada, and the havoc caused by arsonists in both the Vancouver and Seattle areas.

9. The story was in the news media a few years ago about a man who loaded his revolver, walked next door, rang the doorbell, and killed his neighbor. The angry man argued that he had to do what he did because the neighbor's dog always barked and disturbed him.

10. There are, however, many differences between a person and a machine. For example, while the component parts of a machine can be taken apart separately, fixed, replaced and put back again, this may not always be done successfully with an individual. There are many dimensions to an individual—beyond the physical body parts and organs—that cannot be peeled off in separate strands, fixed, replaced and fitted back to-

gether again. The wholeness of every person requires that he or she engage in relevant activities that are necessary for the development of the *whole person.*

11. Keep in mind that although this analogy is being used, it is somewhat inadequate. Unlike automobiles, human beings are not inanimate machines that merely respond to mechanical manipulations. In reality, human beings are more complicated than the most complex machines ever designed and manufactured by human engineers.

12. An interesting example is found in the Bible. See, for example, Jeremiah, chapter 1, verse 10. Sustained positive human progress requires an ongoing dealing with habits of the heart, customs, pertinent problems and such that militate against programs aimed at the attainment of the best life for all humanity.

13. Today, no technology has been developed to ensure the total development of both spiritual and moral capital. Yet, little financial resources have been alloted for intensive R&D in these critical areas. It is high time society woke up to reality and began to reconsider its attitude of continual denial and/or repression of these important components of the HF and their daily impact on the performance of every human being. Truly, humanity may never discover any technology and/or invention/innovation that can replace the HF. In view of this observation, it is therefore fruitless to pursue technological inventions and innovations and yet be extremely bankrupt in the necessary HF. Maybe the time has come for society to finance research programs aimed at discovering whether or not it is important to create departments and/or faculties in all institutions of learning to develop both spiritual and moral capital.

14. Say, for instance, human energy may be devoted to the development of technology whose sole objective will be to destroy other people—as is usually done in war time.

REFERENCES

Adjibolosoo, S. 1993. "The Human Factor in Development." *The Scandinavian Journal of Development Alternatives* 12 (4): 139–149.

Adjibolosoo, S. 1994. "The Human Factor and the Failure of Development Planning and Economic Policy in Africa." In F. Ezeala-Harrison and S. Adjibolosoo, eds., *Perspectives on Economic Development in Africa.* Westport, Conn.: Praeger.

Adjibolosoo, S. 1995a. *The Human Factor in Developing Africa.* Westport, Conn.: Praeger.

Adjibolosoo, S. 1995b. "A Human Factor Perspective on Failing Social Institutions and Systems." Unpublished discussion paper, Trinity Western University, Langley, B.C., Canada.

Adjibolosoo, S. 1995c. "Achieving Optimal Quality and Productivity: The Passions." In D. J. Sumanth, J. A. Edosomwan, R. Poupart and C. G. Thor, eds., *Productivity and Quality Management Frontiers—V.* Norcross, GA: Industrial Engineering Press.

Husain, Z. 1969. "The Never-Ending Pursuit of Learning." In D. Toppin, ed., *This Cybernetic Age.* New York: Human Development Corporation.

Korolev, F. F. 1969. "Rounded Development of the Human Personality." In D. Toppin, ed., *This Cybernetic Age.* New York: Human Development Corporation.

Kouzes, J. M. and Posner, B. Z. 1991. *The Leadership Challenge: How to Get Extraordinary Things Done in Organizations.* Oxford: Jossey-Bass Publishers.

Moyers, B. 1989. *A World of Ideas: Conversations with Thoughtful Men and Women*

About American Life Today and the Ideas Shaping Our Future. New York: Doubleday.

Peter, L. J. 1977. *Peter's Quotations: Ideas for Our Time.* New York: Bantam Books.

Smyth, D. M. 1969. ''The Community for Human Development.'' In D. Toppin, ed., *This Cybernetic Age.* New York: Human Development Corporation.

3

Educating Sub-Saharan African Students to Participate in National Development Programs: The Role of Indigenous African Writers

John A. Anonby

INTRODUCTION

It would be difficult to overestimate the significance of the influence of indigenous African writers in the challenging and complex process of nation-building. Even though writers may not necessarily represent the prevailing popular opinions of a particular time or place, they are likely to be among the most articulate voices in the land, and the issues raised by their literary works have the potential to become widely disseminated, not only within their own countries but abroad.

While the outside world of the international community attempts to evaluate the development of African nations in broad economic, sociological and political terms, indigenous African writers—strategically placed within their own societies—are endowed with the unique opportunity to transmute these issues into human terms. Mere statistics do not have the capacity to stir hearts; it is only as these broader issues are incarnated into the human factor (HF) and intertwined with the lives of ordinary men and women, that the fruits of long-range development can be secured.[1] Good literature translates abstract issues into vibrant realities, filtered through the sensibilities of the characters on the stage in drama and in the pages of short stories and novels.

FUNCTIONS OF THE EFFECTUAL WRITER

The function of an effectual writer can be viewed, like the points of a star, as five-fold, each involving an awesome responsibility. The first of these is the mandate to articulate the aspirations of one's society. For this reason, it is particularly the indigenous African writer whose voice needs to be heard. Even as sympathetic an author as Alan Paton was to the millions of disenfranchised blacks in South Africa, he could not represent South African national goals in their fullest measure.

Secondly, an effective writer should function as a kind of national conscience—a responsibility that places demands upon the author's society and on the writer. Frequently, a nation is beset with overwhelming social and economic problems as well as blatant inequities—in Africa and on other continents. The enticements of patronage and prospects of personal advantage put enormous temptations in front of aspiring authors to ignore issues that need to be addressed and redressed. There is also a great temptation for the most powerful participants in a society to repress ideas that may be deemed a threat to the status quo, as indicated by the widespread censorship laws of South Africa over the past few decades. The conscience of a nation must be allowed to express itself, and this might well be through the pen of the perceptive writer.

The third responsibility of the writer is to depict his or her country or region with accuracy. Travel brochures frequently focus on the grander features of a nation's landscape, its larger cities, and its unique customs, but the real lives of people are often hidden from tourists' eyes; it is at this point that the skilled writer, thoroughly immersed in his or her culture, is able to reveal the essence of people's struggles, as in Ngugi wa Thiong'o's *Secret Lives* (1975), a collection of short stories set in Kenya.

Another essential mandate of the literary artist is to preserve the memory of the cultural heritage of a particular people group, whether of a clan, tribe or nation, as Chinua Achebe has done so successfully in *Arrow of God* (1964) in connection with the Ibo peoples of Nigeria and as Thiong'o has similarly accomplished for the Kikuyus in his exquisite novel, *The River Between* (1965). In the changing African continental scene, with the burgeoning growth of cities and the accompanying population movements, along with international impacts of every kind, regional particularities are susceptible to transformation and even obliteration. Literature has the capacity to preserve the flavor of a particular time and place, and the intellectual heritage of the past could well become a precious legacy for the future.

The fifth—and possibly the greatest—challenge to the aspiring writer is to present a vision of what his or her nation might become if its internal conflicts can be addressed positively rather than negatively. The ancient adage, "Without a vision, the people perish,"[2] is as true in social and political terms as it is in its initial spiritual application. The writer who is able to offer a glimpse of the potential greatness that might be realized if a nation can transcend its internal differences is a gift no society can afford to squander. Thiong'o, for instance, in *A Grain of Wheat* (1967), attributes the successful overthrow of colonialism in Kenya to the ever-expanding vision of the freedom fighters who had foreseen a unified land stretching "from one horizon touching the sea to the other resting on the great Lake" p. (11).

Table 3.1
African Writers and Their Concerns

Writer	Book(s)	Issues of Concern (i.e., the problem)	Year of Publication
Chinua Achebe	*No Longer at Ease*	self-gratification, bribery and political corruption	1963
	Man of the People	political opportunism	1966
	The Trouble with Nigeria		1983
Ngugi wa Thiong'o	*Petals of Blood*	Political and economic exploitation	1977
R. L. Petini	*Hill of Fools*	clan feuds and folly of violence	1976

SELECTING REPRESENTATIVE INDIGENOUS WRITINGS FOR THE STUDY

Selecting representative indigenous writings from sub-Saharan Africa in relation to the issues mentioned above is no easy task, as the number of noteworthy works have proliferated impressively since Achebe's stellar work, *Things Fall Apart* (1958), appeared on the literary landscape of West Africa. Achebe has not only been adulated as "Africa's most celebrated writer" (Abrahams, 1986, p. 83), but he has achieved international acclaim as "one of the master novelists of the twentieth century."[3] *Things Fall Apart* is a penetrating analysis of the points of incompatibility between the traditional beliefs and customs of the Ibo people of Eastern Nigeria and the Christianity introduced by European colonialists and missionaries, but two subsequent Achebe novels, *No Longer At Ease* (1960) and *A Man of the People* (1966), are more pertinent to the HF relating to national development, both prior and subsequent to the achievement of political independence (see Table 3.1).

Picturing sub-Saharan Africa as a triangle with its points in West, South and East Africa, this chapter will start with a selection of a South African indigenous writer. To concentrate on the HF, the focus will be on a comparatively obscure but skilled Xhosa novelist, R. L. Petini, who departs from the politically popular theme of racial conflicts between the blacks and the whites in South Africa in order to portray representative clan factions within the tribal communities. Published in Capetown and London in the same year (1976), Petini's *Hill of Fools* exposes the futility of resorting to violence as a means of solving social tensions.[4]

The situation in East Africa has a closer resemblance in its historical development to West Africa than to South Africa, and Thiong'o's novels, like those

of Achebe, are penetrating analyses of the transition from colonial to independent status, though Thiong'o's works emphasize the struggle and the violence
in this process to a greater extent than Achebe's. The novel most analogous to
Achebe's *No Longer at Ease* and *A Man of the People* is Thiong'o's *Petals of
Blood* (1977), in which Thiong'o explores some of the political options facing
East African nations such as Kenya and places the responsibility for their future
on their own decisions.

ISSUES OF CONCERN TO AFRICAN WRITERS: ACHEBE

Returning to Achebe, it should be noted that while *No Longer at Ease* and
A Man of the People are not didactic novels in an overt sense, they are nevertheless highly illuminating, instructive and sobering works that highlight some
of the HF that is shaping African nations such as Nigeria. With a narrower focus
than either *Things Fall Apart* or *A Man of the People*, *No Longer at Ease* is,
on the surface, a simple and straightforward narrative of a young man, Obi
Okonkwo, who has returned to his own country, Nigeria, after successfully completing his B.A. in English at a British university with a sponsorship by a union
in his hometown, the Umuofia Progressive Union. Achebe's title, *No Longer At
Ease*, is taken from a resonant phrase in T. S. Eliot's "Journey of the Magi,"
a poem in which Eliot depicts the sense of alienation felt by the Magi upon
returning to their own land and its idols, subsequent to their encounter with the
Christ Child. Obi's protracted time abroad has reshaped many of his values and,
like the Magi, he finds himself ill at ease in most of the situations he encounters
back in his homeland. While some critics of African literature such as Eustace
Palmer (1979) consider *No Longer at Ease* as "inferior" to *Things Fall Apart*
in "range of conception and intensity of realization" as well as in plot and
insight,[5] David Cook (1977) maintains "that there are levels beneath levels in
the book which together make up a complex analysis of the issues"[6] addressed.

The central issue in *No Longer at Ease* is the intense conflict between personal
integrity and self-gratification which is played out in the life of the protagonist,
Obi. At the age of "twelve or thirteen, he had passed his Standard Six examination at the top of the whole province," and he had subsequently graduated
from a prestigious secondary school with "the Cambridge School Certificate
with distinction in all eight subjects" (Achebe, 1963, p. 7). His exceptional
potential was recognized by some of his fellow villagers, who had formed "their
union with the aim of collecting money to send some of their brighter young
men to study in England" (p. 6). Obi was the recipient of the first scholarship
under this plan, but there were strings attached. The 800 pound scholarship had
to be repaid within four years of his return—a financial obligation that was to
place Obi under considerable financial duress, with concomitant pressures,
throughout the course of the novel.

With his university degree, however, Obi has obtained "the philosopher's
stone" that can transmute "a third-class clerk . . . into a senior civil servant. . . .

it raised a man from the masses to the elite'' (Achebe, 1960, p. 84). Obi does, in fact, receive a posting in the Civil Service, just as he had hoped. In spite of all these glorious prospects, however, Obi's future is a clouded one—as the reader discovers, rather surprisingly, on the first page of the novel. The story opens with Obi awaiting his sentence for accepting a bribe of twenty pounds, and his apprehensions are confirmed when he is sent to prison—to the great dismay of his sponsors, who had hired a lawyer to defend him.

By means of a fascinating retrospective technique, Achebe constructs virtually the entire narrative as a kind of flashback that, in effect, answers the reader's question as to why a highly intelligent and advantaged young man would jeopardize an entire future by sacrificing his integrity for a bribe. It is evident from his choice of subject in this novel that Achebe is not merely cognizant of, but concerned with, the ubiquitous and rampant scourge of bribery, which has been estimated as consuming 60 percent of the wealth of at least one of the countries of West Africa (Achebe, 1983, p. 40). The cost of bribery in terms of the loss of integrity and trust is clearly evident, but there is also a hidden cost in terms of the denial of genuine merit, which Achebe astutely recognizes as "a form of social injustice which can hurt not only the individuals concerned but ultimately the whole society" (p. 21).

A writer less skilled than Achebe would have exposed Obi's culpability in bold censorious terms. The plausibility of *No Longer At Ease* is due largely to Achebe's sensitive and realistic depiction of the circumstances and protracted pressures that Obi faced prior to his courtroom appearance. Even though Obi is not an appealing or winsome character—at times he is even depicted as antipathetic—his circumstances extract a measure of understanding, if not sympathy, from the reader. This can partially be accounted for by Obi's initial disapproval of bribery when he returns to Nigeria after his university studies in England. He censures the corruption of the "so-called experienced men at the top" of the Civil Service, while rather idealistically maintaining that young university graduates "come straight to the top without bribing anyone" (Achebe, 1960, pp. 17–18). When Obi, himself, is being interviewed as a possible candidate for the Civil Service, he feels insulted when the interlocutor overtly raises the issue of taking bribes.

In another later episode, Obi expresses his indignation towards two policemen who had almost accepted a bribe of two shillings from a lorry driver at a road block. The driver, however, in effect, tells Obi to mind his own business. On another occasion, Obi discovers that one of his close friends, Joseph, has lost his job at the post office, ostensibly "for sleeping while on duty"; the real reason was that the chief clerk who had hired him "had been looking for a way to deal with him since he had not completed the payment of ten pounds' bribe which he had promised when he was employed" (p. 71). Having successfully attained the coveted status of a civil servant, Obi gets an opportunity to test his commitment to his ideals. A young man, Mr. Mark, learns that Obi is the secretary of the scholarship commission, and he broadly hints that he would offer "kola" (p. 80) if Obi would be willing to use his influence in connection with Mark's sister's application to study in England. Politely, but firmly, Obi states that there is no "point in continuing this discussion" (p. 79).

Gloating over the facile manner with which he has handled this affair, Obi is nevertheless forced to acknowledge to himself that he has not been immune to the temptation to accept Mr. Mark's bribe. Besides the heavy obligation to repay the scholarship that made possible his degree, other unwelcome financial obligations begin to mount: his brother John's school fees, vehicle insurance, his mother's medical expenses and an abortion for his lover Clara, whom he has planned to marry in spite of the obdurate disapproval of his parents. These pressures, culminating in Clara's abandonment of Obi, leave him dispirited and vulnerable, and he finally yields to bribery—reluctantly, but routinely. The novel abruptly ends with his arraignment, which brings the reader, full circle, back to the events that open the novel.

Reprehensible as bribery is, with its capacity to paralyze national development programs, the issue is not solely one of personal integrity, though this factor looms large in *No Longer at Ease*. Achebe has also interwoven into the fabric of this novel the salient factor of communal responsibility. Obi's fellow villagers, who had sponsored him, had an agenda of their own, relating to their special interests. They "wanted him to read law so that when he returned he would handle all their land cases against their neighbors" (p. 6). Obi, in effect, has been "bribed" to return favors to his villagers. It is also expected by the community that the person who has risen from their ranks into a position of political power will represent them appropriately by displaying his automobile, living in an acceptably impressive dwelling, or by demonstrating comparable tokens of prestige—all of which place acute financial pressures on civil servants such as Obi. The attitude of the president of the Umofia Progressive Union is particularly revealing in relation to Obi's arrest: "I am against people reaping where they have not sown. But we have a saying that if you want to eat a toad you should look for a fat and juicy one" (p. 5). The shame Obi's fellowmen feel has less to do with the bribe than with the paltry amount of twenty pounds for which Obi had risked his reputation and their honor.

Achebe's courageous endeavor to function as a kind of national conscience is even more impressive in *A Man of the People* than in *No Longer at Ease*. *A Man of the People* is a bold attack on the great threat to a nation's well-being represented by unprincipled political opportunism. The relevant message in the novel was widely recognized when its publication almost coincided with the January 1966 *coup d'etat* in Nigeria. Set in "the highly political times" (Achebe, 1966, p. 1) following the achievement of independence from the colonial powers, the novel offers a comic, yet penetrating, analysis of the corrupting powers of privilege, position, and money" (Palmer, 1979, p. 73). In his literary innovativeness, Achebe presents the career of "Chief the Honourable M. A. Nanga, M. P.," the "most approachable politician in the country" (Achebe, 1966, p. 1), but he does so through the consciousness of the protagonist, Odili, whose first person narration colors all of the events in the book. While Odili's initial admiration for Chief Nanga turns to disillusionment, Odili subsequently modifies his negative attitude when Nanga expresses his serious intention to sponsor Odili for a university graduate program in England. These bright prospects disintegrate, however, when Odili discovers that his girlfriend, Elsie, has been easily seduced by Nanga. Odili's sense of shame, combined with his implacable fury, propels him to challenge Nanga at the polls. While Odili is not successful in this endeavor, Nanga's brutal electioneering tactics create so much unrest in the country that a military *coup d'etat* overthrows the government, whereupon Nanga and his fellow ministers are locked up to await trial.

The major irony in the narrative is linked to the recurring similarities the reader detects between Nanga, the unscrupulous and opportunistic politician, and his unrelenting critic, Odili, whose love of adulation, physical comforts and attractive women subtly but clearly indicates comparable propensities—the major difference being that Nanga has achieved his goals, whereas Odili has not. Achebe is, therefore, simultaneously satirizing the unprincipled behavior of elected political figures and exposing the hypocrisy of the cynical masses who elect them: "Tell them that this man had used his position to enrich himself and they would ask you . . . if you thought that a sensible man would spit out the juicy morsel that good fortune placed in his mouth" (Achebe, 1966, p. 2).

While political turpitude manifests itself in many ways in *A Man of the People*, Achebe singles out three areas of paramount concern: unprincipled opportunism, incompetency and intimidation. Chief Nanga was an unknown back-bencher in the governing People's Organization Party (P.O.P) prior to his sudden emergence into prominence due to some rather bizarre events. A slump in the international coffee market, coinciding with an imminent election, induced the prime minister to order the National Bank to print fifteen million pounds rather than drop the price of coffee for the many farmers who supported the P.O.P., against the sound advice of the minister of finance, who was "a first-rate economist with a Ph.D. in public finance" (p. 3). The minister of finance and the many cabinet members who supported him were promptly sacked and publicly denounced as "conspirators and traitors who had teamed up with foreign saboteurs to destroy the new nation" (p. 3). Seeing his opportunity, Nanga shouts from the back benches, "they deserve to be hanged" (p. 5). He is subsequently appointed as minister of culture.

Nanga, whose academic achievements are far more modest than Odili's, is so far out of his depth that someone else has to write his speech for him at an exhibition of works by local authors. He embarrasses himself as well as the writers present, as he does not even know their names. Odili, who is also at the event, sardonically muses to himself, "I had expected that in a country where writers were so few they would all be known personally to the Minister of Culture" (p. 61). Nanga, nevertheless, received applause when he "announced in public that he had never heard of his country's most famous novel" (p. 65).

By anecdotal episodes such as these, Achebe's satire is directed not only towards suave politicians but the unreflecting masses who elect them (see Table 3.1).

Political opportunism and incompetency, albeit deplorable, are eclipsed by the even more sinister evil of intimidation tactics. As a "born politician," Chief Nanga "could get away with almost anything he said or did. . . . He had that rare gift of making people feel. . . . that there was not a drop of ill will in his entire frame" (p. 65). This description introduces the chapter when the irresolvable disagreement over Elsie occurs, and from this point Odili is singled out by Nanga as a threat with which to deal. When Odili announces that he is contesting Nanga's seat, strange occurrences transpire. Villagers pretend to greet Odili, and suddenly knock off his cap and kick him. At a political rally held in Nanga's honor, Odili is sighted and mauled before being taken to the hospital. A friend of Odili, Max, is run over by a jeep and killed. Vengeful tactics such as these, engaged in by Nanga and some of his party members, demonstrate that Nanga is not devoid of ill will. Nevertheless, the sudden toppling of the entire government indicates Achebe's conviction that political irresponsibility is likely to contain the seeds of its own disintegration. Personal and corporate integrity are essential antidotes against economic instability and political unrest.

ISSUES OF CONCERN TO AFRICAN WRITERS: PETINI

Moving to the southern point of the sub-Saharan triangle, the setting is shifted from West Africa to South Africa. Petini's *Hill of Fools,* as assessed by Barnett (1983) in *A Vision of Order: A Study of Black South African Literature in English (1914–1980)*, is "an unpretentious, interesting and touching story told by a talented writer" (p. 156). Set in the South African "homeland" of Ciskei, the narrative hints only peripherally at the larger political picture in the country. The mobility of blacks is, for example, carefully controlled by the "influx control laws" (Petini, 1976, p. 42), making it very difficult, and sometimes impossible, for people to maneuver themselves out of their dilemmas. The obvious, but effectively depicted, Romeo and Juliet theme in the novel is reinforced by the crisis faced by the pregnant Zuziwe and her lover, Bhuka, who do not have the freedom to move to Port Elizabeth, away from their feuding clans. As a result, Zuziwe undergoes a risky abortion, and dies.

The dominating literary image in the novel, clearly displayed in the title, is the Hill of Fools, a highly visible landmark in the territory occupied by the Hlubi village of Kwazidenge. Across the Xesi River lies the land of the rival Thembu clan, where Bhuka resides. Early in the novel, Zuziwe, while relaxing by the river, meets Bhuka who falls in love with her at first sight. Had this encounter transpired in an earlier era, there would have been no problem; in fact, "large stepping stones for crossing the river and facilitating communication between the two villages" (Petini, 1976, p. 5) were still ensconced in the river. For many years, however, the Thembu and the Hlubi clans have been in a state of hostility, though the origins of their mutual hatred have been lost in the mists of obscurity. Periodic eruptions of "faction fights" (p. 147) have taken their toll of lives, leaving a legacy of grief and fear.

The Hill of Fools, in particular, is the rallying place for the young warrior class of the Hlubis, a group of young men who enflame each other with their hatred of the Thembus. The blowing of a horn from the hill is the time-honored signal for another attack on the Thembu community. The nomenclenture of the "Hill of Fools" indicates, rather blatantly, Petini's uncompromising stance on the issue of violence (see Table 3.1). It is, for Petini, folly of the worst order and, as developments in the narrative make clear, it resolves nothing. Even prior to her initial encounter with Bhuka, Zuziwe describes as "nonsense" (p. 3) the argument of her fellow villager, Deliza, who has categorically stated that "a Thembu boy has no right to set foot on Hlubi soil" (p. 2). Petini's scrutiny of the mentality that prompts Deliza's outburst is particularly revealing:

I hate them because I must. I was brought up to hate them. I know that a Thembu boy must be attacked and hit very hard and be killed. Don't ask me why I must kill them. Ask the sun and the moon and the stars. . . . If I didn't believe that a Thembu boy must be destroyed, I would not be a true Hlubi boy. (p. 3)

Petini's castigation of mindless traditions such as this is implicit in Zuziwe's disgust: "She walked on, hoping that he would go back to the Hill of Fools with his madness" (p. 3).

The tragic irony of the story lies in the fact that it is Zuziwe who, in spite of her abhorrence of violence, becomes its chief victim. While her love for Bhuka increases in its intensity, she encounters the strong disapproval of her elder brother, Duma, whose antipathy towards the Thembus is cut from the same cloth as Deliza's. She also incurs, understandably enough, the jealous rage of Ntabeni, a man considerably older than herself whom she is supposed to marry. When she conveys to him her inclination to break off their engagement, he becomes furious and beats her vehemently with his walking stick. This assault proves counterproductive and even partially alienates Ntabeni from Zuziwe's parents, who frankly rebuke him for using "the language of violence" (p. 67). This hypocritical character, though a lay preacher and deacon of the Presbyterian Church of Africa, has "an unquenchable thirst for home-made beer and a short temper" (p. 45)—but his vengeful nature manifests itself in a far more sinister manner. Realizing that he can never regain Zuziwe's favor while Bhuka is alive, he resorts to the desperate measure of enticing the young warrior men who have assembled at the Hill of Fools to kill Bhuka by stealth when he again appears at the river. This devious plan miscarries, however, as Bhuka is merely wounded by the stones thrown at him. His call for help from his fellow Thembus, how-ever, leads to a full-scale faction fight with the Hlubis and results in the death of Zuziwe's cousin, Katana, who was apparently killed by Bhuka. The inten-sified bitterness between the clans makes further contact between Zuziwe and Bhuka virtually impossible. This plunges Zuziwe into despair; she has an abortion and dies, having lost her will to live, and leaves her family and Bhuka to mourn.

Petini's inescapable message in this stirring novel is the pointlessness of the tragedy that engulfed Zuziwe; as her father clearly states, "violence does not solve anything" (p. 66). The futility of the devastation is also highlighted by the fact that some of the people in the opposing clans are related to each other; Zuziwe makes periodic visits to her paternal aunt in the Thembu village and is treated as a daughter. Furthermore, Zuziwe's mother, Mrs. Langa, is "tormented by the violent clashes between the Hlubis and the Thembus" (pp. 33–34) and she devoutly prays that God will intervene: "why was there so much hate between man and man, between family and family, between nation and nation?" (p. 33). As these questions are considered, it becomes clear that Petini is depicting the rival clans as a microcosm of the tribal conflicts of the country, or even the continent, as a whole (see Table 3.1). If South Africa's racial problems are ever to be solved, surely the rivalry between tribes needs to be replaced by an awareness that their potential—or even survival—is contingent on their willingness to unite for the common good, as was recently demonstrated in the coming together of Nelson Mandela and Chief Mangosuthu Buthelezi in the first free elections in South Africa. It is in such a spirit of amicability and common purpose that real national development can take place.

ISSUES OF CONCERN TO AFRICAN WRITERS: THIONG'O

Focusing on the East African scene, Thiong'o's *Petals of Blood* depicts postcolonial Kenya. Unlike Achebe's *A Man of the People*, which appeared shortly after Nigeria's transition towards independence, Thiong'o's novel was completed more than twenty years subsequent to Kenya's achievement of independence in 1963. Parts of it were written in Kenya and the United States, and it was completed while Thiong'o was a visiting guest in Russia in 1975, though it was not published until 1977. It is a powerful, resonant and intricately structured novel, with a fascinating retrospective plot arrangement, similar to Achebe's *No Longer at Ease* but more complex. The novel is comprised of a series of flashbacks on the part of four closely linked characters who, at the opening of the novel, are all separately summoned by the police for questioning in connection with a large fire in which three of the most prominent citizens in the town of Ilmorog have been burned to death. As in a detective novel, the suspense is sustained throughout most of the narrative; the identity of the arsonist is not disclosed until the reader has had many glimpses into the hidden lives of the four protagonists, thereby leading the reader to a plausible conclusion.

Like *A Man of the People*, *Petals of Blood* is a powerful expose of the political and economic corruption of a post-colonial nation, but unlike its counterpart, Thiong'o's novel is almost completely devoid of satire. *Petals of Blood* is an intensely serious and scathing denunciation of the capitalistic "imperialism" (Thiong'o, 1977, p. 342), which has taken the place of the colonial imperialism that held sway prior to independence. Though clearly propagandist in its message, this novel is sustained by a variety of masterful imagistic techniques. The title, *Petals of Blood*, for instance, borrowed from a phrase in Derek Walcott's poem, "The Swamp," becomes a multifoliate metaphor for the blossoming of violence in a land that should be savoring the fruits of freedom. The symbol can also be viewed in positive terms, suggesting vitality and sustenance, or it can be an image of destruction, like the tongues of flame, "forming petals of blood" (p. 333), which burned down Wanja's whorehouse. This destruction, however, motivates Wanja to change her direction in life, thus prefiguring the possibility of a new and better society rising, Phoenix-like, out of the old.

Thiong'o's central theme—political and economic exploitation—is filtered through the traumatic life experiences of the four major characters. Munira, the first protagonist to appear in the novel, is a respected schoolmaster who has seen the tiny village of Ilmorog transformed into the thriving town of New Ilmorog, an industrial and tourist center aptly described by Palmer (1979) as a "microcosm of Kenyan society as a whole" (p. 156). Munira has always felt alienated from his family and particularly his father, a devout Christian who, years before, had refused to take "the Mau Mau oath for African Land and Freedom" (Thiong'o, 1977, p. 341). However, he is quite willing to take an oath "to protect the wealth in the hands of only a few" (p. 341)—the current politicians who are lining their own pockets and disregarding the plight of the working masses. Also estranged from his wife, who lives near his parents in Limuru, Munira has some isolated affairs with Wanja and Lillian. Eventually, Lillian becomes a Christian fanatic, but her "talk about new worlds with Christ" (p. 314) captures the imagination of Munira, whose new faith finally gives him a focus in his life.

One of Munira's close acquaintances is Abdulla who, as a youth, was a freedom fighter for the Mau Mau and had lost his cousin, Nding'uri, in the conflict. Though merely a poor fruit seller, he adopts a homeless waif, Joseph, whom Wanja helps to sponsor as a student in a prestigious school. Abdulla earns a temporary but widespread fame when he, an amputee with only one leg and a donkey, leads a small delegation to Nairobi to publicize the drought that is devastating Ilmorog. This delegation consists of Wanja, Munira, Joseph and himself, along with an acquaintance of Munira named Karega, an itinerant worker who eventually is hired to teach in Munira's school. As events unfold, Abdulla discovers that Karega is the brother of his cousin, Nding'uri, who had been hanged for assisting the Mau Mau. It is also discovered that Nding'uri had been betrayed by Kimeria—a suave and heartless man who also had seduced Wanja and almost ruined her life. Wanja's life had also been fragmented by the cleavage in her family, between the supporters of the colonial regime and those sympathetic to Mau Mau, such as her mother and her grandparents.

This network of interconnections ties into one main strand, which is the characters' realization that their links with Mau Mau have not benefited them personally, whereas opportunistic and treacherous individuals such as Kimeria, who had worked against the freedom fighters, are now thriving in post-colonial Kenya. Their bitter awareness of this irony propels them into different courses of action that, in effect, demonstrate the options Ngugi sees as available to developing countries in Africa: exploitation, escapism and revolutionary activism.

The first of these, exploitation, is Wanja's choice, though not initially. In search of a new beginning, she joins her grandmother, Nyakinyua, on the latter's small shamba (plot of land) near Ilmorog. Wanja inspires the women of the area to cultivate the land "in common" (Thiong'o, 1976, p. 200), and their success prompts them to undertake another communal enterprise, the brewing of an intoxicating traditional drink made from the theng'eta plant, which has four tiny red petals. The economic transformation of the community attracts the attention of some big business magnates from Nairobi such as Mzigo, who purchases their enterprise and, through deception, assumes control of the franchise to produce the popular brew. This episode, typifying for Thiong'o the national and even international economic measures that have invaded Kenya's traditional tribal lands, so embitters Wanja that she abandons communal endeavors in favor of exploitive measures. Cynically concluding that "you eat or you are eaten" (p. 294), she becomes "the most powerful woman in all Ilmorog" (p. 281) and a wealthy owner of houses, *matatus* (taxicabs), transport lorries, and Sunshine Lodge, a whorehouse located, suggestively, near All Saints Church.

Escapism as an option is imaged in the responses and actions of Munira. This character, described by Robson (1979) as a "fragment" rather than "a fully rounded character" (Thiong'o, 1977, p. 99) is, to be sure, somewhat of an enigma, but Robson's view that Munira detracts from the novel is, arguably, off target. It is precisely because Munira is such an alienated, rejected and fragmented character that he decides to purify this world by setting fire to Wanja's whorehouse to "save" Karega from the embrace of Wanja, who has turned her affections away from Munira. Karega, in fact, has been highly resistant to Munira's persistent "talk about new worlds with Christ" (p. 314). Munira "had been so convinced that this world was wrong, was a mistake, that he wanted all of his friends to see this and escape in time. . . . He followed Wanja; he followed Abdulla; he followed Karega. But it was Karega in whom he was most interested" (p. 332).

For Karega, however, "religion, any religion, was a weapon against the workers" (p. 305). He believes in a "human kingdom" (p. 303) and a "world in which the wealth of our land shall belong to us all" (p. 327), as he affirms to Wanja. He takes comfort from the revolutions that have taken place against imperialistic regimes and is apprehended as a suspect in the burning of Wanja's house of prostitution because of his attempts to form a powerful workers' union. Karega's communication of his political and social convictions to Wanja has a powerful effect, and Wanja carries out her ideological and personal revenge against Kimeria by hacking him to death in her brothel—an action that is never detected by anyone, as his body was burned in the fire that obliterated Sunshine

Lodge that very night. Her narrow escape from the burning ruins, facilitated by Abdulla's timely rescue, images her emergence into a better way of life.

Thiong'o's hope for the future of the world is epitomized in Joseph, the young waif rescued from oblivion by Abdulla, sponsored in school by Wanja and influenced by Karega. Joseph's goal is to complete his school and university studies so he can "contribute to the liberation of the people of this country" (p. 339). Inspired by the example of the Mau Mau and his reading of history, he has noted the "people's revolutions in China, Cuba, Vietnam, Cambodia, Laos, Angola, Guinea, Mozambique" (pp. 339–40).

Thiong'o's overtly leftist interpretation of history, with his myopic disregard of the countless millions whose blood was spilt to "purge" societies in order to "create . . . a new earth" (p. 294), seems somewhat ironic in view of the subsequent collapse of the communist bloc and the unfolding events in Joseph's list of emancipated countries. Nevertheless, Thiong'o's vision of a society— national or international—free of exploitation demands sober reflection (see Table 3.1). The proliferating slums in so many of the large cities of the world, and the colossal disparities that exist between the "have" and "have not" nations, are intrusive evidences that all is not well in our global village.

LESSONS AND POLICY RECOMMENDATIONS

In the representative writings scrutinized, it is apparent that Achebe, Petini and Thiong'o have candidly exposed some of the more acute problems in their respective regions of the African continent. It is, however, also evident that virtually all of the issues addressed are similar (or parallel) to problems in many other parts of the globe, these are human problems—and humanly created difficulties are amenable to human solutions. While most of the selected novels tend to accentuate the problems rather than their resolutions, some of the necessary remedial measures are implicit.

Achebe's *No Longer at Ease* demonstrates, for example, the folly of pursuing a course of self-gratification or yielding to the pressures of bribery. The work clearly implies that aspiring societies and the individuals within them stand to gain much more in the long run by resisting these debilitating practices (see Table 3.1). Similarly, the political shenanigans satirized in *A Man of The People*—with its unprincipled political opportunism, incompetency and intimidation—heighten awareness of the need for a society to institute strict measures of political accountability.

In *Hill of Fools*, Petini unequivocally denounces the irrationality of clan or tribal conflicts that are being perpetuated simply because of historical enmities. Instead of the futility of violence, he suggests that the citizens of his country should emulate Zuziwe, the heroine of his novel, who views members of opposing tribes as individuals much like herself and is willing to establish meaningful relationships with them, in spite of the prejudices of her own clan. For Petini, human worth takes precedence over tribal differences (see Table 3.1).

Thiong'o, in *Petals of Blood*, is primarily concerned with the political and economic exploitation that perpetuates, and often exacerbates, the disparities that exist between the rich and the poor (see Table 3.1). The only viable course for Ngugi is an ongoing revolutionary activism that will eventually usher in a classless, communalistic society. Unfolding events in Eastern Europe would seem to indicate, however, that Thiong'o's vision of an egalitarian order is more likely to be realized by expanding free trade alliances among nations, and even continents, throughout the world.

CONCLUSION

African writers such as Achebe, Petini and Thiong'o are not able to provide all of the solutions desired, but their candid and penetrating analyses of some of the societal and political problems they have detected have arrested their readers' complacency and enlarged their scope of awareness.

Since the HF is crucial to the attainment of progress in Africa (Adjibolosoo, 1995, chapter 5), and since indigenous literature is a valuable vehicle for analyzing the interconnections between significant national issues and the human beings who must wrestle with them, progressive measures should be taken to encourage the effective use of African literature to facilitate HF engineering and sustained human-centered development among youth. Some feasible suggestions might include:

1. The inclusion of representative works by the nation's best writers in both secondary and post-secondary curricula.

2. The offer of prizes (medals or monetary) to the best essays exploring significant national issues relating to these works.

3. The offer of prizes (medals or monetary) to the best writer of fiction in a regional school, using the name of a significant national writer (e.g., "The Chinua Achebe Literary Prize").

4. University entrance scholarships for students who have demonstrated superior prowess in handling their national literary heritage.

Measures such as these would foster the awareness of the fine quality and international significance of the literature of a number of African nations. Such measures would also heighten the realization that the most relevant solutions to pressing issues might well emerge from a nation's own citizens rather than from abroad.

NOTES

1. See Chapter 2 for a detailed definition and discussion on the role of the HF in development.

2. *The Holy Bible* (Proverbs 29:18).

3. See Achebe (1990), p. 40.

4. The very recent dismantling of apartheid has created a new scenario in South Africa, and forthcoming literary works are likely to explore a variety of new directions.

5. See Palmer (1972), p. 63.

6. See Cook (1977), p. 83.

REFERENCES

Abrahams, C. A. 1986. *Essays on Literature.* St. Laurent, Quebec: AFO Enterprises.

Achebe, C. 1958. *Things Fall Apart.* Nairobi, Kenya: Heinemann.

Achebe, C. 1966. *A Man of the People.* Nairobi, Kenya: Heinemann Kenya.

Achebe, C. 1974 [1964]. *Arrow of God.* Nairobi, Kenya: Heinemann.

Achebe, C. 1983. *The Trouble With Nigeria.* Nairobi, Kenya: Heinemann Kenya.

Achebe, C. 1988 [1963]. *No Longer at Ease.* Nairobi, Kenya: Heinemann Kenya.

Achebe, C. 1990. "African Literature as Celebration." *New African* (March): 40.

Adjibolosoo, S. 1995. *The Human Factor in Developing Africa.* Westport, Conn.: Praeger.

Barnett, U. A. 1983. *A Vision of Order: A Study of Black South African Literature in English (1914–1980).* London: Sinclair Browne; Amherst, Mass.: University of Massachusetts Press.

Cook, D. 1977. *African Literature: A Critical View.* London: Longman.

Palmer, E. 1972. *An Introduction to the African Novel.* London: Heinemann.

Palmer, E. 1979. "Ngugi's *Petals of Blood.*" *African Literature Today* 10: 153–166.

Petini, R. L. 1976. *Hill of Fools.* London: Heinemann Kenya.

Robson, C. B. 1979. *Ngugi wa Thiong'o.* London: Macmillan.

Thiong'o, N. wa. 1965. *The River Between.* Nairobi, Kenya: Heinemann.

Thiong'o, N. wa. 1967. *A Grain of Wheat.* Nairobi, Kenya: Heinemann.

Thiong'o, N. wa. 1975. *Secret Lives.* London: Heinemann.

Thiong'o, N. wa. 1977. *Petals of Blood.* Nairobi, Kenya: Heinemann.

4

Preparing for Effective Constitutional Democracy in Africa: Political Education and Training

Mike Oquaye

INTRODUCTION

The winds of change currently blowing in Africa are primarily geared not against foreign domination but internal oppression. It is a quest for change from one-party rule, neo-patrimonialism and military dictatorship to multiparty politics, constitutionalism and civilian rule through free and fair elections. It aims at formatting, generally, the political system and/or tradition in Africa on the established Western democratic model. This process is linked with the concept of good governance, which refers to efficient and effective government character-ized by reciprocity between the rulers and those ruled (Hyden, 1992, pp. 1–26). Good governance is perceived in terms of the accountability of political lead-ership; the management of public funds; transparency in the awarding of con-tracts, making of appointments and investment of public funds; predictability in dealing with society at large; and operating within the rule of law (Jaycox, 1992, p. 1). Mandatory democratization has been tied to economic aid since the World Bank identified the lack of good governance as the root cause of Africa's lack of development (World Bank, 1989, pp. 1–10).

In the post-independence era, only four countries—Botswana, Mauritius, Na-mibia and Senegal—committed themselves to multiparty politics. Following the footsteps of Ghana, Tanzania, Kenya, Guinea and other nations, Zimbabwe zeal-ously sought a one-party state upon attaining majority rule until 1991 (multiparty democracy is now pursued in these countries). A change has occurred, however. Ranging from Kaunda's loss of power in Zambia (as a civilian incumbent) to Rawlings' continuation in office in Ghana (as an example of the transformation of military rulers into civilian "democrats"), no nation on the continent—with the possible exception of Libya—has remained insulated from the new wind of multiparty democracy sweeping across the continent. Indeed, constitutionalism and political pluralism have become prescriptions in contemporary African politics.

The guarantees as to the ultimate success of this process are, however, constricted. There is no insurance that the democratization process is immunized from military adventurism, for example. Since the demand for "good governance" was essentially the dictate of Western powers, it is pertinent to ask: Is the current democratization drive merely an attempt to satisfy foreign donors? To what extent can the pockets of internal resistance withstand the onslaughts—overt and covert—of African governments? A central theme of this work is that if the political culture in Africa is taken for granted, the continent could be overtaken by events and the democratization process could become a nine-day wonder. In order to solidify current gains, Africa should conceptualize the democratic ethos with greater clarity and effectively develop attendant institutions and mechanisms. In my view, the usefulness of constitutional and institutional devices must be perceived against the backdrop of meaningful political education and training. This is made mandatory by the negative effects of abject ignorance and illiteracy—political oppression, misery, disease and lack of development. The employment of education and training as mechanisms for effecting constitutional democracy in Africa constitutes the essence of this chapter.

A basic ingredient of democracy is the effective participation of the populace in the governmental process. Africa is characterized by a practice where rulers make decisions without consulting the people. Even thereafter, such decisions are not debatable by those very persons whose lives are to be affected by them. In addition, military intervention in politics and the use of warfare to settle political scores have seriously endangered the security of the continent. Africa can only make positive strides towards democracy and development if it is able to establish the conditions and institutions necessary for resolving the crises that stem from the lack of individual freedom, social justice and the provision of basic human needs. Formal and informal education should seek to remove the incidents of deprivation and equip the individual for effective membership in society. Such education will pay special attention to social relationships between different individuals and between individuals and society as a whole. In this connection, education becomes a vital tool for social transformation in the removal of reactionary and repressive traits and tendencies. The aim should be a system where the majority of citizens acquire adequate knowledge of themselves, of their environment and of the tangible and intangible forces that tend to control their lives.

This chapter is divided into three main parts. The first part explains some fundamental characteristics of democracy and the role of education in the achievement of democratic goals. Part two examines specific areas that should be addressed by education to bring about attitudinal change. These encompass traditional practices and/or ethnicity, human rights, social justice and civil society. Part three deals with certain recommendations and conclusions.

DEMOCRACY AND EDUCATION

Democracy defies easy definition. There is no agreed upon definition of the term, and the defenders of all kinds of regimes including communism, fascism and Nazism have claimed to be democratic. This is largely because of the prescriptive connotations that the expression has assumed. Wars have been fought in its name. The French, American, Russian, Chinese, Cuban and Libyan Revolutions were all justified in the name of democracy. Invariably, opponents in those conflicts claimed to be fighting on the side of democracy. President Woodrow Wilson led the United States to fight in World War I in 1917 in order to make "the world a safe place for democracy." The term has become, in effect, more "honorific" with a "laudatory meaning" (Lively, 1975, p. 1).

Despite the variance between the Marxist interpretation of democracy (which emphasized economic issues as against the "bourgeois" rights associated with liberal democracy), the salient aspects of democracy may be seen in terms of the following: (1) sovereign power belongs to all the people; (2) citizens are basically equal in political matters; (3) a prescribed and viable system of representative government, leadership selection by universal adult suffrage and a control mechanism to ensure participation and accountability; (4) constitutionalism, which provides for a set of rules and institutional arrangements that serve as a check on legislative and governmental power; (5) separation of powers and judicial independence; (6) observance of the rule of law, which demands the absence of arbitrariness in determining and disposing of the rights of individuals; (7) fundamental human rights; and (8) economic and social development of the individual and society as a whole.

It is necessary to comment on political education and then make a linkage between education and democracy. Education is an instrument by which every society seeks to perpetuate itself. Children are brought up by their parents/family by being taught the skills necessary for earning a living. They are also taught the rudiments of proper behavior and service to the community. By these methods, society is rejuvenated through the process of the young being trained to take the place of the old. This is what education entails—an instrument of stability and continuity. Education is, however, also an agent of change. It is necessary to ask: What is education for? First, education may be perceived as an instrument of social development. Second, it provides for individual development. Third, it is a means of political development. Education in this connection cannot be restricted to the new generation only. In Africa, there is a compelling need to open wide avenues for education because a large proportion of adults is uneducated. They live in the rural areas that are afflicted by isolation, illiteracy and lack of enlightenment. Accordingly, civic, adult and nonformal education techniques have a vital role to play.

Political education for the African people is also important because of their colonial heritage and the fact that their experience with democratic government has been minimal since the colonial era. This is pertinent to the democratization process in Africa because democratic behavior is not genetically conditioned, inborn or an inherent faculty—it is learned. The practice of democracy must, therefore, be taught to its practitioners so it can be instilled into the cultural patrimony of the people (Gitonga, 1988, p. 21). Democracy comprises a set of values and attitudes. It is not only a compendium of principles but also a way of doing things. Education must teach the rudiments of freedom, equality, justice and human dignity. Human beings cannot achieve any goal without being guided by a fountain of ideas. Before a democratic system of government can take root in Africa, a mental liberation is imperative. This can be realized through political education.

It has been feared that since most people are politically inept and unrestrained in Africa, democratic government is unsuitable. Such a defect, however, can be cured through the development of the people's moral, intellectual and civic sense of responsibility. From one perspective, democracy is more than just a method of delivering material goods. It is an embodiment of nonmaterial values—moral and ethical. It describes a state of affairs where humankind can actually enjoy the freedom to realize, develop and utilize higher potentials such as the development and effective use of intellectual abilities (Masolo, 1988, p. 39). The achievement of this goal requires education. Since the majority of people do not have a clear understanding of politics, Plato and Aristotle discredited democracy and advocated an elitist form of government epitomized by Plato's philosopher king. Machiavelli theorized that in order to obtain, maintain and expand power, the prince should not only keep his subjects well fed but also ignorant, since most people are more interested in satisfying the physical appetite than the things of the mind (Machiavelli, 1970, pp. 46–48). What the two authors did not appreciate was the popularization of democracy through education, not of an elite class but of the broad masses. In supporting the right of the people to be involved in government, Oruka (1981, p. 7) wrote: "Government is something which is supposed to help secure and deliver the goods for its subjects. Yet not one individual or group is capable of knowing exactly what such goods are. The people themselves must as a collectivity determine what their goods must be. And this can be done only through democracy."

Political accountability is a vital element of good governance/democracy. It sets the democratic state apart from the military junta, one-party dictatorship, etc. It is synonymous with political responsibility and answering to the populace and requires the ruler to justify by rational arguments the decisions taken in an official capacity. However, accountability to people who do not appreciate the issues on which account is being made is an exercise in futility. There is also the need to teach people that rulers, unless encouraged or even compelled to be responsible by institutions, rules and conventions, could pursue private interests at the expense of the public good. People must be educated to appreciate that rulers are not angels but can be just as selfish, fallible, arbitrary, self-seeking and vindictive as other human beings. Citizens should be schooled in the intricacies of sanctions to ensure accountability. Responsible conduct in public affairs has been guaranteed in other nations through political, administrative and judicial sanctions. These have been buttressed by processes of socialization that school the citizens to uphold the principles that ensure accountability. The supreme political sanction inheres in free election. In all nations where the rulers are obliged to regularly submit themselves for reelection or rejection by the people, provided the electoral mechanisms are free and fair, the leaders will be reasonably accountable. Governments are compelled to explain their policies and actions while in office and in preelection campaigns. An educated citizenry, alone, has the capacity for ensuring effective analysis of public issues in this connection.

POLITICAL CULTURE

The development of a political culture consistent with democratic practices is imperative in Africa. There cannot be an adequate appreciation of the HF in politics without an appreciation of the subjective dimension in politics. This is rooted in the ideas, beliefs, values, sentiments and symbols existing in the society. It is a thrust of my thesis that political education should address issues pertaining to African political culture in order to attain modernization and democratic governance. Several viewpoints of political culture have been offered by various writers that are instructive. These need careful examination, because unless there are well-conceived rules governing the political process, which are accepted and insisted upon by rulers and the ruled alike, the practice of democracy will remain an illusion. Ball (1989, p. 53) perceived political culture as comprising "the attitudes, beliefs, emotions and values of society that relate to the political system and to political issues." Macridis (1961, p. 40) saw it as "the commonly shared goals and commonly accepted rules." Beer and Ulam (1958, p. 32) identified the components of the culture as values, beliefs, and emotional attitudes about how government ought to be conducted and about what it should do.

Dahl's analysis is very pertinent to the African situation, particularly as it relates to political opposition. The salient aspects, which should serve as an educational manifesto for Africa, are: (1) orientations of problem-solving—are they pragmatic or rationalistic? (2) orientations to collective action—are they cooperative or noncooperative? (3) orientations to the political system—are they allegiant or alienated? (4) orientations to other people—are they trustful or mistrustful? (Dahl, 1966, pp. 352–355). These aspects constitute a viable agenda for political education. Finer (1962, chapters 7–9) dwelt on the legitimacy of rulers, political institutions and procedures. These are aspects of the crisis of good governance in Africa. Writing with reference to new states, Pye (1962, pp. 122–124) related political development to political culture. The relevant factors include the scope of politics, the relationship between political ends and means, the standards for the evaluation of political action and the values that are salient for political action.

Cultural orientations are predispositions to political action. They are determined by such factors as traditions, historical memories, motives, norms, emotions and symbols. These orientations may be broken down into their component parts as follows: cognitions (knowledge and awareness of the political system), affect (emotional disposition towards the system) and evaluation (judgment about the system). An individual's view of him or herself as a political actor, and his or her views of other citizens and perception of the organs of government including the legislature, executive, the judiciary, political parties and pressure groups are viable political objects (Kavanagh, 1972, pp. 1–20).

The importance of shaping a democratically oriented political culture cannot be over emphasized. Almond and Verba (in Kavanagh, 1972, p. 11) identified the cognitive, affective and evaluative aspects of political attitudes in order to develop a typology of ideal political cultures—participant, subject and parochial. Where orientations are positive to all the objects (as in Britain, the United States and Scandinavia), the political culture is participant. Where the citizens are passive and obedient in their relationship to the state (as in the socialist countries and most of Africa), the system is the subject type. Where individuals hardly relate to the political system and have very little knowledge of same (as in most traditional societies), the political culture is parochial. These being ideal types, the state of progress in a given society will be determined by the level of political education.

It should not be taken for granted that the traditional African society was democratic and that democratic practices would dawn naturally on Africa without a meaningful educational drive. In a recent debate on aspects of democracy in Ghana, two scholars expressed divergent views in this regard. To Drah (1987, chapter 2), concrete checks and balances existed in the Akan traditional system that militated against autocracy and leaned towards a measure of democracy. These included the powers of the council of elders, the Queenmother and youth. Ansa-Koi (1987, chapter 3) wrote, however, that there is an erroneous conclusion that the traditional system was democratic because of two main factors: first, earlier writers tried to glorify Africans by identifying their system with the rudiments of the now universal norms of democratic rule; and secondly, there was a desire to prove that democracy—the ideal form of rule—is not peculiar to Europe and that traditional African societies had also aspired towards that ideal.

There are inherent difficulties in the African traditional system that must be tackled through the educational process. For example, the system encourages patrimonialism while discouraging pluralism. The deification of political leaders stems partly from the belief that a chief is sacrosanct. Children are brought up in Africa not to challenge the views of their elders, however anachronistic. Hence, to the Akan of Ghana, for example, the ideal child has a cool and quiet disposition—*ne ho dwo*.

Political education in Africa must, *inter alia*, aim at removing apathy. The majority of people trouble themselves so little about public affairs that they willingly leave virtually all such activities to be dealt with by a few. No people can be free who approach freedom with apathy. Freedom is invaluable; it can only be obtained at great cost and, when obtained, must be carefully preserved and zealously guarded. A thorny issue in Africa is military intervention in politics and attendant economic mismanagement. In Ghana, an era of national decadence was marked, for example, during 1972–1979, and a nomenclature emerged that described cheating, hoarding and profiteering as *kalabule* (Adjibolosoo, 1995, pp. 53, 69–70). The vital issue is that during this period, Ghanaians complained bitterly in private but were reluctant or unable to protest against the systemic corruption that allowed such deviant practices. Simultaneously, most people failed to report the cheaters to the authorities as they resorted to misplaced optimism: *ebe ye yiye*—it will be well. Civic education should aim at attitudinal changes that will remove such tendencies.

Similarly, political corruption in Africa has a cultural dimension that should be tackled through an educational process geared towards cultural reorientation. The person with a high position in Africa is besought with requests for favors from the extended family. All eyes wait upon this leader when the annual festival in his or her hometown occurs. The leader, who is the panacea to all the family's maladies and wants, is taxed and tasked till all the extended family needs are satisfied and is pressed for favors till all possible privileges are exploited and abused, leading steadily to his or her fall and disgrace.

Political education should also aim at the elimination of sycophancy. Undue adulation of leaders in African countries has been part of Africa's woes. Africans have praised their leaders when there was no need for praise; approved and concurred when they needed to question and caution; and flattered and cajoled until they have almost lost their heads. Africans must learn to question rather than succumb to their leaders. The people must perceive those who stand up to their leaders not as rebels but as promoters of the right to insist on accountability.

An important aspect of the African traditional system that requires attention is the communalistic concept of life versus individualism, which has been a catalyst in the development of Western civilization. Halevy (1955, p. 504) observed that "in the whole of modern Europe it is a fact that individuals have assumed consciousness of their autonomy, and that everyone demands the respect of all others, whom he considers as his fellows or equals: society appears . . . as issuing from the considered will of the individuals which make it up." Nevertheless, even in Europe, individualism took time to attain its present dimensions. As de Tocqueville (1955, p. 158) wrote, "our fathers did not have the word 'individualism,' which we have coined for our use, because in their time there was indeed no individual who did not belong to a group and who could be considered as absolutely alone."

By a systematic process of acculturation, aspects of Africa's communalistic approach to social and economic organization must give way to the doctrine of individualism, which has been seen as "the shining light of evolution" (Commons, 1959, p. 34). The idea of individualism permeated not only the principles of private enterprise and *laissez-faire,* but also advanced the thesis that private accumulation led to the public welfare. Respect for private property and the rights of the individual, generally, are inextricably interwoven.

In Africa, the competitive attendant to political pluralism has often generated acrimony and violence because of the lack of development of the competitive spirit. As a result, the work of district councils, assemblies and parliaments has been disrupted. Even in clubs and associations, contests for offices have degenerated into bitterness. Political education should focus on the establishment of a broad political matrix in which divergent views could be accommodated in an atmosphere of healthy competition. This should aim at attaining Bryce's concept of the American sense of individualism: "However much at odds on specific issues, the major political traditions have shred a belief in the rights of property, the philosophy of economic individualism, the value of competition; they have accepted the economic virtues of capitalist culture as necessary qualities of man" (Bryce, 1954, p. viii).

The worth and dignity of every individual must be taught and preferred to meaningless collectivism. Kwame Nkrumah, Sekou Toure and other African leaders justified preventive detention in terms of the communal interest. This should be repudiated and, on the contrary, Africans should be educated to appreciate the view that "man is too noble a being to serve simply as the instrument for others" (Rousseau, 1925, p. 22). Kant (1956, pp. 95–96) emphasized that human beings should be treated "never simply as a means, but always at the same time as an end." There is the need to escape from collectivism in order to survive. As Reisman (1954) wrote, "to hold that conformity with society is not only a necessity but also a duty" is to "destroy that margin of freedom which gives life its savor and its endless possibility for advance." Society, therefore, should "give every encouragement to people to develop their private selves—to escape from groupism—while realizing that, in many cases, they will use their freedom in unattractive or 'idle' ways" (pp. 26–27).

The African concept of development has been plagued with collectivism for far too long. State enterprises have drained scarce resources in several African countries and encouraged parasitic dependence upon the state. In order to promote the requisite development, which in turn fosters democracy, the notion of self-development must be learned. To emphasize the qualitative—as opposed to the numerical—value of the individual, this lesson from Rousseau (1782, p. 33) needs to be taught: "I am made unlike anyone I have ever met; I will even venture to say that I am like no one in the whole world. I may be no better, but at least, I am different." Political education will bring to the fore not only the difficulties inherent in the traditional African society but also those inherent in Marxist philosophy. Marx perceived self-development in a communal context: "Only in community with others has each individual the means of cultivating his gifts in all directions. . . . individuals obtain their freedom in and through their association" (Marx and Engels, 1964, pp. 431–432). Marx (1963, p. 76) perceived communism as advantageous because it does not only transcend "personal independence, based on dependence on things" but also ensures "free individuality based on the universal development of individuals and on their joint mastery over their communal, social productive powers and wealth." Communism has, however, failed to promote development and human liberty. However, this is not to accept unbridled individualism and attendant capitalism. It's important not to be oblivious of the fact that without the group people cannot exist as individuals. The aim is to emphasize regard for the individual and the protection of his or her life, liberty and property in a new democratic order.

HUMAN RIGHTS AND SOCIAL JUSTICE

The discussions above flow into considerations of human rights and social justice. The world today is concerned with human rights. The United Nations has, however, observed that vast numbers of people are unaware of their rights as human beings. Many suffer as a result of this lack of basic knowledge of human rights. Even though the existing laws and institutions—national and international—in many cases defend victims and counter abuses, people must first know where they should turn for help (United Nations, 1989, p. 1). Without appropriate education, human rights cannot be effectively upheld. This is because (1) people who are aware of their rights stand the best chance of realizing them; (2) knowledge of human rights, spread widely in the community, is the first and surest defense against the danger that these rights will be destroyed; and (3) learning about one's own rights builds respect for the rights of others and points the way to more tolerant, peaceful societies (United Nations, 1989, p. 1). This belief in knowledge accounts for the launching of the United Nations' World Public Education Campaign for Human Rights, as a drive for awareness, information and education.

The disregard for human rights in Africa is shameful. In Uganda, for example, Amin ordered the murder of 3,000 Acholi and Langi tribesmen who were suspected of being loyal to ex-president Obote. Macias Nguema of Equatorial Guinea turned his country into the concentration camp of Africa. He incredibly murdered ten of the twelve ministers in his original cabinet and declared himself president for life. His reign of blood took the lives of some 50,000 Guineans and drove about 150,000 people—one-third of the remaining population—into exile. In Ghana, under the revolutionary Provisional National Defence Council (PNDC) government, detention, torture and murder were employed as part of the regime's control mechanism. Throughout Africa, political opponents—actual and imaginary—have been eliminated in bizarre ways by both civilian and military regimes.

An educational process should be developed in an attempt to promote human rights in Africa partly because of conceptual differences as to exactly what these rights entail. The Western concept of human rights derived from Cicero's idea that human rights are not created by the state but exist independent of it; they antedate the state and are founded on natural law, the basis of which is morality that is common to all men, universal, everlasting and unchanging. When any human law is inconsistent with natural law, therefore, that human law is void (Cicero, 1929, p. 213). Locke's (1924, chapter 6) teachings on the natural right of man to life, liberty and property as well as Rousseau's (1977, chapter 1) argument that the powers of government are held only to safeguard the inalienable rights of citizens should bring out useful lessons. The Marxist perception must be distinguished in that it is a denial that the individual could have any rights separate and apart from the group to which he or she belongs. Marx (1963, p. 24) ridiculed human rights as the rights of "egoistic man, of man separated from other men and from community."

Turning to Africa, it is important to ask the question: "Did Africa have an autochthonous formulation of human rights?" Bayart (1986, p. 109) argued that the "ideas of democracy and human rights are the products of Western history. They derive from the value placed on the idea of the individual (as opposed to the person) which pre-colonial societies did not share, and which were introduced in the wake of colonial rule." The tendency has been to emphasize economic and social rights in Africa and justify violations of fundamental human rights as governments seek to promote economic development. This is untenable. Rather, it should be taught that economic development must move together with fundamental human rights including the right to life, personal liberty, freedom of conscience, freedom of expression, assembly, association and movement and protection from discrimination, inhumane treatment and deprivation of property. Despite the limitations of the traditional society examined earlier, it had certain virtues that should be taught. The widely held view that life is sacrosanct is reflected in the Akan saying *onipa nnye aboa*—man is not an animal. Under Akan tradition, a person could not, therefore, be killed, imprisoned or punished without just cause and due legal process. The accused was publicly tried before any punishment was meted out. Procedures of trial were developed, and witnesses had to be called and examined in public. Such lessons should encourage Africans to repudiate secret trials by revolutionary regimes.

Constitutional mechanisms have been devised to protect human rights as part of the search for democracy. These include provisions for national institutions such as the Commission for Human Rights and Administrative Justice (CHRAJ) in Ghana established in 1993 under its 1992 Constitution. The Commission has power, inter alia, to receive complaints of violations of fundamental human rights, injustices, corruption, abuse of office and unfair treatment by any public officer in the performance of his or her duties. Such an institution cannot operate meaningfully within a fog of human ignorance. The CHRAJ noted that the depth of ignorance about human rights, both on the part of officials and citizens, constituted the major obstacle in its work. Noting that the police engaged in excesses and brutalities largely out of ignorance, the Commission organized a number of seminars to alleviate this anomaly. Attention was drawn to the deplorable conditions in police cells and prisons, such as poor ventilation, inadequate toilet facilities and unsanitary conditions.[1]

The Ghanaian experience studied by this writer is very instructive. It revealed that despite strenuous efforts made by the Commission, public ignorance affected responsiveness. By the end of October 1994, only 2,040 petitions had been received by the Commission. Out of this figure, 740 were labor-related cases mainly from urban areas, representing about 36.3 percent of the total number of petitions that were received. Further, 451 petitions out of the 740 labor-related cases had to do with wrongful dismissals of educated officials, representing 61 percent of administrative justice cases (Domaakyaareh, 1994, pp. 9–10).

Human rights abuses cannot be overcome by total reliance on constitutional devices nor conflict resolution techniques. A vital educational role exists in order to effect attitudinal changes in discriminatory practices. A Commonwealth Secretariat publication recognized the role of education thus: (1) without the requisite education and information, the necessary awareness of human rights (its scope, objectives and implications) is often lacking; (2) without education, politicians and public officials who want to come up with solutions of human rights problems are sometimes unsure of how to proceed; and (3) individuals and groups, particularly the indigent and disadvantaged, are prejudiced in that they remain unaware of their rights (Hatchard, 1993, pp. 77–78).

Civil Society

Civil society in Africa may be perceived as organized groups outside government that are committed to challenging autocratic regimes to liberalize the political system. They often comprise intellectuals, artists and professional associations of lawyers and doctors, university students and organized labor. They have also included associations of farmers, fishermen, women, cultural and recreational clubs, human rights groups and political parties. They, however, exclude ethnic and social organizations that are generally primary units of society (Gellner, 1991, p. 500). Emphasizing the importance of civil society, Bayart (1986, pp. 109–125) stated that the future of Africa lies in civil society.

The conscious development of civil society through an educational process is imperative for liberalization of politics, fostering of the pluralist ethos and enhancement of enlightened political leadership. It is important to ask: "Does civil society exist in Africa?" If so, what can be done about it? Expressing optimism, Bratton (1989, pp. 410–411) wrote:

At first glance, African societies seem to possess few intermediary organisations to occupy the space between the family (broadly defined by effective ties of blood, marriage, residence, clan and ethnicity) and the state. . . . (But) I argue that political scientists should devote more attention to the associational life that occurs in the political space beyond the state's purview. . . . Far from being stunted in sub-Saharan Africa, it is often vibrant.

Civil society in Africa has been increasing in magnitude since most countries achieved political independence. This is evidenced by the fact that popular uprisings brought down an oppressive regime in Sudan in 1985. In the same vein, popular movements were at the root of the collapse of autocracies in Benin, the Congo, Zambia and Madagascar.

Even if the optimism towards the effectiveness of civil society in Africa is well founded, it is noteworthy that the activities have revolved around a few educated and/or enlightened people. In Sierra Leone, for example, the bar association successfully withstood Siaka Stevens' dictatorship while the private press resisted censorship to become "the voice of criticism and opposition to government policies and programs" (Hayward, 1989, pp. 178–179). In Ghana, the professionals' and students' revolt under the umbrella of the Association of Recognized Professional Bodies (ARPB) triggered off the collapse of General Acheampong's military dictatorship (Oquaye, 1980, pp. 55–56).

Civic education is necessary to broaden the base of civil society participation if effectiveness is to be maximized. Unless the farmers, fishermen, women and ordinary workers become active agents in civil society, the search for democracy in Africa will remain an illusion. This is especially because when civil society activities are limited to a privileged few, they are more easily crushed by dictators, particularly military oppressors. In Sierra Leone, the sheer brutalities of soldiers have silenced the hitherto voices of dissent. In Ghana, the attempts of professionals and students to regroup against Jerry John Rawlings, as they did against General Ignatius Kutu Acheampong, were met with the arrest, detention and untold brutalization of their leaders as well as closure of the universities. Several people were forced into exile. Even Nigeria is plagued with this problem, despite its size, apparent might and potential. Perceived as having the most "vibrant, resilient and expansive civil society" in West Africa, the inability of civil society to maximize its effectiveness was explained by Drah in terms of ethnicity (Drah, 1994, p. 9). It is pertinent to add that not only will civic education narrow the tribal barriers, but it will produce an enlightened society that will be able to conceptualize and focus on the real issues at stake. This will also mean that military dictators will have the broad majority, and not a small minority, of the people to intimidate. Africa is replete with satellite organizations set up by governments that effectually aim at negating the impact of civil society.

LESSONS AND RECOMMENDATIONS

The history of civic education in Africa carries vital lessons that are pertinent to study. First, government-sponsored agencies may not promote the rights of citizens, since the protection of individual rights is necessarily a check on governmental power. Secondly, it should be appreciated that education cannot take place in a vacuum. Those who can best solve a problem are the people who should be involved. Therefore, civic education can best be undertaken by voluntary organizations and identifiable groups whose interests are affected by various issues. Through a means of socialization, civic education should be distinguished from indoctrination, which essentially involves overt and covert inculcation of ideas. Civic education is not ideological education.

It has been observed that Kwame Nkrumah, for example, used every educational process to promote his political ideology. Nkruma's ideological education was essentially aimed, however, at projecting his own image (Agyeman, 1977, pp. 10–14).

The answer to the problem of governmental interference is to empower independent segments of society to engage in civic/political education. It is desirable to have autonomous national institutions determine the content of civil education and the methods for its dissemination. Membership of a policy formulation body should include representatives of the main political parties, the ministry of education, the press commission, the media, the universities and religious bodies. Another method is to leave civic education entirely in the hands of political parties and voluntary groups. The problem here is that this could result in the promotion of too many conflicting and sectional viewpoints. The *laissez-faire* approach works best in a developed political system where the content of education has become an integral part of the accepted norms and culture of the society.

Africa needs a continuing education program akin to the system that has proved very beneficial in Asia. This should entail all those activities of educational institutions that are designed to meet the educational needs of the broader society apart from the formal teaching programs of such institutions. Learning should not be confined to childhood and adolescence but should be carried through adult life. Lifelong education should be emphasized to attain the benefits associated with the system. First, it caters to the explosion of knowledge, enabling trained personnel to benefit from the ever-increasing flood of new information. Second, it provides an overflow that benefits untrained personnel as they interact with their trained counterparts. Third, it allows nationals to benefit from global changes in ideas. In order to operate as a democracy, a nation's citizens should have some knowledge about the nature of scientific discoveries and technological developments to be empowered to make critical judgments. These affect the polity, economy and society. The success of democracy rests on people who have acquired the appropriate human factor. Fourth, it fosters higher expectations of life and thus encourages political participation. Fifth, it helps to correct imbalances in the educational system.

The Conference on Continuing Education and Universities of the Asia and Pacific Region, held in Madras in 1970, set the following main objectives for lifelong education: (1) to promote the optimum functioning of individuals so that they realize their full potential and also contribute effectively to society; (2)

to encourage the development of decision-making and leadership skills; (3) to promote the optimum functioning of social, economic and political institutions so as to maximize their contribution to individual and social development within the context of a democratic society; and (4) to help the individual participate effectively in a society characterized by rapid social change (Pant, 1972, p. 4).

Forms of continuing education include the following: (1) general and functional literacy programs; (2) remedial education for those insufficiently educated; (3) refresher and updating courses in vocational and professional fields; (4) reconversion courses for those who need such education and training; (5) opportunities for participation in the analysis of social and economic problems;[2] (6) opportunities to cultivate skills necessary for citizenship in plural societies; (7) opportunities for cultural enrichment and creative use of leisure (Pant, 1972). Program types include courses in: (1) scientific and technical areas; (2) human relations and decision-making processes; and (3) the humanities, social sciences and liberal arts, as well as the training of leaders in continuing education, community development and voluntary organizations.

Finally, some lessons may be learned from Denmark. First, there is a "train the trainers" program that establishes a viable network for public education. Second, several types of adult education have been devised that are worthy of emulation. These include the general liberal adult education program, also known as popular enlightenment. The major part of this program is under the Leisure-time Instruction Act, and is organized mainly by educational associations. Additionally for young people (aged 14–18), there is the youth school. There is also the well-known and unique folk high schools (for adults above age 18), which offer liberal, general, nonvocational education. No qualifications are demanded for getting accepted as a student but neither are credits obtainable. The aim is to provide personal development and enrichment.

CONCLUSION

Democracy refers to a system of government that ensures the effective participation of the governed in the government of their country; accountability of public officials to the electorate; and protection of the people's fundamental human rights. These human rights include freedom of thought, expression and association and the provision of fair opportunities for the realization of the aspirations and potentials of the individual, in order that "we may bring from the souls of men and women their richest fruition" (Laski, 1917, p. 25). Democracy, itself, provides an opportunity for human development but guarantees nothing. How to empower citizens to maximize success and minimize failure should be the concern of political education.

Empowerment of the people to make rational choices and be meaningful partners in responsible and accountable government is of paramount concern. Democracy cannot survive unless people are empowered to express their will and are meaningfully able to choose and change their leaders. The role of education in enabling people to exercise such powers remains a focal point in the search for democracy.

This chapter stressed the need for education to enhance human rights. Before anyone can meaningfully exercise any rights that will promote social justice, he or she should understand the source of those rights, appreciate the world around him or her, communicate with others and receive, transmit and compare information and experiences. Neither can cultural perspectives be ignored if attitudinal changes are desired. In Africa, a high status is necessarily ascribed to age, and strict adherence to the status quo is always prescribed.

Knowledge about the rudiments of government and administration—the legislature, executive, judiciary, local government, civil service and the media—should be the prerogative of every citizen. Among other things, he or she should possess a good understanding of the constitution—the fundamental law of the land—in a local language. In this connection, people should opt to be bound by law and not by any one individual or group of persons. As Jefferson stated, "Free government is founded on jealousy and not in confidence. . . . In questions of power, then, let no more be heard of confidence in man, but bind him down from mischiefs by the chains of the constitution" (quoted in Crabbe, 1981, p. 67). The legal machinery should be perceived as the best means of human management in all spheres (i.e., political, social and economic). Force has been employed for far too long as a control mechanism in Africa. It was applied in the initial colonization and subsequent domination of the continent. These contours were deepened by neo-patrimonial leaders and military dictators. Education should help to revise this.

There is the need to develop the culture that resolves conflict by instrumentality of law. This, in itself, rules out military intervention in the resolution of political differences. Courts should be instruments of liberation. It should be taught that as a unit of government, the judiciary is not an institution subordinate to any other branch of government. Africa should create an atmosphere in which the people as a whole come to look upon the members of the judiciary not as employees of the government of the day and not as civil servants, but as the bulwark of independence. In this, citizens should insist that no government seeks to impose its political philosophy on the judiciary. As the famous U.S. Justice Robert H. Jackson once said, "The legal profession in all countries knows that there are only two real choices of government open to a people. It may be governed by law or it may be governed by the will of one or of a group of men [and women]. . . . Law as the expression of the ultimate will and wisdom of a people, has so far proven the safest guardian of liberty yet devised. . . . We commend it to your notice, not because . . . it is perfect, but because it is an earnest effort to fulfill those aspirations for freedom and the general welfare which are a common heritage of (mankind)" (Crabbe, 1981).

Education encompasses knowledge about economic realities. It is a means of broadening and strengthening civil society, promoting social justice and protecting human rights. It is a useful agency for reshaping (not necessarily abandoning totally) obsolete cultural and traditional practices to satisfy the needs of a global democratic order. Operationally, civic and/or political education is best left in private hands empowered by civil society and other independent agencies. The role of government lies in the provision of the appropriate climate for the attainment of optimum results. Such measures should help stabilize the second winds of change.

NOTES

1. Interview with Emile Short, commissioner, CHRAJ, in Ghana, 1994.

2. In 1963, a system known as the Radio Rural Forum was introduced in Ghana. It was a social club consisting of a cross section of the people in a village who wished to listen to and use radio broadcasts in an organized way to start discussions among themselves, increase their knowledge and information and put into practice the things they learn. It comprised a cross section of the people (i.e., literates and illiterates, teachers, farmers, masons, tailors and others). Every forum had a chairperson and a secretary/convenor. The latter had to be literate and was the coordinator of the forum. He or she organized the group to listen to the programs and drew up listeners' questions and comments for transmission to Broadcasting House. Once a month, representatives of the forums visited Broadcasting House to take part in broadcasts so they could give their own views and comments. In its operations, the Broadcasting House liaised with appropriate government departments/ministries and other organizations. Even though agriculture was the emphasis, health, civic education and social issues were also featured. The results were quite admirable as people began to meaningfully discuss local and national issues and undertake self-help projects pursuant to their learning experiences. Although the program suffered from governmental interference as a result of tight government control over broadcasting, it could be employed through independent operators and with the help of NGOs.

REFERENCES

Adjibolosoo, S. 1995. *The Human Factor in Developing Africa.* Westport, Conn.: Praeger.

Agyeman, D. K. 1977. "Ideological Education and Nationalism: The Ghanaian Experience." Unpublished manuscript, Department of Sociology, University of Cape Coast.

Ansa-Koi, K. 1987. "A Historical Outline of Democracy in Ghana." In K. A. Ninsin and F. K. Drah, eds., *The Search for Democracy in Ghana.* Accra: Asempa Publishers.

Ball, A. 1989. *Modern Politics and Government.* London: Macmillan.

Bayart, J. F. 1986. "Civil Society in Africa." In P. Chabal, ed., *Political Dominations in Africa: Reflections on the Limits of Power.* Cambridge: Cambridge University Press.

Beer, S. H. and Ulam, A. B., eds. 1958. *Patterns of Government: The Major Political Systems of Europe.* New York: Random House.

Bratton, M. 1989. "Beyond the State: Civil Society and Associational Life in Africa." *World Politics* 41 (3): 407–430.

Bryce, J. 1954. *The American Political Tradition.* New York: Vintage Books.

Cicero, M. 1929. *Loeb Classical Library, Vol. 16.* Cambridge, Mass.: Harvard University Press.

Commons, J. R. 1959. *Institutional Economics: Its Place in Political Economy.* Madison: University of Wisconsin Press.

Crabbe, V. C. R. A. C. 1981. "Government of the People, by the People, for the People." In P. K. Fordjour, ed., *Citizen Participation in Government.* Accra: Institute of Adult Education.

Dahl, R. A., ed. 1966. *Political Opposition in Western Democracies.* New Haven, Conn.: Yale University Press.

Dolphyne, F. 1991. *The Emancipation of Women.* Accra: Universities Press.

Domaakyaareh, A. 1994. "The Commission for Human Rights and Administrative Justice." Paper delivered at a conference on Administrative Justice in an Emerging Democracy, Accra, November 8.

Drah, F. K. 1987. "Aspects of the Akan State System: Pre-colonial and Colonial." In K. A. Ninsin and F. K. Drah, eds. *Political Parties and Democracy in Ghana's Fourth Republic.* Accra: Woeli Publishing Services.

Drah, F. K. 1994. "Civil Society and Democratisation in the West Africa Sub-Region." Paper delivered at a conference on Democratization in Africa organized by the Friedrich Ebert Foundation, Ghana.

Finer, S. E. 1962. *The Man on Horseback.* London: Pinter.

Gellner, E. 1991. "Civil Society in Historical Context." *International Social Science Journal* 129 (August): 495–510.

Gitonga, A. 1988. "The Meaning and Foundation of Democracy." In W. O. Oyugi et al., eds., *Democratic Theory and Practice in Africa.* London: Heinemann.

Halevy, E. 1955. *Growth of Philosophic Radicalism.* Boston: Beacon Press.

Hatchard, J. 1993. *National Human Rights Institutions.* London: Commonwealth Secretariat.

Hayward, F. M. 1989. "Sierra Leone: State Consolidation, Fragmentation and Decay." In D. C. O'Brien et al., eds., *Contemporary West African States.* Cambridge: Cambridge University Press.

Hyden, G. 1992. "Governance and the Study of Politics." In G. Hyden and M. Bratton, eds., *Governance and Politics in Africa.* Boulder, Colo.: Lynne Reinner.

Jaycox, E. 1992. *The Challenges of African Development.* Washington, D.C.: World Bank.

Kant, E. 1959. *Foundations of the Metaphysics of Morals: And What Is Enlightenment.* New York: Liberal Arts Press.

Kavanagh, D. 1972. *Political Culture.* London: Macmillan Press.

Laski, H. J. 1917. *Studies in the Problem of Sovereignty.* New Haven, Conn.: Yale University Press.

Lively, J. 1975. *Democracy.* London: Oxford University Press.

Locke, J. 1924. *Two Treatises of Civil Government.* London: Dent.

Machiavelli, N. 1970. *The Prince.* London: Hammondsworth Books.

Macridis, R. C. 1961. "Interest Groups in Comparative Analysis." *Journal of Politics* 23 (1): 25–45.

Marx, K. 1963 [1857]. "On the Jewish Question." In T. B. Bottomore, ed., *Karl Marx: Early Writings.* New York: McGraw-Hill.

Marx, K. and Engels, F. 1964 [1845]. *The German Ideology.* Moscow: Progress Publishers.

Masolo, D. 1988. "Ideological Dogmatism and the Values of Democracy." In W. O. Oyugi et al., eds., *Democratic Theory and Practice in Africa.* London: Heinemann.

Oruka, H. O. 1981. "Philosophy and Democracy." Unpublished seminar paper, University of Nairobi, Kenya.

Pye, L. 1962. *Politics, Personality and Nation-Building.* New Haven, Conn.: Yale University Press.

Reisman, D. 1954. *Individualism Reconsidered.* Glencoe, Ill.: Anchor Books.

Rousseau, J. J. 1925. *Julie, ou la Nouvelle Heloise (1761) V lettre 2.* Paris: Garnier-Flammarion.

Rousseau, J. J. 1947. *Les Confessions (1782).* Paris: Bibliotheque la Pleiade (Louis Martin-Chauffier).

Rousseau, J. J. 1977. *The Social Contract.* London: Dent.

Tocqueville, A. de. 1955. *L'Ancien Regime et al Revolution (1856), Book II.* In J. P. Mayer, ed., *Oeuvres Completes.* Garden City, N.Y.: Doubleday.

United Nations. 1989. "World Public Information Campaign for Human Rights." *Fact Sheet,* No. 8.

World Bank. 1989. *Sub-Saharan Africa: From Crisis to Sustainable Growth.* Washington, D.C.: World Bank.

5

Entrepreneurship Development for Industrial Progress in Africa

Francis Adu-Febiri

INTRODUCTION

African societies have always had a good supply of indigenous entrepreneurs. However, contemporary African entrepreneurship has failed to be a catalyst for socioeconomic development. This chapter argues that a critical factor of this unfortunate situation is the failure of African entrepreneurs to apply crucial human factor (HF)[1] ingredients such as integrity, communal spirit, responsibility, accountability, self-reliance, cooperation and so on. HF aspects such as these constitute the underlying matrix that ties entrepreneurship and socioeconomic development together. Against this backdrop, the chapter (1) examines African entrepreneurship and (2) suggests the inculcation of the HF in contemporary African entrepreneurs through education and training programs and other relevant incentives.

Like Marx (1973, p. 512), it seems contemporary African leaders and developers have more interest in capital than entrepreneurship. Consultants and policy makers of Africa's development have, since the colonial period, tended to concentrate on how to attract foreign capital. They have neglected the need to develop the relevant HF. Yet, it is entrepreneurs with the relevant HF that can generate adequate capital and stimulate socioeconomic development in Africa.

Entrepreneurship played a very significant role in the emergence of the Industrial Revolution in England in the mid-eighteenth century (Heilbroner, 1989). Similarly, entrepreneurship has been central in the socioeconomic development of other Western European countries (e.g., the United States, Germany, Great Britain, Canada and Japan and the newly industrializing countries of Southeast Asia). The development success of great civilizations of Africa—Egypt, Nubia, Ethiopia, Ghana, Mali, Songhai, Great Zimbabwe and many others—could be attributed mainly to the growth of relevant entrepreneurship. In light of these examples, it could be argued, as Trivedi (1991, p. 1) does, that "entrepreneurs are key persons of any country for promoting socioeconomic growth." From this perspective, there is the tendency to make a direct correlation between Africa's underdevelopment and lack of entrepreneurs (McClelland, 1971a, 1971b; Hagen, 1971; LeVine, 1966; Trivedi, 1991). Trivedi (1991, p. 1), for example, asserted that "the socioeconomic development of the country is attained only when the society creates a large number of entrepreneurs from various strata of population."

The arguments and presentations of this chapter corroborate "the necessity-for-entrepreneurship-in-development" argument (Belasco, 1980, p. 169). The chapter, however, argues extensively that it takes entrepreneurs who have acquired the relevant HF, rather than a mere large number of entrepreneurs, to set the forces of development in motion. Flowing from this, is the suggestion to African leaders and developers that they need to reformulate their development policies to create the HF that will enhance the catalyst role of entrepreneurship.

THEORETICAL BACKGROUND

The discussion on the relationship between Africa's underdevelopment and its entrepreneurial deficiency centers on two main issues: achievement motivation (McClelland, 1971; Hagen, 1971) and colonial and post-colonial economic policies and practices (Belasco, 1980; Friedland and Roseberg, 1964).

The achievement motivation theorists believe that high achievement motivation is the determinant of high entrepreneurial performance and consequent development success. This motivation theory emphasizes a psychological or behavioral element of entrepreneurship. It argues that high achievement motivation is prevalent in Western societies because of their "permissive" or "open" social structures (McClelland, 1971a, p. 121). In such societies, individuals can devote their time to developing their careers and businesses. The theory leads to the conclusion that Africa lacks such enterprising individuals because of its "paternal authoritarianism" (McClelland, 1971a, p. 121). It therefore recommends the introduction of a new system of education and Western entrepreneurial ethos that will transform the low achievement motivation of Africans.

This chapter rejects the achievement motivation theory's perception of the African people. Africans are not naturally despondent. Whenever the conditions are conducive, Africans have demonstrated high achievement motivation and extraordinary venturesomeness. The high socioeconomic achievement of African civilizations and the vibrant small-scale entrepreneurship in the informal sectors of contemporary African countries are excellent manifestations of this motivation. It is largely the colonial and neo-colonial economic and sociopolitical arrangements of Africa that have depreciated the critical HF essential for development (see Adjibolosoo, 1995a, pp. 55–72). In fact, Belasco (1980, p.

182) is right in asserting that "achievement motivation or the need for achievement is an ethnocentric conceit veiling the historical process which deforms the use-value of multi-functional leadership, a capacity of all human population, and replaces it with the exchange-value of market-centered entrepreneurship, a specialized role limited to the culture of capitalism."

The historical process has something to do with the decay of African entrepreneurship. In the colonial period, major areas of production were reserved for European, Asian, Lebanese and Syrian entrepreneurs. Thus, during the colonial period, African indigenous entrepreneurs were relegated to small-scale cash crop farming, artisanal activities, petty trading and brokership. Post-colonial policies focusing on state entrepreneurship, according to critics of state participation in the economy such as Friedland and Roseberg (1964, pp. 1–14), have discouraged the development of an indigenous African entrepreneurial class (see Adjibolosoo, 1995a).

This chapter does not dispute the perception that entrepreneurship is a crucial factor in socioeconomic development and that part of the explanation of contemporary Africa's underdevelopment may be an entrepreneurship problem. However, it argues that Africa does not lack entrepreneurs *per se*. What Africa lacks, instead, are entrepreneurs with the right kind of HF; a lack that has resulted from the historical processes of colonialism and neo-colonialism. Africa does not need more entrepreneurs. It instead needs entrepreneurs with the necessary sacrificial and cooperative spirit, who are not only interested in maximizing profits through dubious means for private ostentatious ends, but also consider the improvement of the larger society as a critical part of their entrepreneurial agenda.

ANATOMY OF AFRICAN ENTREPRENEURSHIP

The argument concerning the lack of entrepreneurship with the right type of HF advanced in this chapter is not aimed at reinforcing "the inadequate individual or defective social structure" proposition of modernization theory (Belasco, 1980, p. 177). In fact, Africa does not lack innovators and risktakers. By extension, indigenous African social structures do not necessarily discourage propensity to innovate nor create barriers to risktaking. The innovativeness and risktaking spirit of Africans are evident in their economic activities in the pre-colonial, colonial and post-colonial periods.

In the pre-colonial times, various African societies had vibrant trade links among themselves and with the Arab world and the Mediterranean coast of Europe. African commodities exchanged included gold and other precious minerals, salt, ivory, kola nuts, liquor, textiles, jewelry, agricultural implements, weapons and, of course, slaves. In colonial Africa, Africans produced and exchanged minerals and cash crops such as cocoa, coffee, tea, cotton, sisal, palm oil, and copra. These activities continue in post-colonial Africa. For example, Africa is the number-one producer of cocoa. In recent times, African commod-

ities such as salted and dry fish, cassava and plantain powder, cane products
and traditional fabrics and clothes are produced and exported by Africans to
Europe, Asia and North America to meet the demand of Africans in the diaspora.
In addition to the above economic activities, there have been vibrant informal
sector manufacturing activities taking place in various parts of Africa. Typical
examples are *Kokompe* and *Suame Magazine* in Ghana and *Nnewi* in Nigeria
(*Kokompe* and *Nnewi* are automobile part manufacturing centers). These economic activities clearly suggest that Africa does not lack "real entrepreneurs,"
that is, "new men [*sic*]" who introduce "new methods of production, new
sources of raw material, and new products and markets" (Trivedi, 1991, p. 9).
The pertinent question is: Why has it been the case that the flourishing of entrepreneurship in Africa fails to translate into self-sustained socioeconomic development?

AFRICAN ENTREPRENEURS AND UNDERDEVELOPMENT

It is possible to understand the failure of African entrepreneurship to create
viable socioeconomic development from the perspective of the acquired HF of
African entrepreneurs rather than their size. Africans neither suffer from the
"anti-entrepreneurial attitudes" syndrome proposed by Awad (1971, p. 462)
nor lack high "achievement motivation" as proposed by McClelland (1971a, p.
121). On the contrary, there seems to be even more entrepreneurs than is necessary. Africa has many cash crop farmers, small-scale manufacturers, brokers,
artisans and traders who take risks in organizing production and distribution of
goods and services. In fact, the informal economic sector, which constitutes the
hub of these indigenous entrepreneurs, occupies more than 60 percent of the
economies of many African countries.

In effect, if Africa is not developing as it should, it is hardly because of the
small size of African entrepreneurial class as purported by Trivedi (1991, p. 1).
The explanation rather lies in the quality of African entrepreneurs. The following
problems permeate African entrepreneurship: getting rich quick through fair or
foul means; squandering business profits in ostentatious living rather than reinvestment; failing to pull resources together to create more viable ventures;
caring more for profits than entrepreneurial values—profits through short-term
measures; and lacking community spirit. In short, for entrepreneurship to be a
catalyst for development, there must be entrepreneurs with the right attitudes
and values. Contemporary Africa lacks entrepreneurs with the appropriate HF.

Unscrupulous Entrepreneurs

Many contemporary African entrepreneurs seem to be more interested in maximizing and harvesting their profits in the shortest possible time. This is not a
bad thing if they legitimately use innovative means. Rather, these entrepreneurs
specialize in using dubious means for this end. Their philosophy seems to be

"the end justifies the means," as has been the case in the United States. What they, perhaps, do not realize is that the use of unproductive methods to maximize profits does not stimulate sustained economic development in society. The *kalabule*[2] system of Ghana, particularly during the 1970s, illustrates this point. The so-called businesspeople concentrate on buy-and-sell businesses and create artificial shortages through hoarding of commodities to reap windfall profits. Some of them major in manipulating or forging import licenses to import goods at state subsidized prices. These commodities are then sold at inflationary prices. Such activities do not promote economic development because they hardly ever add any value to the production process.

The few African entrepreneurs who engage in manufacturing activities also suffer from the *kalabule* syndrome. They are not quality conscious. They poorly imitate and/or copy foreign products and yet sell them at prices as high as the originals. Sooner or later, consumers see through the smokescreen and stop patronizing these goods. Industries built on this shaky foundation do not stay in business for long. Typical examples are the African cosmetic and electronic manufacturers. In view of these cases, Sharma's (1980) work about Indian entrepreneurship cited by Trivedi (1991, pp. 14–15) is relevant to the African situation. Sharma (1980), according to Trivedi (pp. 14–15), argued that entrepreneurs are much more engrossed with profit maximization than being true to traditional entrepreneurial values. As such, their primary objective is to increase their own short-term wealth rather than long-term development in their societies. This kind of entrepreneurship, reminiscent of irresponsibility, does not have the capacity to create sustained economic development.

African Entrepreneurs and the Misuse of Acquired Profits

An important hallmark of effective entrepreneurship is the ploughing back of a substantial portion of earned profits into the enterprise to generate more profits and/or increased investment in other productive business ventures. There seems to be a conspicuous absence of this quality in many contemporary African entrepreneurs. Although many African entrepreneurs make enough profit from their business activities, they tend to spend a chunk of this profit on ostentatious living. There are several instances where business profit is used to acquire many wives, luxurious automobiles, mansions and expensive clothes and to conduct glamorous funerals. With this kind of life-style and attitude, it is no wonder that larger industrial establishments owned by African entrepreneurs are a rare scene on the African economic landscape.

African entrepreneurs need to realize that the reinvestment of profits is a necessary requirement for entrepreneurial growth. As Trivedi (1991, p. 10) rightly observed, the Gujaratis and Marwaris of India experienced entrepreneurial growth when "a group of self-made entrepreneurs began to emerge, who, by ploughing back their high profits into their small workshops, could build-up larger industrial establishments." African entrepreneurs cannot hide behind the facade of lack of capital to justify their failure to achieve growing and sustained entrepreneurship. It does not take any huge start-up capital to be successful in entrepreneurship. The experience of the Marwaris of India supports this claim. According to Trivedi (1991, p. 11), "the Marwaris emerged as big investors and industrialists from the status of petty-shop keepers and moneylenders."

In fact, there is no shortage of petty traders and artisans in Africa. A cursory observation of African cities, towns and villages would demonstrate that there is even an overabundance of these categories of people. The problem of these African entrepreneurs is their failure to reinvest their profits in productive economic activities. This is not a cultural problem, for pre-colonial African entrepreneurs achieved tremendous successes through the ploughing back of their profits into their ventures. It is a HF issue. Many contemporary African entrepreneurs do not seem to have the sacrificial spirit characteristic of traditional African entrepreneurs and leaders. Contemporary African entrepreneurs should learn that nothing sacrificed, nothing gained.

The Uncooperative Spirit and African Entrepreneurship

Many African entrepreneurs concentrate their activities on small-scale enterprises. This is not because they lack the skills to manage large enterprises, but mainly because they lack the requisite financial and physical capital (Adu-Febiri, 1994). This problem of insufficient capital could be solved by creating cooperative and joint-stock enterprises. In traditional African societies, people pull their resources together in the areas of labor, capital and organization. For example, the cocoa industry in West Africa benefitted a great deal from such cooperative efforts, particularly at the extended family level (Hill, 1970, pp. 21–29). This system of economic organization works mainly because of the existence of strong principles of mutual trust. Unfortunately, the cooperative spirit has waned under the onslaught of colonization, particularly through the state formation process (Adu-Febiri, 1995). The failure of African entrepreneurs to pull their resources together is manifested in the fact that most African entrepreneurs are sole proprietors: partnerships and joint-stock enterprises are exceptions. Mutual distrust seems to be at the root of this lack of cooperation among African entrepreneurs.

Lack of Community Spirit

Contemporary African societies have millionaires who acquired their wealth through successful entrepreneurship. However, their wealth fails to have growth impacts on the economies of their societies. The reason is not only because they concentrate on the sphere of circulation (Febiri, 1991, pp. 45–50), but also because they seldom invest in community development projects. There are only a few instances in contemporary Africa where indigenous businesspeople substantially contribute to the building of schools, libraries, health and sanitation facilities and research projects in universities.[3] Rather, whenever possible, many a businessperson will exploit community resources to build personal wealth, power and prestige. It is in this connection that Nyerere's (1964) emphasis on the need for Africans to change their selfish attitudes becomes relevant. Nyerere (p. 242) suggested that "Our first step, therefore, must be to re-educate ourselves; to regain our former attitude of mind. In our traditional African society we were individuals within a community. We took care of the community, and the community took care of us."

Perhaps it is because of the blind adoption of Western values that many contemporary African entrepreneurs attune more to the venturesomeness and profit motivation aspects of entrepreneurship than the leadership aspect. This does not auger well for African societies that are fundamentally communalistic. In the African context, therefore, more attention should be given to the development of entrepreneurship as a multifunctional leadership that will encourage the exercise of entrepreneurship not only for personal gain but also for communal ends (Asad, 1972, p. 86; Diamond, 1974, p. 135; Belasco, 1980, p. 182).

STRATEGIES FOR PREPARING AFRICAN
ENTREPRENEURS FOR INDUSTRIAL DEVELOPMENT

The entrepreneurial skills and knowledge base of African farmers, traders and small-scale industrialists promise to be a dynamic force that can contribute greatly to the continent's economic and social development. Of late, some African countries seem to have realized this need. Hence, they are now attempting to encourage the development of private entrepreneurship through the promotion of nontraditional export products. These efforts are, however, not likely to yield much fruit given the prevailing value orientations of many African entrepreneurs. There is the need for African leaders and developers, therefore, to reactivate traditional African entrepreneurial values such as honesty, loyalty, integrity, accountability, responsibility, sacrifice, modesty, mutual trust, cooperation and community spirit, which have been depreciated by the forces of colonialism and neo-colonialism. Entrepreneurs of contemporary Africa need to be trained to cultivate these necessary entrepreneurial values. The lack of these values, rather than inadequate capital and deficient managerial, supervisory and organizational skills, are the critical bottlenecks of African development.

Africa should, therefore, commit more financial and managerial resources to foster the development of the appropriate HF in its entrepreneurs if there is to be a modern African industrial revolution. Africa could accomplish this by rigorously training its entrepreneurs in the HF and offering them adequate incentives. The underlying reasons for suggesting these methods of effecting the appropriate HF are that (1) training is a time-honored vehicle for systematic and sustained change in human society and (2) usually people respond positively to incentives. When Africa is able to inculcate the HF in its general populace, the entrepreneurs that emerge will more likely possess the appropriate HF for progressive entrepreneurship.

The education system designed for training African entrepreneurs should include adopting a HF-focused curriculum at all levels of the formal education system and organizing periodic seminars on HF for African entrepreneurs, as well as formulating and implementing comprehensive HF civic education programs for politicians, bureaucrats, chiefs, soldiers, the police, local leaders and the general public.

Since the transmission of cultural values such as the HF begins at infancy, the HF education should begin at home. Parents should socialize their children to internalize the appropriate HF. The ministries of education, social welfare and culture must design workable HF educational programs for parents. The night school system and continuing education and training programs would be effective in this direction.

The curricula of elementary, secondary and post-secondary schools should reinforce and consolidate the HF education that starts at home. Business administration programs in African polytechnics, business schools and universities must have a high content of not only the usual entrepreneurial skills and values such as creativity, originality and imagination, but also moral and spiritual values. One way of fostering the HF in students of the school system is by teaching social studies courses that concentrate on both past and contemporary local, national and international entrepreneurs who are successful in business, critically evaluating the magnitude of their HF. Business administration students should do internships under acclaimed entrepreneurs with the relevant HF.

The teacher training education system should have a curriculum that could produce teachers who are fully equipped to impart the HF. African governments and private educators should establish institutes of HF studies, with all teacher trainees and other professionals having to spend at least six months of their training period in these institutes. As part of their professional development projects, African university professors should undergo periodic training in these institutes of HF studies.

African governments and business associations must periodically organize and fund seminars with specific HF agenda for entrepreneurs. Organizers of these seminars should ensure that they are participatory, providing forums for various entrepreneurs to share innovative ideas and techniques on HF development. Also, organizers of such seminars should include in the package received by attendees a list of local businesses that have exhibited the HF in their business operations and/or activities.

With regard to civic education, African governments should use their national television and radio stations as channels of propagating the HF to the target groups mentioned above. Governments must ensure that the innovative organizational ideas and technologies of African entrepreneurs and intellectuals are celebrated by the mass media. For example, morning and evening news should always feature successful entrepreneurs who always adhere to HF principles in their businesses. Local communities should set up information services offices to collaborate the HF educational efforts of the national media and the ministries of education, social welfare and culture. This type of civic education is aimed at providing a supportive environment for entrepreneurship. Thus, it should strive to instill in Africans that entrepreneurship based on the HF is a common societal good towards which all members of society must work.

Turning to the use of incentives for entrepreneurship development, governments and local communities must create practical and adequate incentive systems that would stimulate entrepreneurs to apply the necessary HF to their businesses. In this respect, the chapter proposes the following strategies:

1. Organize an annual HF development week to honor entrepreneurs who adhere to HF principles in their business. The honor should be in the form of concrete prizes such as cash and plaques as well as traditional clothes and crafts. The national television, radio, magazines and newspapers should publicize these celebrations of new entrepreneurship.

2. Name schools, institutions, streets, historic buildings and monuments after entrepreneurs and other nationals who demonstrate extraordinary responsibility, accountability, integrity, community spirit, innovativeness and national loyalty.

3. Discourage the importation of goods that local entrepreneurs could produce by imposing high sales tax on those commodities. The revenue that would accrue from such a tax should be loaned to local entrepreneurs investing in the production of those items.

4. Make fully tax deductible investments in HF and community development projects.

5. Give substantial loans and tax breaks to entrepreneurs who invest in areas such as food and raw material production, food processing, manufacturing, mining, textiles, arts and crafts, alternative tourism and sanitation.

6. Give special loans to entrepreneurs who, by entering into partnerships and joint-stock enterprises, demonstrate effective cooperation and continuously plough back some required minimum amount of financial resources into their businesses. Tax incentives must be given to these enterprises.

7. Sponsor a number of deserving entrepreneurs on short-term scholarship trips to visit foreign businesses that show the positive effects of continuing HF application.

8. Publicize through the mass media donations made by entrepreneurs to charity, university research and scholarship funds. Also make these donations tax deductible.

The implementation of the above suggestions on incentives would go a long way to reinforce the HF educational programs.

CONCLUSION

African countries are going through a serious development crisis (Onimode, 1988), and in the coming years, this crisis is likely to become more intense if African leaders and developers do not take effective measures to arrest it. The hope lies in Africa making the development of entrepreneurs its top priority. HF decay, particularly in the area of entrepreneurship, is the main underlying factor of Africa's underdevelopment. Lack of high achievement motivation, capital, modern technology and managerial skills are symptomatic of underdevelopment. The experiences of the advanced industrialized nations and the newly industrializing countries underscore this assertion. They have achieved economic development mainly because they created the entrepreneurs with the appropriate HF. This, in turn, generated the other necessary ingredients of development.

Africa needs similar entrepreneurs to remove itself from current socioeconomic doldrums. Since entrepreneurs with the HF are made, African countries are capable of creating this type of entrepreneurship. Herein lies the hope for contemporary African societies. This hope would, however, remain a mere dream unless African leaders, developers and educators get serious about training all entrepreneurs to acquire the HF and give them adequate incentives to apply the acquired HF to their enterprises.

NOTES

1. The Human Factor (HF) is given a new meaning by Adjibolosoo (1994), pp. 25–37. According to Adjibolosoo, it is an unchanging fact that "to be effective and efficient in the production process, the people of a nation must also acquire unique human qualities and/or characteristics that encourage and promote economic progress (such as discipline, dedication, responsibility, accountability, integrity, and the like). It is these attributes and many others akin to them that contribute to a successful or unsuccessful utilization of acquired knowledge and skills. Human capital is, therefore, a small segment of the HF."

2. *Kalabule* is a system of exploitation of the masses by Ghanaian businesspeople in the 1970s. It involves the creation of artificial shortages through the hoarding of essential consumer items. By manipulating the simple economic principle of supply and demand, prices are effectively inflated and windfall profits reaped. See a detailed analysis and discussion on *kalabule* in Adjibolosoo (1995a), pp. 53, 69–70.

3. Many African entrepreneurs donate money to churches during harvest feasts but not to concrete community projects such as schools, market buildings, sanitation projects, water projects, libraries and research projects. They must be encouraged to extend some of this generosity to meaningful community programs and/or projects.

REFERENCES

Adjibolosoo, S. 1994. "The Human Factor and the Failure of Development Planning and Economic Policy in Africa." In F. Ezeala-Harrison and S. Adjibolosoo, eds., *Perspectives on Economic Development in Africa*. Westport, Conn.: Praeger.

Adjibolosoo, S. 1995a. *The Human Factor in Developing Africa*. Westport, Conn.: Praeger.

Adjibolosoo, S. 1995b. "The Genesis of Entrepreneurial and Commercial Decline in Africa." Unpublished discussion paper, Trinity Western University.

Adu-Febiri, F. 1994. "Tourism and Ghana's Development Process: Problems of and Prospects for Creating a Viable 'Post-Industrial' Service Industry in a Non-

industrial Society." Unpublished Ph.D. Thesis, Department of Anthropology and
Sociology, The University of British Columbia, Vancouver, Canada.

Adu-Febiri, F. 1995. "Culture as the Epitome of the Human Factor in Development: The
Case of Ghana's Collectivistic Ethic." In S. Adjibolosoo, ed., *The Significance
of the Human Factor in African Economic Development.* Westport, Conn.: Praeger.

Asad, T. 1972. "Market Model, Class Structure, and Consent: A Reconsideration of
Swat Political Organization." *Man* 71 (1): 45–51.

Awad, M. H. 1971. "The Supply of Risk Bearers in the Underdeveloped Countries."
Economic Development and Cultural Change 19 (3): 461–68.

Belasco, B. I. 1980. *The Entrepreneur as Cultural Hero: Preadaptations in Nigerian
Economic Development.* New York: Praeger.

Diamond, S. 1974. *In Search of the Primitive, A Critique of Civilization.* New Brunswick,
N.J.: Transaction Books.

Febiri, F. A. 1991. "Marxism, Social Class, Ethnic and Gender Inequalities in Contemporary African Societies." *The African Review* 18 (1–2): 39–56.

Friedland, W. H. and Roseberg, C. G. 1964. "Introduction: The Anatomy of African
Socialism." In W. H. Friedland and C. G. Roseberg, eds., *African Socialism.*
Stanford, Calif.: Stanford University Press.

Hagen, E. E. 1971. "How Economic Growth Begins: A Theory of Social Change." In
P. Kilby, ed., *Entrepreneurship and Economic Development.* New York: Free
Press.

Heilbroner, R. L. 1989. *The Making of Economic Society.* Englewood Cliffs, N.J.: Pren-
tice Hall.

Hill, P. 1970. *Studies in Rural Capitalism in West Africa.* Cambridge: Cambridge University Press.

LeVine, R. 1966. *Dreams and Deeds: Achievement Motivation in Nigeria.* Chicago: University of Chicago Press.

Marx, K. 1973. *Capital, Vol. I.* New York: International Publishers.

McClelland, D. 1971a. "The Achievement Motive in Economic Growth." In P. Kilby,
ed., *Entrepreneurship and Economic Development.* New York: Free Press.

McClelland, D. 1971b. *Motivational Trends in Society.* Morristown, N.J.: General Learning Press.

Nycrcrc, J. K. 1964. "Ujamaa: The Basis of African Socialism." In W. H. Friedland
and C. G. Rosberg, eds., *African Socialism.* Stanford, Calif.: Stanford University
Press.

Onimode, B. 1988. *A Political Economy of the African Crisis.* London: Zed Books Ltd.

Sharma, K. L. 1980. *Entrepreneurial Growth and Development Programs in Northern
India: A Sociological Analysis.* New Delhi: Abhinav Publications.

Trivedi, M. 1991. *Entrepreneurship Among Tribals.* Jaipur, India: Printwell.

6

Education and Training for Effective Leadership Development and Productivity and Quality Management in Africa

Senyo B-S. K. Adjibolosoo

INTRODUCTION

For many years, African businesses have been deeply involved in the productivity and quality revolution. Although great successes have been achieved, there is yet much to be done. The methods whereby continuing productivity and quality enhancement could be achieved are not always obvious to business leaders and managers. The crucial point to note is that it is the availability of the relevant human factor (HF) that provides the necessary leadership qualities for efficient organizing, managing and controlling of the existing productivity and quality management programs. The HF, through the commitment and integrity it creates, directs and motivates employees to accomplish tasks required for continuing improvements in productivity and quality. In this chapter, I argue that regardless of the magnitude of the resources put into productivity and quality enhancement programs, the results may not be longlasting without adequate development of human qualities and characteristics (i.e., the HF). A model for preparing productivity and quality managers in African countries (ACs) is developed and presented.

For several years, African leaders and business managers have made relentless efforts to achieve improved factor productivity and product or service quality. Although African leaders and managers seek expert advisors who are steeped in productivity and quality enhancement knowledge, problems of low productivity and poor quality goods and services continue to plague social, economic and political institutions in Africa.

It seems to me, therefore, that in many cases, productivity and quality enhancement programs fail because they ignore the fact that for continuing success, HF engineering must be made the primary core of these programs. The desire for quick fixes usually leads to the institution of ad hoc productivity and quality enhancement programs at every level of the business organization. In what follows, this chapter argues that unless African leaders and business managers view HF engineering as the integrating core of the productivity and quality education and/or revolution, very little will be achieved in terms of positive changes in factor productivity and product or service quality.

The HF is the primary requisite for effective and continuing human performance for all nations. It is in view of this that it is critical that HF development be made the basic foundation for leadership development of the work force, productivity and quality improvement in ACs. Education and training for leadership development and enhanced productivity management has to begin with programs solely aimed at the total development of the HF.

OBSERVED QUALITY OF THE AFRICAN LEADERSHIP AND WORKFORCE

A recent survey of 805 business managers in the city of Vancouver, British Columbia, and its surrounding municipalities concluded that there exists a set of necessary qualities that people must possess to be effective leaders, productivity managers and employees (Adjibolosoo, 1995b). These results are summarized and presented in Table 6.1. The results reveal what managers perceive to be the critical human qualities that the labor force must possess to be effective and efficient on the job. These qualities play a critical role in leadership effectiveness, managerial success and improved employee productivity in the twenty-first century. African leaders and productivity and work force managers must be problem solvers who relentlessly pursue excellence in leadership, productivity and management. In a speech delivered in the late 1980s, Konosuke Matsushita, founder of Matsushita Electric Industrial company, noted that the increasing complexity and escalating global competitiveness of business require that every company must have all its employees entirely committed to be successful. The intellectual capacities and total commitment of the work force is critical to company survival and success (see Townsend and Gebhardt, 1992, p. 12).

As such, the quality of the workforce cannot be brushed aside when African firms search for continuing success. Matsushita's view suggests that business companies and/or nations cannot achieve significant successes without a well-prepared and disciplined labor force. By focusing on and emphasizing the HF, necessary leadership will be developed in Africa. Leaders who have been assisted to develop all their potentials will turn out to be assets for African productivity management and turnaround. The existing crisis in Africa calls for responsible, accountable, committed leaders and loyal employees. Where the leadership lacks vision, conscience, character, integrity and foresight, it will be almost impossible to develop. In view of this, it is very important that education and training programs in African countries must focus on helping students to

Table 6.1
Ranking of Human Qualities as They Affect Worker Effectiveness, Efficiency and Productivity

Human Quality	Description	Mean	Standard Error
Responsibility	Acting without detailed guidance	7.9	1.8
Commitment	Binding onself to a course of action	7.6	2.0
Integrity	Uprightness and honesty	7.7	2.3
Knowledge	Theoretical and/or practical understanding of a subject	7.4	2.1
Accountability	Answerable for one's actions	6.8	2.2
Judgment	Good sense of discernment	6.4	2.2
Creativity	Originality and imagination	5.6	2.4
Sensitivity	Degree of susceptibility to others or stimulation	4.8	2.6
Courage	Acting on one's convictions	4.0	2.5
Humility	Having modest opinion of one's importance or rank; meekness or showing high regard for others	3.2	2.5

Source: Adjibolosoo (1995b).

develop integrity and personal trust. By successfully achieving this goal, the African education and training systems will produce good leaders. Thus, ACs that will be successful in the twenty-first century will be those that are currently investing huge financial resources in HF development. Each country must identify the necessary human qualities lacking in its leadership, managers and employees and assist them to develop the pertinent HF.

GROOMING AND MANAGING THE PEOPLE

As we enter the twenty-first century, a primary concern of every sub-Saharan AC is the implementation of economic development programs and policies that will improve living conditions. To permanently improve human welfare, labor productivity must increase—a demand that raises the following two questions: (1) How can average labor productivity be increased under prevailing conditions? and (2) Is the objective of feeding, clothing and housing sub-Saharan Africans feasible and sustainable?

The goal for increasing labor productivity is attainable only if sub-Saharan Africans can be motivated to change current labor practices, methods and cultural mind-sets (Adjibolosoo, 1995a, pp. 190–191). They must acknowledge that the attempt to increase productivity requires efficient management of every social, economic and political institution. These institutions, however, need people-managers with a strong work ethic to implement programs on productivity enhancement. As the vehicle of economic development, a society's labor force must be well-groomed and managed.

Many businesses, organizations and countries are fond of introducing programs that will enhance labor productivity or improve product quality. These programs must be designed to promote and develop worker confidence in management.

Presently, resources are poured into education and training programs that do not meet the needs of changing sub-Saharan African societies. Many of these programs are not only ineffective, but also not relevant to the economic development process (see chapter 1). Sub-Saharan ACs need education and training programs that will produce skilled and principled workers who can increase their average labor productivity and also adapt to ever-changing national and global situations. In terms of primary, secondary and university education, many sub-Saharan ACs have made some advancements. In recent years, the number of students who have had primary education has steadily increased (Cornia and de Jong, 1992, pp. 246–271). Furthermore, many of these students have pursued post-secondary education, earning master's and Ph.D. degrees in their chosen fields. In most cases however, primary education has not been accorded the priority it deserves, since a number of the graduates have not increased their labor productivity. This discovery raises the question of whether or not existing sub-Saharan African education and training programs can produce the HF necessary for economic development.

To be successful, all efforts to increase the mean labor productivity and economic development in sub-Saharan ACs must focus on total development of the HF and welfare enhancement. Many economic development plans and social, economic, educational and political policies have failed because of the negligible attention paid to the development of the HF. Existing plans, policies and programs have done little to increase competence for they do not progressively enhance labor productivity. The success of labor productivity enhancement programs and economic development plans depends not only on the availability of economic resources and acquired human capital, but also on the people who have acquired the appropriate HF. No nation can successfully achieve economic development without developing its HF first.

The main objective of the social, economic, educational and political planning machinery of every sub-Saharan AC must begin with relevant research into discovering the relevant HF. By acquiring adequate knowledge, sub-Saharan Africans will be able to successfully restructure and manage their institutions in order to achieve dynamic progress in economic development. Ulrich (1991, p. 144) noted that the effective and efficient functioning of an organization or a specific department requires excellent human resource management. As such, procurement, manufacturing, distribution, marketing, sales and service departments cannot achieve any successes without operating through people. The creation of competitive advantage requires successful management of people.

Similarly, Schuler and Jackson (1989, p. 44) observed that the successful pursuit of competitive strategy requires the ability to manage and select well-qualified and highly skilled people who are furnished with the necessary resources to perform. For sub-Saharan ACs to expand their industry, develop the economy and build confidence in their governments, they must equip the labor force to manage all institutions. Their planning and policy machinery must articulate solutions to all problems of economic underdevelopment. To solve existing problems, these institutions must adapt and adopt what is known about using human resources in developed countries. Furthermore, these characteristics should be thoroughly researched to determine what they actually are and how they affect economic development.

A MODEL FOR ENGINEERING THE HF AND MANAGING THE LABOR FORCE

The following discussion proposes a model for grooming and managing the sub-Saharan African people to acquire the necessary HF that will help increase average labor productivity. The model in Table 6.2 suggests that the grooming and managing processes must begin by identifying the basic embodiments of the existing HF (stage I) and by asking the following questions: What is the current state of the HF in each sub-Saharan AC? What skills are available? What are the orientation and the morale levels of the labor force? What ethos and universal principles are being followed? Do sub-Saharan African people

Table 6.2
A Model for Grooming and Managing the HF

Stage I	Stage II	Stage III
Identify the embodiments of the existing HF	Groom the HF-appropriate education, training and socialization programs	Accomplish the management process by planning, organizing, integrating and measuring

have and practice a sound work ethic? Whatever the answers to these questions may be, the planners must proceed to stage II, which involves grooming people through education, training, mentoring and other socialization programs.

Brown and Comola (1991, p. 48) observed that "training from the viewpoint of the company must involve three major attributes: acquisition of skills necessary for performance, optimization of system performance through education, and attitude alteration of the worker toward objectives of the company. Failure of any one of the three can result in total failure."

These programs must be directed at developing the human personality, acquiring the appropriate HF, gaining attributes and abilities and cultivating productive systems based on universal principles: creativity, the spirit of responsibility and accountability, self-efficacy, self-management, entrepreneurship and so on. Although such programs may be expensive to pursue initially, they must be instituted because the long-term benefits are bound to outweigh the initial time and financial costs. At the end of the grooming process, if the people acquire communication, behavior, analytical, quantitative, and decision-making skills, the program will have achieved its objectives. The acquisition of these skills will enable the people to commit themselves to excellence and to encouraging higher productivity.

A deliberate grooming of the people is important because "it produces an educated electorate, a competent workforce, and innovations to develop the future" (Brown and Comola, 1991, p. 57). The design of the HF preparation process must encourage personal improvements that will in turn generate increased labor productivity. If the model is properly implemented, it will produce visionaries, educators, entrepreneurs, engineers, administrators, scientists, managers, a creatively self-motivated work force, and so on. Grooming programs require sensitivity to educational needs. Vaizey and Debeauvais (1961, p. 43) noted that

the education system should be sufficiently flexible to allow it to respond fairly rapidly to the changing needs of the economy. . . . Education should therefore be relatively abundant, flexible, and capable of producing people with a high general level of culture, which makes them more adaptable to changing economic and social conditions. An increasing emphasis on adult education is necessary if the adult workforce is to be prepared to face the risks inherent in the process of economic growth.

The final stage of the model in Table 6.2 is the completion of the management process. Managers of both public and private corporations have to plan, organize and use the skills, talents and qualities of those people who were adequately prepared and have acquired the necessary HF. They must effectively integrate the labor force with other existing co-operant factors to enhance labor productivity. At each stage, they must install safety mechanisms to monitor performance and deal with bottlenecks. These monitoring mechanisms may not be necessary in the long run if the labor force has gained the required HF.

When people are schooled to develop themselves around universal principles, work ethics and acceptable social ethos, labor productivity will rise without continuing supervision. People will frequently perform at their highest level of potential because their work ethics, principles of living and social ethos will demand it. From this perspective, as the grooming program matures, neither productivity enhancement programs nor strict supervision will be required. Programs designed for improving worker productivity must, therefore, focus on personal development and revolve around universal principles, social ethos and work ethics. Having identified these principles and defined the social ethos and relevant work ethics, education, training and mentoring programs must then foster an environment that will adequately prepare people to attain the necessary HF.

Proper transformational education and training will help the labor force meet the needs of its society. Individuals must be appropriately trained, socialized, educated and equipped to become problem solvers who are loyal, dedicated, responsible and accountable. Although many different methods for accomplishing this goal may exist, sub-Saharan ACs need to take a more detailed look at their institutional structures and social norms, since these usually exert strong impacts on performance, social character and individual ability.

Achieving a turnaround in the economic development process cannot happen through mere cosmetic changes in goals, policies, ideologies and programs; rather, it requires a massive internal overhaul of the existing social character and cultural mind-sets. This overhaul requires changes throughout the country and in the working of existing institutions and other entrenched social rent-seeking practices that may destabilize economic development plans and social, economic and political policies (see Adjibolosoo, 1995a, chapter 3). The changes would positively affect the role of the people in the process of economic development. To achieve higher average labor productivity and economic development, mandatory changes may include modifying or, perhaps, abandoning certain aspects of the existing culture, their negative rent-seeking behavior and their inefficient institutional structures.

In the past, attempts to develop the available human resources failed to produce individuals who had acquired necessary human qualities. The model for grooming and managing the required HF (see Table 6.2) must correct this deficiency and produce people who will be determined and willing to raise their labor productivity.

This process must deal with existing social practices that militate against higher labor productivity. Properly developed, HF will equip sub-Saharan Africans with the positive embodiments outlined in Table 6.3. If sub-Saharan Africans attain these positive HF aspects, programs to enhance productivity, economic development plans and policies will have a higher chance of success. In the absence of such attributes, ACs must institute grooming programs such as those listed in part B of Table 6.3. Having developed the required HF in the labor force, sub-Saharan ACs will find the management and leadership functions easier to accomplish. Part C of Table 6.3 provides a list of management objectives; managers (whether private, public, military, etc.) must work relentlessly to reach these goals. Labor productivity in sub-Saharan Africa will rise if the model is successfully implemented.

ENHANCING MANAGERIAL AND LEADERSHIP EFFECTIVENESS

Management effectiveness is evident in the extent to which a society develops the relevant HF in its people. In terms of the embodiments listed in part A of Table 6.3, managers, educators and trainers must successfully identify and appropriately deal with any observed bottlenecks. Careful attention must be paid to management objectives by properly grooming, controlling and managing those who have developed the required HF. The acid test of success in this economic program will be marked by accompanying growth in average labor productivity, based on the HF approach to development.

Management must devise ongoing reinforcement programs that boost worker productivity by providing rewards for performance. For example, workers may be rewarded for the following: making personal sacrifices that lead to productivity increases; accepting and accomplishing overtime work requests; and developing programs or ideas to raise average output. Whatever form rewards take, they must be offered when any worker achieves an extraordinary output goal. Commendations and honors conferred upon selected individuals may encourage others to follow.

Although it may be difficult to set up such programs, African managers and leaders can benefit from the ideas of Sims and Lorenzi (1992, p. 46) who noted that:

The specific timing of rewards creates schedules of reinforcement. Rewards/disincentives can be distributed based on a time period (interval) or on the occurrence of the desired behavior (ratio). Rewards/disincentives can be awarded on a continuous basis or (more commonly) on an intermittent basis. For intermittent schedules, the pattern can be consistent (fixed) or irregular (variable). That is, if rewards are not continuous, they are intermittent. Intermittent schedules include fixed interval and fixed ratio as well as variable interval and variable ratio.

Table 6.3
The HF: Embodiments, Grooming and Management Objectives

A. Embodiments	
Positive	Negative
Integrity	its opposite
Responsibility	. . .
Self-sufficiency	. . .
Self-management	. . .
Accountability	. . .
Dedication	. . .
Devotion	. . .
Commitment	. . .
Ability to achieve	. . .
Motivation	. . .
Initiative	. . .
Innovativeness	. . .
Inventiveness	. . .
Technical ability	. . .
Conceptual skills	. . .
Personal relations skills	. . .
Positive attitudes and abilities	. . .
Others	. . .

B. Grooming Programs

Education, training, socialization (i.e., seminars, conferences, internships, role playing, field trips, etc.).

C. Management Objectives

Clarify goals
Communicate effectively
Empower employee
Encourage participative management
Encourage and reward hard work
Promote management/employee relations
Educate everyone on time management techniques
Pay attention to quality of work life
Achieve reduction of material waste
Deal with employee morale and absenteeism
Achieve cooperative employee involvement
Avoid effort duplication
Establish conditions for higher productivity
Facilitate individual and group performance
Deal with negative rent-seeking activities

The incentive format each sub-Saharan AC uses will depend on the local situation and the behavior to be rewarded. Sims (1979) showed that different reinforcement schedules have varying impacts on employee behavior. For example, continuous reinforcement provides the fastest means for influencing worker behavior. The main problem with this schedule is that the rewarded behavior can quickly disappear if reinforcement is discontinued before a new pattern is permanently established. Conversely, although a slower process, intermittent reinforcement not only encourages the gradual formation of behavior, but guarantees its durability. To enhance the performance of sub-Saharan African workers, each manager must determine which of these reinforcement schedules best encourages productivity increases in a specific environment. When properly used, schedules of reinforcement could lead to the development of a productive and long-lasting work ethic. This will encourage each employee to perform at his or her best regardless of existing reinforcement schedules or other employee monitoring systems. The development of a positive work ethic is the ultimate goal of the HF model for grooming and managing people. When workers learn to manage themselves independently and when all resources, requirements and specifications for the production process are in place, productivity will increase and ensure managerial effectiveness.

PRODUCING EFFECTIVE AND EFFICIENT MANAGERS AND LEADERS

In training sub-Saharan African leaders and business managers for either national government or productivity and quality management, it is necessary to follow effective use and careful control of the management process (i.e., planning, organizing, leading and controlling resource use—the four major categories of management functions).

In the education and training process, emphasis must be placed on the acquisition of proper and productive skills and other relevant dimensions of the HF. Effective management requires: (1) technical skills—the ability to utilize expertise to effect goals, (2) human skills—the ability to work in cooperation with others (i.e., human relations skills), and (3) conceptual skills—the ability to identify problems and opportunities to solve these problems analytically and/ or take advantage of them. Yet, these skills cannot be utilized successfully without having developed the other critical dimensions of the HF (see details in Chapter 2 of this book).

In the case of technical skills, it is necessary that both business and engineering schools provide the integrated education and training necessary for equipping prospective productivity and quality managers. Training must emphasize not only the acquisition of technical skills, but also the utilization of these skills to achieve productivity and quality goals. For example, students must not only learn about marketing techniques, accounting processes, manufacturing procedures, designs, etc., but also learn how to apply the acquired managerial and technical expertise in a more productive way. In a sense, a mutual relationship between business and engineering institutions on one side and the businesses on the other must provide the required environment where a new generation of leaders and managers can learn about the technical aspects of leadership and productivity and quality management. By so doing, this new breed of national leaders and productivity and quality managers will learn to combine technical, engineering and managerial expertise to foster successful governance and productivity growth.

The Japanese have been highly successful at combining technical and managerial learning. In addition to achieving this goal through business and engineering schools, they also provide appropriate job environments for their employees that enable them to acquire relevant human qualities and skills by spending part of their working years in different functional areas of the business. Employees are able to obtain first-hand information and learn to apply it effectively. While engineering students must be provided with the opportunity to develop skills for managing, communicating, organizing, etc., business students must also learn to understand technical and/or engineering processes. An educational provision that facilitates the attainment of this goal will help develop productivity and quality managers for sub-Saharan African businesses.

Similarly, it can hardly be denied that successful business activities and labor productivity growth require managers with intense and effective conceptual skills and excellent human qualities. These skills and human characteristics can easily be provided through formally instituted integrated business and engineering education. It is thus necessary for business and engineering schools to identify the manufacturing needs and expectations of production managers. To produce effective future national leaders and productivity and quality managers, practical education and training cannot be neglected; that is, institutions must give trainees the opportunity to make frequent visits to production centers (i.e., the factories) and get first-hand information and/or knowledge about the businesses' needs and problems. When visiting production sites, students will learn about problems currently being faced in design and manufacturing. As this becomes a perpetual and integral part of the training process, future productivity and quality managers will gradually develop the necessary conceptual skills required for effective productivity and quality management.

Although case studies may be helpful, they are not always the best way for helping students develop conceptual skills and human qualities. In many cases, for example, case studies deal with issues that have already been resolved; they are just studied after the fact. Telling students how such problems were resolved does not necessarily help them develop the necessary conceptual skills and characteristics required for effective and efficient productivity and quality management. Robinson (1985, p. 116) noted that

many case studies dealing with the practical problems of specific organizations are available from a variety of sources, but the use of these does of course restrict trainees of studying situations which are not always easily related to their own problems and indeed may never be repeated elsewhere. There are therefore advantages in using case studies derived from the experiences of the group's own organization, where there is first-hand information about its successes and failures.

Visiting factories, learning about actual designing and manufacturing problems and thinking up solutions to them would help sub-Saharan ACs develop effective productivity and quality managers. As business problems and needs change, it is necessary that sub-Saharan Africa's traditional educational methods and/or procedures also change to effectively address new demands of society (Adjibolosoo, 1993a).

In the West, business and engineering schools are making meaningful progress through co-operative education. This type of training can provide for greater conceptual skill acquisition than the case study method of business education. Co-operative education can be a strong link between classroom studies and practical business. In a sense, it is capable of bringing business and engineering schools and business together. In both Canada and the United States, many business and engineering schools and corporations are engaging in fruitful education/business cooperation.

Co-op education, as it is usually called, can aid business and engineering students develop conceptual skills by providing them with the environment and/or opportunities through which they can obtain practical experience. In this way, co-op students can put into practice theories learned at school. Co-op education, however, is very selective and is available only to students who make good grades. Unfortunately, the program forgets that other students of average intelligence should also develop their potential for becoming excellent productivity and quality managers in the future. It is necessary that co-op education programs be extended to all students at participating institutions regardless of their grades. Let each student prove him or herself. It will come as no surprise when co-op programs, which include all students, turn out better productivity and quality managers than those restricting opportunities to ''A''-average students (Adjibolosoo, 1993b).

Not only must practical workshops be included in this type of training, but also global dimensions of business. Since schools are educating sub-Saharan Africa's future productivity and quality managers for a globally competitive marketplace, education must also be global in vision. To accomplish this, sub-Saharan African business and engineering schools, in addition to cultural, language and international studies, must also include international co-op internships. Such internships must be carefully designed to provide opportunities for each student to work abroad, in order to develop the global skills and/or experience required for successful management of worldwide business ventures and competition. International co-op and/or practical workshops must form part of the core of business and engineering education in all sub-Saharan African schools.

It is necessary for business and engineering schools to be in constant dialogue with men and women in the business environment. Professors of these institutions must continually be in touch with business and engineering firms. It is hoped that this will allow business and engineering professors to decipher current business needs. It should not be out of place for businesses to organize seminars at their facilities for explaining their current industry problems and pressing needs to professors and students. Businesses must also contribute to the development of business and engineering curricula. Programs can be designed to meet the specific needs of both businesses and students. Furthermore, business and engineering students must be permitted to design their own study programs. This would provide them with valuable opportunities to decide what is best for their education and training.

CONCLUSION

Commitment is the key to accomplishing these objectives. When businesses and business and engineering schools commit themselves to the educational approach put forward in this chapter, productive and encouraging results will be attained. The role of integrative education in business and engineering schools is of crucial importance in the preparation for increased productivity and quality enhancement. When sub-Saharan African leaders and managers learn to be passionately committed to the goals, ideologies and principles underlying effective management, the war against declining productivity and quality will be won. Ideologies, principles and values help prepare managers for steadfastness, dedication, integrity, responsibility, accountability and sacrifice in order to achieve productivity and quality enhancement goals. As noted by Rogow and Lasswell (1963) and reiterated by McFarland (1982), an ideology helps in attempts to solve problems by intellectually stimulating the individual in many different ways. Ideologies, however, do not accomplish tasks in themselves. People, using ideologies, do (Adjibolosoo, 1995a).

Sub-Saharan African businesses need people who have the qualities to lead the work force into the productivity and quality revolution in the twenty-first century. Since values are not only useful, but also are developed over a long period of time, formal business and engineering education in sub-Saharan African schools must educate and train men and women properly for this job. If these issues are left to time and chance, sub-Saharan Africans will be disappointed in the long run. It is an undeniable fact that managers who are committed to productivity and quality improvement must be men and women of character who are groomed to pursue national goals of development.

Sub-Saharan Africans need to educate and train management personnel who are not only married to jobs and/or positions, but also are adaptable and devoted to duty. They must be nurtured to commit totally to the company's productivity and quality management for effective results. Managers must also pursue character and personality development to acquire the necessary HF. It is thus necessary that business and engineering schools produce high caliber men and women who do not only have the skills required by business, but also have the human characteristics that are necessary for perpetual productivity growth and quality enhancement. Sub-Saharan African managers and leaders must be dedicated to strong moral and ethical principles and/or systems. This requires character and personality; the ability to use knowledge and/or information; ambition and commitment, steadfastness and single-mindedness; dedication and sacrifice—the HF. Armed with such men and women at the forefront of sub-Saharan African business, improvement in productivity and quality will be easily accomplished.

Although it seems as if sub-Saharan ACs are unable to solve the problems of economic underdevelopment, hope still exists. As this chapter reveals, the average labor productivity in sub-Saharan ACs can be enhanced. For this progress to occur, however, sub-Saharan ACs must develop programs to deal with the deficiencies in their existing HF.

Sub-Saharan African educators need to realize that the world is changing moment by moment. The implication is that ideas, theories, principles, and so on that worked a few years ago may not necessarily be applicable to the present era. In view of this, it is necessary that the curricula of sub-Saharan African business and engineering schools be continually updated to be relevant and to prepare people to adequately face present-day challenges. If sub-Saharan African countries fail to do so, they will produce educated elites who may be equipped to solve the problems of yesterday but yet, unfortunately, will be incapable of dealing with those of the present and future. The model developed in this chapter can be extended to other subject areas.

REFERENCES

Adjibolosoo, S. 1993a. "The Human Factor in Development." *The Scandinavian Journal of Development Alternatives* 12 (4): 139–149.

Adjibolosoo, S. 1993b. "Productivity and Quality Enhancement Model for African Managers." In D. J. Sumath et al., eds., *Productivity and Quality Management Frontiers—IV.* Norcross, Ga.: Industrial Engineering and Management Press.

Adjibolosoo, S. 1995a. *The Human Factor in Developing Africa.* Westport, Conn.: Praeger.

Adjibolosoo, S. 1995b. "Achieving Optimal Quality and Productivity: The Passions." In D. J. Sumath et al., eds., *Productivity and Quality Management Frontiers—V.* Norcross, Ga.: Industrial Engineering and Management Press.

Brown, J. H. U. and Comola, J. 1991. *Educating for Excellence: Improving Quality and Productivity in the 90's.* New York: Auburn House.

Cornia, G. A. and de Jong, J. 1992. "Policies for the Revitalization of Human Resource Development." In G. A. Cornia, R. van der Hoevan and R. Mkandawire, eds., *Africa's Recovery in the 1990's: From Stagnation and Adjustment to Human Development.* New York: St. Martin's Press.

McFarland, D. E. 1982. *Management and Society: An Institutional Framework.* Englewood Cliffs, N.J.: Prentice-Hall.

Robinson, R. K. 1985. *A Handbook of Training Management.* London: Kogan Page.

Rogow, A. A. and Lasswell, H. D. 1963. *Power, Corruption, and Rectitude.* Englewood Cliffs, N.J.: Prentice-Hall.

Schuler, R. S. and Jackson, S. E. 1989. ''Linking Competitive Strategies with Human Resource Management Practices.'' In F. K. Foulkes, ed., *Strategies with Human Resource Management Practices: Readings.* Englewood Cliffs, N.J.: Prentice-Hall.

Sims, H. P., Jr., and Lorenzi, P. 1992. *The New Leadership Paradigm: Social Learning and Cognition in Organizations.* London: Sage Publications.

Townsend, P. L. and Gebhardt, J. E. 1992. *Quality in Action: 93 Lessons in Leadership, Participation, and Measurement.* New York: John Wiley.

Ulrich, D. 1991. ''Using Human Resources for Competitive Advantage.'' In R. H. Kilmann and I. Kilmann and Associates, eds., *Making Organizations Competitive: Enhancing Networks and Relationships Across Traditional Boundaries.* San Francisco: Jossey-Bass Publishers.

Vaizey, J. and Debeauvais, M. 1961. ''Economic Aspects of Educational Development.'' In A. H. Halsy, J. Floud and C. A. Anderson, eds., *Education, Economy and Society: A Reader in Sociology of Education.* Glencoe, Ill.: The Free Press.

7

Human Factor Development and Labor Productivity Growth in the Agricultural Sector in Africa

Harold J. Harder

INTRODUCTION

In recent years, there has been growing concern about availability of adequate food supplies in many African nations. Some of these concerns can be directly related to problems arising out of conflict situations, to changing weather patterns or to other disruptions of normal human activity. However, as populations in Africa continue to grow, it remains necessary to increase food availability for the growing populations, as well as to improve the diet of those people that currently are inadequately fed. This must be done with minimal environmental degradation, since harm to ecological balance may reduce the potential for future generations to feed themselves. Therefore, this chapter presents the need for research and training for improved agricultural production that values those involved and seeks to show that persons from different levels of society need to work cooperatively in order to solve these urgent problems.

THE NEED TO INCREASE FOOD PRODUCTION IN AFRICA

That there are frequent food shortages in Africa should come as no surprise when one realizes that over the last few decades, per-capita food production has been declining in Africa. Figure 7.1 illustrates the problem of declining per-capita food production and shows that this decline has occurred despite increases in total food production, because population growth has been more rapid than that of total food production.[1] The trend in Africa is different from the world-wide trend as illustrated in Figure 7.2. Worldwide, during the same time period, total food production has grown more rapidly than has population, resulting in an increase in per-capita food production. Figures 7.1 and 7.2 show values as

Figure 7.1
Africa: Food Production and Population Trends

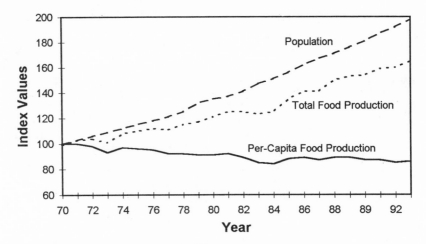

Source: FAO Production Yearbook, 1980–1993.

index values with 100 being the average level at the reference point (1969–1971), in order to compare trends in several factors. It will be necessary to increase food production at a rate greater than the population growth rate in order to improve on the current situation, as well as to keep up with the food needs of a growing population.

In addition to recognizing the changing total food requirements for a growing population, it is important to realize that agriculture itself is dynamic, since it deals with living things—plants, animals and microorganisms—which change, adapt and live in a changing environment. New pests—insects, microorganisms or disease—as well as other changing environmental factors can diminish existing food production and storage capacity if no effort is given to deal with these continual challenges.

In view of the need for increasing food production at a rate greater than the population growth rate and dealing with naturally occurring changes in food production capacity, it would seem reasonable that increasing food production at the local level—where it would be available for the majority of the people—would have been a development priority in African countries; dealing with food production and distribution must be priority since people can live without some of the amenities gained from modern industrial production, but not without food. Yet, it seems that in many cases attempts at industrial expansion have taken priority over development of food production capacity for consumption by the people. Even when attention was given to improving agricultural production, many of the efforts at agricultural development focused on developing large-scale agriculture for export crops or for production of a few staple foods (Huss-

Figure 7.2
World: Food Production and Population Trends

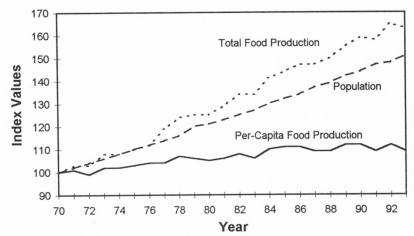

Source: FAO Production Yearbook, 1980–1993.

Ashmore, 1989; Hyden, 1986; Keller and Mbewe, 1991; Moock, 1986; Shipley, 1987). Yet, increased production for export or large-scale production of marketable staple foods seldom increases food availability for the majority of the population who cannot afford to buy it. On the other hand, increasing food production at the small-farm level deals not only with the need to increase total food production, but also with the problem of food distribution to those who need it.

FINDING SOLUTIONS FOR THE PRESENT

One response to the increasingly apparent problem of failed development projects has been to look for answers in traditional African life as it is thought to have been before colonialism (Adu-Febiri, 1995). Indeed, the colonial and the post-colonial periods have been very difficult times for many African people, and many useful things can be learned and adapted from pre-colonial African history. However, it must also be remembered that the situation in Africa today is very different from what it was before colonialism and that new solutions must be found for today. The present situation differs in several significant ways from that of pre-colonial times. There is now a much greater total population, and a rapidly growing population, hence the need for food and other agricultural output is greater and is increasing rapidly. Today, we live in a community of nations that is different from what it was a few centuries ago. That means that people's expectations and the dynamics of interaction with people of other nations are different. Furthermore, the nature and extent of communications have changed drastically, so that expectations of people in Africa are influenced by what is perceived about people in nations in other parts of the world, even if those perceptions are inaccurate or incomplete (e.g., assuming that all people in some nation live like a few of the wealthy who are portrayed on television or in the movies). Solutions to today's problems must therefore be "made in Africa" solutions for current African conditions. They may draw on lessons from former ways of life, as well as on knowledge of modern technology as used in other parts of the world, but must be solutions fit for today's realities in Africa.

Therefore, to improve food availability for existing populations and provide for a growing population requires continual effort including changes in attitudes and in the way of thinking about food production, storage and distribution. It is no longer possible to remain complacent, simply say all will be well in the future if things continue as in the past and assume it is appropriate to just import unmodified technologies for food production from other parts of the world. This provides a challenge for training people, a challenge that goes beyond technical training for specific changes in agricultural production technologies. Rather, it deals directly with the human factor (HF), with the way people work together and how they view their contribution if the necessary agricultural development is to occur (see Chapter 2 in this volume for a detailed discussion and characterization of the HF).

DEVELOPMENT, A PROCESS OF CHANGE

Development involves a process of change in people. It is not something that is done to, or for, people by outsiders. Therefore, training for development in agriculture as in other endeavors must give due consideration to the HF—building those necessary human qualities in the process of agricultural advancement that will enable a people to maintain the progress that occurs and continue to improve their situation. This will require dedication, commitment, honesty, self-confidence and a willingness to work together for improvements needed now. Agricultural development and training must therefore seek to bring changes that enable the people of a nation to deal more effectively with the problems before them.

Use of new technological knowledge and/or management practices may be necessary to bring about needed increases in appropriate food production, but this will not be sufficient. People must accept the necessary changes and implement them effectively. These changes will often come as enhancements to the systems in place (Huss-Ashmore, 1989). Without the committed involvement of the food producers, effective changes cannot be longlasting. New machinery or the economic models of planners cannot be sufficient to bring about the needed changes that will benefit the poor who are most in need of change.

A NEW PERSPECTIVE IS NEEDED

That development is a process of change in people and that it is therefore necessary to build the requisite HF in order for development truly to occur has been clearly articulated by Adjibolosoo (1993, 1995a, 1995b). To bring about development for the majority of small-scale farmers will require a change in outlook and in methods of training for agricultural production. Many former efforts at increasing agricultural production in Africa were focused on increasing cash crop production for export in order to gain foreign currency for imports or for debt repayment, rather than on improving agricultural production for local consumption among the many small food producers. This approach has tended to bypass the needs of the majority of the population, many of whom are small-scale farmers. They have suffered much by this approach, since the desired economic growth and its expected trickle-down effect has not occurred and their needs have not been addressed. In fact, the poor majority has had to bear the brunt of the burden of losses and the effects of structural adjustment programs without participating in many of the benefits of economic development.

In addition to emphasis on increasing production for export crops, efforts at agricultural development and extension (training) have often been focused on production of a few staples considered important for national self-sufficiency (Keller and Mbewe, 1991; Shipley, 1987) but ignoring the needs of the small-scale producers, many of them women. In many African countries, women often take responsibility for producing a significant part of the food used for consumption by family members (Huss-Ashmore, 1989; Keller and Mbewe, 1991; Shipley, 1987). Efforts at agricultural development that focus on export crop production and production of a few staple crops may actually work against providing self-sufficiency at the local and regional levels, because they may detract from the importance of food production of a great variety of foods by family members for consumption by the family.

Some models for economic development have not clearly recognized the role of labor, especially family labor in low-resource regions (Harwood, 1989). Instead of simply treating family labor as a cost input for production, it is important to recognize that the opportunity cost of family labor may be very low and that providing local opportunity for more labor to increase production may be a benefit rather than a cost in production. There may indeed be social costs to not utilizing labor that is available (Harwood, 1989). Much agricultural development effort has been more suited for considerations in large-scale farming than in small-scale farming. Many of the planners and modelers of development have been more accustomed to dealing with problems in high-resource, capital-abundant, labor-poor situations. This trend is not true for Africa alone. Vaughn (1992) points out a claim that the U.S. agriculture extension service stopped trying to reach the very small farmer after World War II. If concepts and methods that have been used in agriculture extension service in the West are simply transferred to African countries, there is great danger that the real problems in African countries will not be dealt with and that solutions will not be appropriate to the situation.

People involved in training for agricultural development must recognize the importance of the HF in order to focus their efforts where needed. Speaking from their experience of working with *campesinos* (peasants) in Honduras in

Central America, Flores and Sanchez (1992) state that "if the mind of a Campesino is a desert, his farm will look like a desert." The problem that must be dealt with is people, their attitudes and their way of thinking about development. It is not enough to deal with technological questions of agricultural development. In a recent conversation with a development worker in Nicaragua, I was told a similar story. People must be taught that they are able to do something about their situation and that they must seek solutions in the situation around them. Many farmers think in terms of finding yet another export crop in the hope of improving their income, rather than looking for ways to build self-sufficiency at the local level.[2] Yet, self-sufficiency at the local level provides much more stability in food supply than does dependence on the uncertainties of either trade or aid. Dependence on trade and aid may make people vulnerable to a change of fortunes at the whim of political or economic changes in other countries or regions of the world over which those affected have no control. It is therefore important to consider the HF in programs aimed at raising agricultural productivity in Africa.

TRAINING FARMERS

Training for improved agricultural production must be much more than training in the operation of particular technologies. Flores and Sanchez (1992) suggest several necessary ingredients, including the need to "practice what you preach" and to "start small." They observe that the most effective extension agents have been those who practiced what they advocated. When persons hired as extension agents to share new ideas with farmers speak from their own experience and demonstrate that they are able to successfully use the methods they encourage others to use, farmers will be much more likely to accept the suggestions. Similar observations were shared with me in a recent discussion with a development worker in Nicaragua.[3]

The value of cooperation between peasant farmers, extensionists and researchers was well illustrated in programs that I was involved with in Bangladesh.[4] I will refer to two of those program methods: use of a demonstration garden in extending vegetable cultivation and the cropping systems method. In introducing vegetable production to small-scale farmers, an effective method was to make packages of available good-quality vegetable seed along with easy-to-understand instructions, to provide well-illustrated diagrams (since many of the farmers were illiterate or had very limited reading ability) and to link this program with demonstration gardens at the extension offices. These demonstration gardens permitted farmers to observe what extension agents were doing and what results their methods produced. This simple method proved to be highly effective in increasing vegetable production in the regions where we were involved. Though the strength of this method may seem obvious, too often extensionists see themselves as educated people who "tell" the farmers what to do, rather than doing it themselves and showing what to do.

Another method that we found to be successful in many cases was the cropping systems approach, or in its more general form, the farming systems approach. The particular strength of this method is that it involves farmers throughout the process. Work begins with careful observation of the situation within a defined region. This is called site description. After learning to understand the social, economic and agricultural aspects of life and agricultural production in a region, researchers and extensionists test new crop varieties and cropping practices that seem to have potential for bringing improvement. At all stages, the local farmers are included in the process by providing information about their real needs, participating in testing new ideas and responding to proposed changes. What is especially significant in this approach is that it involves the farmer in trying to improve farm management. It recognizes that farmers (even traditional, small-scale farmers) are innovators who can play an important role in the process of agricultural research and extension. This process also gives the farmers a sense of ownership in what is being tested; and when successful improvements to cropping practices or suitable new varieties of plants are observed, farmers do not need to be told to try them in their own fields, they are ready to incorporate these practices in their own farming. They have been involved in the process of testing the ideas, they feel a part of it and have observed what works, and what does not.

In reporting on the cropping systems program described above, Webster (1982, p. 51) wrote:

Bangladesh's agricultural potential can be best realized through an integrated effort that addresses the many factors limiting food production and farm income. The farming community is acutely aware of the constraints, and is best helped by a sensitive team of researchers and extensionists who recommend improvements that are within the farmers' means. This is the key to a successful cropping or farming systems program.

When farmers participate and observe, they will be more willing to try new ideas in their own fields than if they are simply told what to do. By starting small and including farmers in the testing of new ideas and practices, it is possible to have rapid acceptance of good ideas and to let inappropriate ideas die before they have become practiced on a widespread scale.

ADVANCED EDUCATION

An area of international cooperation in training for increased agricultural production has been to provide opportunity for African (and other) students to enhance their education and training by studying, especially in graduate schools, at universities in more developed countries (MDCs). The purpose has been to develop a cadre of educated and trained persons who could then give leadership in finding solutions to problems in their home environment. Too often, students are enamored with technology they observe and work with in their host country, then are frustrated when they return home and find they cannot continue with research on the same problems or with the same technologies. It is fundamental that students recognize that people in MDCs are working on problems they are concerned about and using and developing necessary technologies to deal with those problems.

I have tried to observe how persons with a foreign graduate education have been able to successfully adapt when back in their own country. One individual, who made a very successful transition to dealing with relevant problems in his own country and working within the conditions present there, told me that a significant factor in his preparation while doing graduate study in the United States was learning as much as he could about related fields of knowledge. He realized that when he returned to his country, he would not have the same supporting group of researchers around him in related fields of knowledge, so he needed to prepare well. My observation was that he also approached his work in his own country with commitment, dedication and a genuine determination to solve significant problems by available means, more than to advance his own position. These were requisite human characteristics needed to make a successful transition and a significant contribution to his own country. Students can learn much about the techniques and technologies used during their study and research programs in other countries. If willing to draw on that knowledge while working on problems relevant to the situation in their own country, they may be able to effectively deal with various real problems. Those who have learned this well have been able to be more effective in their work after returning to their own country.[5]

SUGGESTIONS FOR AFRICA

To provide solutions to development problems in Africa and appropriate training for development in agriculture and other endeavors, it is important to realize that improving a situation is not something that outsiders can do for, or to, insiders. Rather, it is something that a people must do for themselves. This requires the appropriate HF. Outsiders may be helpful and make major contributions to facilitate development by giving encouragement and good advice, sharing their understanding of technology and showing how they seek solutions. They may even share some of their means as inputs to finding "made in Africa" solutions for Africa's problems. However, an outside agent of change may be a great help but will not bring long-term change by "doing it for them." Growth must come from within. The solution to agricultural production problems in African countries must be indigenous—something suitable that is accepted and workable by the people living in the situation.

This approach to development or positive change requires recognition of the importance and value of each person—the poor and the rich, the uneducated and the educated, those of "my" family, nation or tribe, and those of another; and the local person with traditional ideas and the person from outside with new ideas. Each must be seen as a person who can make valuable and needed contributions.

In agriculture, this will lead to a new kind of cooperation for the common good. It will include highly educated researchers, administrators and extension agents cooperating with uneducated small-farm operators. Each will have a valuable contribution to make. Highly advanced current research techniques will be needed to develop new plant types for specific environments and capable of producing for current and future needs.[6] The traditional farmer, though not formally educated, may be able to contribute traditional knowledge (Harwood, 1989; Huss-Ashmore, 1989), and will need to help find solutions that are appropriate and that work in the present, since the traditional farmer will need to be a part of the change that must occur for true development. Each person must first ask, ''What can I contribute?'' rather than ''What can I get others to do for me?'' Training for small farmers needs to arise from solutions tested in the local setting. People need to be shown what has been found to work, encouraging them to participate in the process and to try that which is suitable for them.

In Africa, these suggestions will need to be implemented by means suitable to the society involved. It may involve discussions and training sessions for farmers that allow them to contribute their understanding and ideas, as well as to listen to advice from ''experts.'' Involving small-scale farmers in learning and sharing may help build the commitment, dedication and confidence to bring about change as people gain hope and realize that they can contribute meaningfully to the betterment of their society. By seeing others cooperate, they will recognize they cannot get the maximum benefit for themselves without concern for the welfare of others.

To bring about effective change requires ideas, practices and technologies that are appropriate[7] to the time, the need and the social setting. It also requires exercise of the necessary HF. Effective change requires the cooperation of the people involved.

CONCLUSION

Self-sufficiency in food and other essentials will come by cooperation and by building the strength of a nation's many food producers, rather than by promoting highly specialized production of a few cash crops for export and a few staples to satisfy the assumptions of economic planners. Hope and stability come from strength within, rather than by excessive dependence on outside agents through international aid and trade that make people vulnerable to economic and political instabilities or whims in other parts of the world.

This approach requires a high level of development of the HF—of humility, of commitment to the common good and of a sense of personal value. The wealthy and the poor, the uneducated and the educated, the people of powerful and of weak tribes, nations or families, need to see themselves as part of a highly interdependent body, with different people having different functions but all contributing their part to the proper functioning of the whole.

NOTES

1. This issue has been discussed at greater length in Harder (1995b), pp. 199–208.

2. Conversation with Daniel Malenfant, a Canadian working on development problems in the Matagalpa region of Nicaragua (June 1995).

3. Ibid.

4. I was involved with the Mennonite Central Committee program in Bangladesh from 1981–1984. Prior to, during and after that time, agriculture development, including an active extension program, was part of the organization's activities.

5. This statement is based on my personal observations of various people in several Asian countries who have done graduate study in the United States.

6. For example, take the new rice plant architecture proposed by the International Rice Research Institute (IRRI) to give further increases in rice yields without further stressing the environment (*IRRI Reporter*).

7. Take, for example, the rower pump, a hand-operated pump developed in Bangladesh for irrigation under conditions present there. Reasons for successful use and dissemination of the pump include that it was appropriate to the needs of a major region of the country and that effort was given to develop the pump in cooperation with farmers and market it through local marketing channels (Harder, 1995a).

REFERENCES

Adjibolosoo, S. 1993. "The Human Factor in Development." *The Scandinavian Journal of Development Alternatives* 12 (4): 139–149.

Adjibolosoo, S. 1995a. "The Significance of the Human Factor in African Economic Development." In S. Adjibolosoo, ed., *The Significance of the Human Factor in African Economic Development.* Westport, Conn.: Praeger.

Adjibolosoo, S. 1995b. *The Human Factor in Developing Africa.* Westport, Conn.: Praeger.

Adu-Febiri, F. 1995. "Is Africa's Development a Basket Case?" *Review of Human Factor Studies* 1 (1): 45–60.

Flores, M. and Sanchez, E. 1992. "The Human Farm: People-Based Approach to Food Production and Conservation." In K. Smith and T. Yamamori, eds., *Growing Our Future: Food Security and the Environment.* West Hartford, Conn.: Kumarian Press.

Food and Agriculture Organization (FAO) of the United Nations. 1980–1993. *FAO Production Yearbook.* Various issues.

Harder, H. J. 1995a. "Not Just a Good Idea—Marketing Bangladesh's Rower Pump." *Waterlines* 13 (3): 28–30.

Harder, H. J. 1995b. "Human Context, a Critical Factor in Technology Transfer for Development." In S. Adjibolosoo, ed., *The Significance of the Human Factor in African Economic Development.* Westport, Conn.: Praeger.

Harwood, R. R. 1989. "Broadening the Food Development Agenda." In P. M. Hirschoff and N. G. Kotler, eds., *Completing the Food Chain: Strategies for Combating Hunger and Malnutrition.* Washington, D.C.: Smithsonian Institution Press.

Huss-Ashmore, R. 1989. "Perspectives on the African Food Crisis." In R. Huss-Ashmore and S. H. Katz, eds., *African Food Systems in Crisis. Part One: Microperspectives.* New York: Gordon and Breach Science Publishers.

Hyden, G. 1986. "The Invisible Economy of Smallholder Agriculture in Africa." In J. L. Moock, ed., *Understanding Africa's Rural Households and Farming Systems.* Boulder, Colo.: Westview Press.

International Rice Research Institute (IRRI) 1994. *IRRI Reporter* September 1991, December 1994.

Keller, B., and Mbewe, D. C. 1991. "Policy and Planning for the Empowerment of Zambia's Women Farmers." *Canadian Journal of Development Studies* 12 (1): 75–88.

Moock, J. L. 1986. "Introduction." In J. L. Moock, ed., *Understanding Africa's Rural Households and Farming Systems.* Boulder, Colo.: Westview Press.

Shipley, K. G. 1987. "Agriculture in Africa." *Agrologist* 1–4 (Winter, Spring, Summer, Fall).

Vaughn, J. H. 1992. "Food Security, Environment, and Agrarian Reform." In K. Smith and T. Yamamori, eds., *Growing Our Future: Food Security and the Environment.* West Hartford, Conn.: Kumarian Press.

Webster, R. M. 1982. "Learning and Teaching Alongside the Bangladeshi Farmer." *Association of Development Agencies in Bangladesh (ADAB) News,* pp. 38–41, 51.

8

Human Factor Development and Technological Innovation in Africa

Benjamin Ofori-Amoah

INTRODUCTION

The role of technological innovation in economic development is a fact that can no longer be disputed (Pederson, 1970; Malecki, 1991). As a collective body of *new* know-how or knowledge systems that a society can employ to produce, distribute and consume goods and services, technological innovation becomes necessary when existing technologies do not allow society to achieve such socially desirable goals effectively and efficiently. Technological innovation does not only allow existing solutions to economic development problems to be perfected, but also provides breakthroughs to unresolved or unprecedented development problems. Technological innovation defines new needs, roles, quantities and qualities of both human and natural resources needed for economic development. It extends the capacities of people to live beyond the strict confines of nature and free themselves from other domineering human groups (Ofori-Amoah, 1994; Malecki, 1991). Consequently, technological innovation is intertwined with a people's liberation and well-being. Societies that are able to innovate technologically are the ones that can also advance materially. Technological innovation cannot fix every economic development problem, but it is indispensable to the process of economic development.

In Africa, however, the tremendous role that technological innovation plays in the economic development process is yet to be seen, except in certain sectors of the South African economy. Thus, not only does the continent as a whole rank lowest as a generator and user of technological innovations in the world, but it is also a region in which the technologies of production, distribution and consumption of goods and services for most people have stagnated, if not retrogressed over time (Ofori-Amoah, 1994). This situation has not been created because African countries do not realize the role of technological innovation in economic development. As evident in the works of Forje (1989) and the American Association for the Advancement of Science [AAAS] (1991, 1992a, 1992b), African governments realize the crucial role technological innovation plays in the development process. Instead, this situation is believed to have been created by a number of obstacles that have made technological innovation in Africa a very difficult venture. Among these obstacles are lack of capital, political will and stability, a scientific and technological community, an appropriate institutional framework for scientific and technological activities and favorable international political and economic systems.

Ofori-Amoah (1994) argued that while these factors are important, the fundamental cause of Africa's technological backwardness lies in its failure to establish a specific technological change strategy. In the absence of this, African governments have desperately followed any new ideas thrown at them without any means of ascertaining whether such innovations would be consistent with their overall development program. By taking this argument a step further, this chapter argues that like all other major components of the economic development process, technological innovation is a human factor (HF) process. This process depends on the "spectrum of personality characteristics and other dimensions of human performance that allow social, economic and political institutions to function and remain functional over time" (Adjibolosoo, 1994, pp. 25–37). Africa's inability to innovate technologically is due to the lack of the appropriate HF that is required to make such technological innovation possible. This chapter shows how the lack of the appropriate HF underlies the problems facing technological innovation in Africa and addresses how the necessary HF could be developed to help African countries take advantage of the benefits of technological innovation.

This chapter is divided into three sections: In the first section, I outline the main theories of technological innovation and how these have played out in Africa. In the second section, I discuss the HF component in technological innovation. In the third section, I propose some possible lines of action for developing the appropriate HF for technological innovation. The underlying assumption of the chapter is that Africa cannot develop economically without technological innovation.

TECHNOLOGICAL INNOVATION THEORIES AND AFRICA

In Schumpeterian economics, technological innovation is one of the three processes of technological change. The other two are invention and diffusion. Schumpeter (1939) considered invention as the development of a new idea, innovation as the first commercial application of the idea and diffusion as the acceptance and use of the idea by many users. As used in this chapter, technological innovation refers to the broad spectrum of processes by which a new technology emerges and becomes accepted. In this regard, we can identify three main trends of technological innovation theories: The first deals with the sources and motivations for new ideas that translate into new technologies. The second deals with the actual strategies for translating new ideas to new technologies, and the third deals with the factors that influence the acceptance and use of new technologies. Each of these is discussed in detail in the following subsections.

Sources of Technological Innovation

Three main theories exist regarding the sources of technological innovation. The first theory, due to Schumpeter (1939, 1943), says that new technologies emerge through "technology-push" activities. Scientific research leads to new ideas, then to inventions, innovations and diffusion. The second theory, due to Schmookler (1966), says that new technologies stem from the demand side. Consumers withdraw their demands from a product. Sellers respond by seeking ways to improve their products through the development and use of new technologies. The third theory, due to Nelson and Winter (1977) and Dosi (1982, 1984), sees new technologies as emerging paradigms, or patterns of possible solutions to technological problems, within which there are many trajectories or possible directions. A technological paradigm emerges from the interplay among a nation's scientific advances, economic factors, institutional variables, cultural factors, physical environmental factors and unresolved difficulties in established technological trajectories (Nelson and Winter, 1977; Dosi, 1982, 1984; Thomas, 1985; Dankbaar, 1990; Porter, 1990; Ofori-Amoah, 1995). Once established, a technological paradigm may initially generate several technological trajectories. Later, such factors as the technology's marketability, economic interests of its developers, public and political forces and priorities and the technology's cost-saving capability and labor-saving potential serve as focusing or selective devices to make some of these trajectories become more established than others (Rosenberg, 1969; Dosi, 1982, 1984; Nelson and Winter, 1977). The limitations of both the technology-push and the demand-pull theories have made this last theory more acceptable.[1]

Strategies For Technological Innovation

If the need for a new technology is established, how does this need become a reality? There are three main theoretical strategies: The first is to develop a new technology. The second is to improve upon an existing technology. The third is to acquire an existing technology from an outside source through technology transfer. In general, developing a new technology requires intensive research and development activity and a high quality of personnel who are motivated and willing to spend long periods of time in research (Adjibolosoo, 1995b). In addition, several methods exist such as imitation and learning by doing through which new technologies can be generated. The very nature of these activities requires large sums of capital and infrastructure in terms of laboratories and equipment. The result is that existing literature on technological innovation generally does not recommend this form of technological acquisition to developing countries.

Improving existing technology is the second way of acquiring new technologies (Ofori-Amoah, 1994, 1988a, 1988b). One advantage is that since the technology already exists, there may be a considerable amount of previous knowledge available, which can lower the expense that goes with developing a new technology from scratch. Another is that since the new technology will be an improvement upon an existing one, it may not be as difficult for it to diffuse as compared to an altogether new technology. However, the disadvantage is that if the problems arising from the existing technology have reached an unresolvable stage, it might be cheaper to develop a new technology, thereby shifting from the old technological paradigm to a new one.

Acquiring a new technology through transfer and adoption or transfer and adaptation is the strategy that has commanded most attention, especially when dealing with developing regions (Fransman and King, 1984; Baranson and Roark, 1985). According to Fransman (1985), the different modes of transfer can be categorized on the basis of whether foreigners are active or passive in the process and whether the process is formal (market-mediated) or informal (nonmarket-mediated). A great deal of research has been done on the transfer modes in the first process with relatively very little on the remaining modes. The results of these studies have been mixed.

In the case of South Korea, the most extensively studied case, these modes seem to have worked. However, elsewhere it seems the cost has been high. Apart from this, questions regarding the quality of the knowledge being transferred have also been raised. Lall (1984) argued that sophisticated products may be transferred while the know-why may not, since the know-why tends to be concentrated in the developed countries. Thus, Baranson and Roark (1985) distinguish technology transfer that impacts among operational, duplicative and innovative capabilities. Technology transfer that results in operational capabilities theoretically permits the recipients to make a product equivalent to that produced by the technology supplier. Duplicative technology transfer allows sufficient know-how to reproduce an entire manufacturing plant or discrete components. Others, including Fransman (1985), believe that sometimes know-how may not be necessary.

Theories of Technological Innovation Diffusion

A new technology does not impact people's lives unless it diffuses. As a result, diffusion of technological innovation has attracted the most attention in the field of technological change, out of which three main theories have come to exist. The first perspective focuses on the demand side of the diffusion process and tries to explain behavior of adopters in terms of their characteristics and the characteristics of the innovation, which I have called the innovation-adopter-characteristic (IAC) approach (Ofori-Amoah, 1990, 1993). Within the manufacturing sector, this perspective has identified profitability, firm size, firm location, availability of capital, age of plant, age of executives, etc. (Mansfield, 1961, 1963, 1968; Davies, 1979). Within the nonmanufacturing sector, factors such as compatibility, congruence, the nature of the change agent and the social system have been identified (Rogers, 1962).

The second set of theories have focused on the supply side of the diffusion process and emphasized the role of suppliers of the innovation. Special emphasis has been given to the strategies followed by these suppliers and their profitability motives (Brown, 1975; Metcalfe, 1981). The third set of theories seeks to combine these two theories into a dynamic framework that focuses on the decision-making processes leading to the various technology choices (David, 1975; Gold, 1981; Gold et al., 1984; Thomas, 1985; Ofori-Amoah, 1990, 1993). This perspective argues that technology diffusion that is observable in any place at any time is a function of technology choices made by firms as well as individuals. The diffusion pattern can best be understood by focusing on the factors that influenced those choices. Ofori-Amoah (1990, 1993) argues that these are complex forces and need to be put in contexts. How does technological innovation in Africa reflect these theoretical trends?

Technological Innovation In Africa

Technological innovation in Africa has followed the general trends identified in the technological innovation theories (Forje, 1989; Thomas-Emeagwali, 1992a, 1992b; Waite, 1992; Ofori-Amoah, 1994). In pre-colonial Africa, there was much focus on developing new technologies and less on transfer and adoption. Then, African societies were mostly self-sufficient and had developed a wide range of technologies for food production, manufacturing goods, medicine, transportation and communication.

Under colonialism, the strategy of technological innovation became more of transfer and implantation of new technologies. European colonialists transferred a selected number of technologies and imposed them on Africa as part of the colonial strategy. These were mainly in the form of products and institutions rather than know-how and know-why. Thus, European currencies were forcibly introduced as media of exchange. To obtain these media of exchange, Africans had to engage in certain activities, mainly cash crop cultivation and mining activities. Over time, this gradually wooed people away from their pre-colonial activities, as the new products and activities quickly diffused among the people. Africans began to look outside for what they needed, an attitude that had become solidly entrenched by the time colonialism ended.

Technological innovation in post-colonial Africa continued with the transfer and adoption strategy. Increasingly, development plans acknowledged the role of science and technology in the development process. Efforts to follow these plans manifested themselves in the adoption of import-substitution industrialization, establishment of scientific and technological research institutes, colleges and universities and modernization of some services (Forje, 1989; Ofori-Amoah, 1994). As the adoption strategy soon proved costly, modified versions of technological innovation strategies began to emerge. The intermediate or appropriate technology (AT) idea became very popular during the 1970s, with a number of AT centers established. However, this did not change the technological change strategy in any significant way.

As it turned out, the AT strategy had a number of difficulties. For example, it still followed a strategy of transferring outmoded or sometimes a poor parallel of advanced technology to Africa. The result was that the AT strategy did not impact in any significant way the lives of the African people. Besides, it came to be largely regarded as technology for rural areas and thus widened the gap between urban and rural areas. As the momentum for the AT slowed down, renewed interest in the need for science and technology in development manifested itself in the establishment of full government departments of science and technology and efforts to formulate technology policies in a number of countries.

The foregoing account shows that, in general, technological innovation in Africa has followed the general trends of technological innovation theories, doing what it was directly or indirectly advised to do—that is, focusing mainly on technology transfer. However, rather than providing a means for a rapid transformation of economies of African countries into replicas of developed countries, some of these projects bequeathed to their beneficiaries heavy debt burdens; agreements that benefit foreign firms more than domestic economic development; white elephant projects—capital items that have broken down and rusted because there are no spare parts or know-how to fix them; and research institutes that are stifled because of funding insufficiencies and personnel and structural problems. Obviously, these raise the questions to why technological innovation in Africa has not been successful and how to remedy the situation. Thus, lack of capital, political will and stability, a scientific and technological community, an appropriate institutional framework and favorable international political and economic systems have been identified as the main reasons for Africa's low technological innovation performance. In the next section, I argue that technological innovation is a HF process and that whether the factors identified above are going to be obstacles or not depends on whether or not the appropriate HF is in place.

TECHNOLOGICAL INNOVATION AS A HUMAN FACTOR PROCESS

Adjibolosoo (1994, p.26) defines the HF as the

spectrum of personality characteristics and other dimensions of human performance that enable social, economic, and political institutions to function and remain functional, over time. Such dimensions sustain the workings and application of the rule of law, political harmony, a disciplined labor force, just legal systems, respect for human dignity and the sanctity of life, social welfare, and so on. As is often the case, no social, economic, or political institutions can function effectively without being upheld by a network of committed persons who stand firmly by them.

Adjibolosoo (1995a, p. 26) argues further that these dimensions and attributes go beyond mere human resource development and human capital acquisition through education and training. Instead, they involve dedication, responsibility and accountability in implementing measures towards development. From this, we define a HF process as any process that depends on the HF for its success. Such a process recognizes the centrality of the HF in guaranteeing the success or failure of all human endeavors.

As a HF process, a successful technological innovation depends on people, their attitudes, dedication and sense of responsibility. First, it takes a dedicated and responsible group of people to be concerned with existing technological problems and recognize the need for a new technological paradigm. Once this need is established, it is again the same group of people who will have to assess the various strategical options available for meeting the need. If the strategy of developing a new technology or improving an existing one is chosen, it will require commitment to long-term societal benefits of such efforts rather than short-term personal benefits on the part of both supporters and researchers in order to succeed. Similarly, once the strategy of transfer is selected, it cannot succeed without the appropriate HF component. As Baranson and Roark (1985) have pointed out, the geographic transfer of very productive forms of physical capital may be of little use unless the appropriate human resources are simultaneously available in the recipient country to provide for the generation, maintenance, repair and upgrading of facilities, as well as the interface with foreign engineers and specialists. More important, problems of hidden international political and economic agendas, issues of international balance of power, and conditionality requirements, which cloud international technology transfer negotiations and purchasing, require people with selfless attitudes and loyalty to their respective societies to negotiate contract agreements that will benefit their societies as a whole rather than their own personal and individual goals. Finally, the diffusion of technological innovation will depend on the attitudes of both the agents charged with the dissemination and the recipients. Agents that are ill-prepared and only interested in personal gain will falter on their jobs, while recipients that hold indiscriminately to certain values for the simple reason of culture and tradition will frustrate any efforts of technological innovation diffusion. Does this mean, then, that capital, political will and stability, institutions and the international political and economic systems are not important?

Technological innovation requires capital, whether the strategy is by indigenous development or by transfer. In the case of the former, it can involve prolonged research, which in turn can lead to heavy capital outlay in terms of equipment, instrumentation and personnel. Thus, it has become an accepted notion that with lack of funds in Africa, there is bound to be problems with technological innovation. However, when, in the midst of this accepted notion, one sees the allocation of Africa's scarce resources to grandiose projects of questionable character (e.g., Bokassa's imperial throne and regalia, Boigny's largest Roman Catholic church in the world, the purchase of expensive weaponry and the funding of foreign personal accounts of certain government officials rather than of scientific and technological research for economic development), the problem becomes more than mere lack of capital.

Lack of political will and stability are also two genuine problems that have set Africa back in its drive for general economic development and, for that matter, a positive technological innovation path. Within their relatively short period of existence, most African countries have seen political turmoil of all kinds and have experimented with almost every development theory and strategy that has been developed on the face of the earth. The rapidly shifting views between ideologies, policies and strategies have denied Africa's economic development efforts the important elements of stability and continuity without which effective planning becomes difficult to achieve. The question, though, is why such turmoil? The answer to this question is a complex one. It is easy to identify Africa's colonial roots, the cold war and international political and economic conspiracy as the root causes of these problems.

Technological innovation requires a well trained scientific and technological population that will be able to generate new ideas and also sift through, and adapt, foreign ideas to domestic conditions. The fulfillment of a greater portion of this requirement is through the educational system, its structure, content and goals. As Bagchi (1988, pp. 69–91) has pointed out, the entire evolution of modern science and technology was rooted in the development of Western culture, and unless there is a detachment of education systems in the Third World from this, many educated Africans will find they can operate better in a Western environment than in their own. The implication of this is that a scientific and technological community needed for technological innovation does not come to exist through the mere schooling of people in the science and technology fields, but by what that schooling does to equip the people to solve the technological problems of their immediate environment. As I have argued elsewhere, the record of technological innovation in Africa seems to indicate that it is rather the people without formal education in science and technology that have been the most successful (Ofori-Amoah, 1994).

Technological innovation theorists place a high value on the role of institutions in the technological innovation process in developed countries (Nelson and Winter, 1987; Freeman and Perez, 1988; Dosi, 1982, 1984; Porter, 1990; Dankbaar, 1990). The most exemplary case given in this regard is that of Japan, where governmental institutions, notably the Ministry of Trade and Industry (MITI) and private institutions such as the Sogososhas, have contributed to the economic and technological advances of that country. Technological change needs institutions of research and diffusion at both private and government levels. Lack of appropriate institutions has often been cited as a problem in Africa, but the fact is, African countries abound in scientific and technological research institutions, at least in the public sector. According to Forje (1989), almost every country in Africa now has a science and technology research institution of some sort, with some countries such as Ghana and Nigeria having a multiplicity of them. The real problem is that these institutions have not been effective by themselves because they are inanimate (Adjibolosoo, 1995a, chapter 5). They do not run themselves; it is people who run them. To be successful, institutions must be run by people who are dedicated to their goals, objectives, ideals and standards.

Finally, on the international scene, technological innovation is more than practical know-how. It is also a symbol of power and a means for control, and is at the core of national sovereignty and territorial integrity. As a result, not all technological innovations may be available on the so-called international technology shelf. If and when information is available at all, it may not be entirely accessible due to codes of secrecy and for strategic and national interest reasons. For the same reasons, domestic efforts at technological innovation may be frustrated directly or indirectly. In spite of all these, the technological innovativeness shown by Japan and Southeast Asian countries indicates that there is always a way to get information, even in this apparent hostile international technological environment. Thus, technological innovation is a task that requires more than a scientific and technological community with capital, institutions and appropriate political commitment and climate. It requires a carefully laid out policy and strategy that can navigate through the narrow passageways and tight corners in the apparent hostile international technological environment and a people who are committed to implementing this strategy.

People are the ultimate resource for a country's economic development and, for that matter, all its component activities such as technological innovation. However, a people without the appropriate HF will engage in activities that will undermine their very existence and eventually self-destruct. Thus, scarce capital will become even scarcer, political will and stability will be difficult to maintain, institutions will exist only in name and unfavorable international political and economic trends will get a free ride. Within the context of technological innovation then, the question is how can Africa develop this appropriate HF for technological innovation? I provide an answer to this in the next section.

DEVELOPING AN APPROPRIATE HUMAN FACTOR FOR TECHNOLOGICAL INNOVATION IN AFRICA

Developing an appropriate HF for technological innovation in Africa must be seen in the context of the overall development of Africa. This is because technological innovation does not occur in isolation. As much as it influences economic development, technological innovation is in turn also influenced by the economic development process itself. Thus, apart from certain specific details,

the appropriate HF required for technological innovation is by and large insep-
arable from that required for economic development as a whole. To this end,
developing an appropriate HF for technological innovation has a two-pronged
approach: one for general economic development and the other for technological
innovation, both of which require a number of reforms and initiatives. In what
follows, a few suggestions are made in regard to the development of the appropriate HF for technological innovation in Africa.

1. There must be a change in the attitude and in the aspiration of Africa's leadership
   (Page, 1995). Africa needs a new kind of leadership that will put the interest and
   welfare of the people first. It needs a new kind of leadership that will be tolerant to
   other views and not drive its educated and trained human resources into self or com-
   pulsory exile. This new leadership must see itself as a servant, not only in name but
   also in action. Its style must be rooted in seeking to serve rather than to be served.
   This new leadership must also seek to protect the scarce resources of African countries
   from both domestic and external looters and ensure proper allocation of these resources to crucial areas of the economy, including technological research and innovation.

2. This change in leadership attitude must result in the institution of national awareness
   programs aimed at educating students, as well as the general public, about the effects
   of the decay of such human characteristics as responsibility, dedication, loyalty and
   institutionalization of such practices as bribery and corruption. This must be undertaken through the use of literature, drama, public fora, discussion groups and the mass
   media (Ofori-Amoah and Adjibolosoo, 1995).

3. This new leadership must show commitment to use domestic experts rather than foreign ones (Ofori-Amoah and Adjibolosoo, 1995). To this end, existing scientific and
   technological research institutes, as well as individuals and groups with scientific and
   technological training, must be challenged to come to grips with domestic technological problems. They must find solutions by providing funding and holding funding
   recipients accountable to provide the results of their research.

4. Incentive systems to encourage and reward local creativity, originality and adaptabil-
   ity, as well as innovativeness, must be established. These can include increased funding, a domestic patent system, organization of national technological shows, a national
   awards day for innovative ideas and assistance with technical information (Ofori-
   Amoah, 1994; Adjibolosoo, 1995b).

5. To provide a base for sustaining this initiative, existing education systems must be
   reorganized (see details in chapter 1 in this volume): (a) more emphasis should be
   given to science and technology education at the middle level through expansion of
   technical and vocational education; (b) the current educational systems that encourage
   rote learning to obtain certificates and degrees must be replaced by ones that create
   in the students an awareness and understanding of problems of their own societies
   and challenge them to think about solutions (see details in Chapter 1, 2 and 11 in this
   volume); (c) in particular, existing indigenous technologies in such sectors as health
   care, food production, storage and processing, as well as the technologies employed
   in small-scale manufacturing activities, must be incorporated into the scientific and
   technological curricula; and (d) interaction between students and the people engaged

in activities employing these indigenous technologies as small-scale industries must also form an integral part of the science and technology curricula (Ofori-Amoah, 1994), in order to explore the problems for improving these activities.

6. Diffusion of new and proven technological innovations should be encouraged through the use of television drama, literature and other forms of mass media (see Chapter 3 in this book for an extensive discussion on this issue): (a) such programs must focus on the advantages, applications and problems of the new innovation compared with an existing one; (b) proven innovations must be given initial subsidies to make them affordable to the people; and (c) universities and technical, vocational and research institutions must establish technological liaisons with the community to educate the general public about new developments and their advantages and use. People must be assisted to use these innovations.

7. Well-designed programs to promote continuing HF development must be implemented (Adjibolosoo, 1995a).

CONCLUSION

Technological innovation plays a very important role in the economic development process. While it cannot fix every economic development problem, it is now widely accepted that it is indispensable to the process of economic development. In Africa, however, this role has not materialized into positive development gains. The situation has been attributed to a number of obstacles that seem to be consistent with the general theories of technological innovation. Thus, factors such as lack of capital, political will and stability, a scientific and technological community and a favorable international political and economic system have been blamed for Africa's lack of development. This chapter has argued that technological innovation is a HF process, and unless the issue is addressed from the HF perspective, it will be difficult to make any significant progress in the area of technological innovation and, for that matter, economic development. African countries must therefore start developing their HF. This must begin with a change in attitude of the current leadership and the general public and a number of reform initiatives in both the formal and informal education systems. It is in this direction that Africa will be able to harness and employ technological innovation for its economic development.

NOTE

1. Technology-push theories have been criticized for being unidirectional in conception and ignoring the complex nature of feedback between the economic environment, variations among industries and direction of technological change. Similarly, demand-pull theories have been criticized for being passive, mechanistic and static and unable to explain why and when certain technologies emerge at the times they do. For a comprehensive review of these criticisms, see Dosi (1984) and Mowery and Rosenberg (1979).

REFERENCES

Adjibolosoo, S. 1994. "The Human Factor and the Failure of Economic Development and Policies in Africa." In F. Ezeala-Harrison and S. Adjibolosoo, eds., *Perspectives on Economic Development in Africa.* Westport, Conn.: Praeger.

Adjibolosoo, S. 1995a. *The Human Factor in Developing Africa.* Westport, Conn.: Praeger.

Adjibolosoo, S. 1995b. "Human Factor Engineering: The Primary Foundation of All Industrial Technology Transfer Programs." Unpublished discussion paper, Trinity Western University, Langley, B.C., Canada.

American Association for the Advancement of Science (AAAS). 1991. *Science In Africa: Achievements and Prospects.* A symposium at the 1991 AAAS Annual Meeting. Washington, D.C.: AAAS.

American Association for the Advancement of Science (AAAS). 1992a. *Science In Africa: Setting Research Priorities.* A symposium at the 1992 AAAS Annual Meeting. Washington, D.C.: AAAS.

American Association for the Advancement of Science (AAAS). 1992b. *Science in Africa: Innovations in Higher Education.* Washington, D.C.: AAAS.

Bagchi, A. K. 1988. "Technological Self-Reliance, Dependence and Underdevelopment." In A. Wad, ed., *Science, Technology and Development.* Boulder, Colo.: Westview Press.

Baranson, J. and Roark, R. 1985. "Trends in North-South Transfer of High Technology." In N. Rosenberg and C. Frischtak, eds., *International Technology Transfer: Concepts, Measures, and Comparisons.* New York: Praeger.

Brown, L. A. 1975. "The Market and Infrastructure Context of Adoption: A Spatial Perspective On the Diffusion of Innovation." *Economic Geography* 51: 185–216.

Dankbaar, B. 1990. "International Competition and National Institutions: The Case of the Automobile Industry." In C. Freeman and L. Soete, eds., *New Explorations in the Economics of Technical Change.* London: Pinter Publishers.

David, P. A. 1975. *Technical Choice, Innovation and Economic Growth.* Cambridge: Cambridge University Press.

Davies, S. 1979. *The Diffusion of Process Innovation.* Cambridge: University Press.

Dosi, G. 1982. "Technological Paradigms and Technological Trajectories: A Suggested Interpretation of the Determinants and Direction of Technical Change." *Research Policy* 11 (3): 147–62.

Dosi, G. 1984. *Technical Change and Industrial Transformation.* London: Macmillan Press.

Forje, J. W. 1989. *Science and Technology In Africa.* London: Longman.

Fransman, M. 1985. "Conceptualising Technical Change in the Third World in the 1980s: An Interpretive Survey." *The Journal of Development Studies* 21 (4): 572–652.

Fransman, M. and King, K. eds., 1984. *Technological Capability In the Third World.* London: Macmillan Press.

Freeman, C. and Perez, C. 1988. "Structural Crises of Adjustment: Business Cycles and Investment Behavior." In G. Dosi et al., eds., *Technical Change and Economic Theory.* London: Pinter Publishers.

Gold, B. 1981. "Technological Diffusion in Industry: Research Needs and Shortcomings." *Journal of Industrial Economics* 29: 247–69.

Gold, B., Pierce, W. S., Rosseger, G. and Perlman, M. 1984. *Technological Progress and Industrial Leadership: The Growth of the US Steel Industry.* Lexington, Mass.: Lexington Books and D. C. Heath and Co.

Lall, S. 1984. "India's Technological Capability: Effects of Trade, Industrial Science and Technology Policies." In M. Fransman and K. King, eds., *Technological Capability in the Third World.* New York: St. Martin's Press.

Malecki, E. J. 1991. *Technology and Economic Development: The Dynamics of Local, Regional and National Change.* New York: Longman and John Wiley.

Mansfield, E. 1961. "Technical Change and the Rate of Imitation." *Econometrica* 29 (4): 741–766.

Mansfield, E. 1963. "Intrafirm Rates of Diffusion of an Innovation." *Review of Economics and Statistics* 45 (November): 348–359.

Mansfield, E. 1968. *The Economics of Technical Change.* London: Longman.

Metcalfe, J. S. 1981. "Impulse and Diffusion in the Study of Technical Change." *Futures* 13 (October): 347–359.

Mowery, D. and Rosenberg, N. 1979. "The Influence of the Market Demand Upon Innovation: A Critical Review of Some Recent Empirical Studies." *Research Policy* (8): 102–153.

Nelson, R. R. and Winter, S. 1977. "In Search for a Useful Theory of Innovation." *Research Policy* (6): 36–76.

Ofori-Amoah, B. 1988a. "Ghana's Informal Aluminium Pottery: Another Grass-Roots Industrial Revolution?" *Appropriate Technology* 14 (4): 17–19.

Ofori-Amoah, B. 1988b. "Improving Existing Indigenous Technologies as a Strategy for the Appropriate Technology Concept in Ghana." *Industry and Development* 23: 57–79.

Ofori-Amoah, B. 1990. "Technology Choice in a Global Industry: The Case of the Twin-Wire in Canada." Unpublished Ph.D. Thesis. Burnaby, B.C.: Simon Fraser University, Department of Geography.

Ofori-Amoah, B. 1993. "Technology Choice and Diffusion in the Manufacturing Sector: The Case of the Twin-Wire in the Canadian Pulp and Paper Industry." *Geoforum* 24 (3): 315–326.

Ofori-Amoah, B. 1994. "Technological Change Strategy for Economic Development in Africa." In F. Ezeala-Harrison and S. Adjibolosoo, eds., *Perspectives on Economic Development in Africa.* Westport, Conn.: Praeger.

Ofori-Amoah, B. 1995. "Regional Impact on Technological Change: The Evolution and Development of the Twin-Wire Paper Machine, from 1950 to 1988." *Environment and Planning, A.*

Ofori-Amoah, B. and Adjibolosoo, S. 1995. "Crises as Windows of Opportunity: Prospects for Africa's Economic Development in the Twenty-First Century." Paper presented at Africa 2000 Conference, Hofstra University, Hempstead, N.Y., October 12–14.

Pederson, P. O. 1970. "Innovation Diffusion Within and Between National Urban Systems." *Geographical Analysis* 2 (3): 203–254.

Porter, M. E. 1990. *The Competitive Advantage of Nations.* New York: The Free Press.

Rogers, E. M. 1962. *Diffusion of Innovations.* New York: Free Press.

Rosenberg, N. 1969. "The Direction of Technological Change: Inducement Mechanisms and Focusing Devices." *Economic Development and Cultural Change* 18: 1–24.

Schmookler, J. 1966. *Invention and Economic Growth.* Cambridge, Mass.: Harvard University Press.

Schumpeter, J. A. 1939. *Business Cycles: A Theoretical, Historical and Statistical Analysis of the Capitalist Process.* New York: McGraw-Hill.

Schumpeter, J. A. 1943. *Capitalism, Socialism and Democracy.* New York: Harper and Row.

Thomas, M. D. 1985. "Regional Economic Development and the Role of Innovation and Technological Change." In A. T. Thwaites and R. P. Oakey, eds., *The Regional Economic Impact of Technological Change.* New York: St. Martin's Press.

Thomas-Emeagwali, G. 1992a. *The Historical Development of Science and Technology in Nigeria.* Lewiston, N.Y.: The Edwin Mellen Press.

Thomas-Emeagwali, G. 1992b. *Science and Technology in African History with Case Studies from Nigeria, Sierra Leone, Zimbabwe and Zambia.* Lewiston, N.Y.: The Edwin Mellen Press.

Waite, G. 1992. *A History of Traditional Medicine and Health Care in Pre-Colonial East-Central Africa.* Lewiston, N.Y.: The Edwin Mellen Press.

9

Accounting Education for Economic Development Management in Anglophone Sub-Saharan Africa

Moses Acquaah

INTRODUCTION

Accounting, which has been called the language of business, is a measurement and reporting information system that covers both micro- and macro-economic activities. It is concerned with individual enterprises, the administration of government activities and macro-economic planning (Enthoven, 1973, 1981). In the case of a nation, well-designed and implemented accounting information systems that cater to the financial information needs of economic planners are essential for resource allocation between the present and future uses. But, as presented in a series of case studies by Enthoven (1977), developing countries (including sub-Saharan Africa) lack adequate accounting information systems, especially at the macro-economic decision level. These systems are the prime source of information upon which sound economic decisions are based. It is, therefore, an indispensable system for the management of the financial and economic resources in any economic system.

However, it should be noted that a well-designed accounting information system will not necessarily result in efficiency and/or effectiveness in the management of financial and economic resources in an economy. This can be achieved if and only if those who are entrusted with the responsibility of implementing and monitoring the system possess the necessary human factor (HF). According to Adjibolosoo (1993, p. 142), the HF

refers to a spectrum of personality characteristics and other dimensions of human performance that enable social, economic, and political institutions to function, and remain functional over time. Such dimensions sustain the workings and application of the rule of law, political harmony, disciplined labor force, just legal systems, respect for human dignity and the sanctity of life, social welfare, and so on.

He further defines the HF as those unique characteristics and qualities of the human personality such as dedication, integrity, honesty, responsibility, commitment and accountability that enable the labor force in an economy to achieve set goals and objectives.

It is the absence of these human characteristics in the accounting profession in Anglophone sub-Saharan Africa (ASSA) that has led to massive misappropriation of funds and mismanagement of financial and economic resources in their public sectors. So, for ASSA countries to exercise effective control and management over their financial and economic resources, an indigenous, dedicated, honest, responsible and accountable accounting profession must be developed. Accounting education and training must therefore be geared toward the provision and inculcation of knowledge, skills, attitudes and values that are needed in the management of financial and economic resources in the process of economic development.

Although ASSA economies are endowed with abundant economic, financial and human resources, significant deficiencies in financial and economic data (i.e., the foundations of effective planning and control at both micro- and macro-economic levels) are prevalent. For instance, deficiencies in the accounting systems include inadequate, unreliable and untimely information systems; ineffective systems of internal controls and checks; lack of "qualified" accountants;[1] unethical behavior of many accountants and auditors (e.g., compromising accounting and auditing standards for self-benefit); and lack of dedicated management personnel. Thus, financial statements and reports that are supposed to be the main indicators of the financial conditions of enterprises and nations fail to provide relevant and reliable information that is needed as a safeguard against misappropriation and embezzlement of funds, fraud, corruption and other malpractices that are commonplace in ASSA economies (Adjibolosoo, 1994; Ghartey, 1985). For example, *The Independent*[2] of July 13, 1994, in a front page article entitled "Scandals," reported that the Auditor General's Report on the public sector accounts in Ghana in 1993 details massive embezzlement and misappropriation of funds. These include a 53 million *cedis* petroleum theft at the Ministry of Defense; the embezzlement of 50 million *cedis* at Juabeso-Bia Education Office; a 53 million *cedis* hospital fees embezzlement at Korle-Bu Teaching Hospital; a 21 million *cedis* fuel theft at Wa Police Station; and an embezzlement of 3 million *cedis* by a court registrar at Bechem.

These embezzlements could not have taken place without the help of the accounting personnel in the various departments. The accounting profession in sub-Saharan Africa is, therefore, facing a crisis of confidence, integrity, responsibility, accountability and credibility. The citizens of these countries and the international community have lost confidence in the ability of the accounting profession to perform its historically unique function of assuring the integrity of financial information on which sub-Saharan African countries rely for the management of economic development (Anderson, 1985).

These deficiencies have rendered the inadequate accounting information systems in ASSA countries useless in controlling and managing financial and economic resources at all levels of government (district, regional and national). In view of these observations, two questions come to mind: "What knowledge, skills, attitudes and values are essential at the workplace for the development and elevation of the status of the accounting profession and accountants in ASSA? How can ASSA countries effectively organize their accounting education and training programs to facilitate the acquisition and transmission of the skills, attitudes and values that best meet the needs of their economies?"

Porter and McKibbin (1988, p. 3), in identifying a fundamental concern for management education and development, posed the following questions that best describe the condition in the education and training of accountants in ASSA countries:

How, as a nation can we best educate and develop those individuals who now have and would have in the future the responsibility for managing, leading, and directing our organizations, particularly those engaged in business type activities? How, in short, can we best make use of available and clearly limited educational resources to enhance the quality of management?

In relating these questions to accounting education and training in ASSA countries, they could be rephrased as follows: "How can we best educate and develop the HF in those individuals who now have and would have in the future the responsibility for managing our financial and economic resources? How, in short, can we best make use of our limited educational resources to promote and enhance the quality of financial management and accountability in ASSA economies?" The operation of effective accounting systems depends on the availability of people who have been thoroughly trained to design, install, implement and maintain them (Chandler and Holzer, 1981; American Accounting Association (AAA), 1986; American Accounting Educational Change Commission (AECC), 1990). Thus, accounting education and training programs that inculcate the human characteristics of dedication, responsibility, integrity and honesty and also promote financial accountability and stewardship are indispensable to the successful management of economic development in ASSA countries. In essence, then, the central issues relating to accounting education and training and economic development management in ASSA countries are related to the contents of the curricula.

In this chapter, the relevance and adequacy of current accounting education and training programs in ASSA countries in fostering economic development management are discussed. A new educational structure that would provide relevant accounting knowledge and skills and promote the development of the HF necessary for economic development management is proposed.

BACKGROUND LITERATURE

Most of the literature on accounting education and training in sub-Saharan Africa can be categorized into two areas: (1) those that deal with the needs of accounting education and training (Wallace and Pendlebury, 1994; Ndzinge, 1994; United Nations, 1991; Briston and Wallace, 1990; Wallace and Briston, 1992) and (2) those that describe the development of accounting education and training (Ghartey, 1978; Osiegbu, 1987; Markell, 1985; Ogundele, 1969). The studies in the first category argue that ASSA countries lack the requisite accounting and financial management humanpower. There are few indigenous professionally and academically qualified accountants per capita in ASSA countries when compared with those in developed countries. Most of these indigenous accountants "who are imbued with knowledge of accounting techniques and theory acquired painstakingly . . . are unable to apply such knowledge effectively in a work environment" (Wallace and Pendlebury, 1994, p. 159). Accounting education and training in ASSA countries should, therefore, be designed to meet the accounting skills needed by the socioeconomic environment. These studies also argue that accounting infrastructure in ASSA countries should be upgraded by designing accounting systems that cater to the financial information needs of economic planners. The studies in the second category are mostly concerned with the historical development of the accounting profession, the structure of accounting education and training curricula and the professional examination schemes. Both categories, however, attribute lack of the requisite humanpower in accounting and financial management to the following reasons:

1. Accounting education and training has not received the emphasis that has been accorded other disciplines such as engineering, medicine, law and many others in the process of national development. Most ASSA countries have established schools for law, medicine and engineering; however, institutions established specifically for the education and training of qualified professional and academic accountants and financial administrators are a rare phenomenon (Ghartey, 1994). This is because there is a general lack of awareness of the potential contribution of accounting in the management of social and economic development (Perera, 1989; Mirghani, 1982).

2. Accounting education and training in ASSA countries are just prototypes of the traditional system for training accountants in the United Kingdom, without any modifications and/or adaptations to include the financial information needs of the local environment. Accountants in ASSA countries are therefore educated and trained under a system that does not serve the needs of the targeted users (e.g., the public sector that comprises a large portion of ASSA economies).

3. There is lack of a blend of theoretical and practical training in the education of accountants as it exists in professions such as law, medicine, pharmacy, etc. The advancement of the accountancy profession in the developed world is due to the widening of the educational background of accountants to make them reasonably comparable to that of other leading professions (Ghartey, 1978).

4. The pass rates in the professional examinations conducted by both the United Kingdom accounting bodies and, recently, the local ones are low. This results in a lot of
repeaters and significantly high dropout rates. The many years of time and resources
devoted to passing these examinations are therefore wasted. This is due to the communications gap among examiners, accounting educators and students. Related to this
problem is the lack of fully qualified accountants in accounting education and training.
According to the United Nations (1991), by the end of 1990, there were only fifteen
fully qualified accountants out of 4,167 in accounting education in Nigeria, which has
the largest number of qualified accountants in the ASSA countries.

The studies reviewed above are most interested in the production of a lot of
indigenous accountants who are educated and trained in the financial information
needs of the socio-economic environment in which they would be using their
expertise. It could thus be argued that the more accountants of a country are
educated and trained, the more likely they are able to perform their duties and
promote effective financial accountability and management. It should, however,
be noted that evidence from some developing countries, with better educated
and trained accountants, suggests that educating and training more people to be
academically and/or professionally qualified as accountants does not necessarily
raise the standard of financial accountability and management.[3] It is not only
the mere acquisition of knowledge and skills that are important in the education
and training of accountants in ASSA countries, but also the ability and willingness of those trained to utilize the acquired knowledge and skills in fostering
financial accountability and management in the economic development process.

THE CURRENT STATE OF ACCOUNTING EDUCATION
AND TRAINING

To qualify and practice as a professional accountant in all the ASSA countries,
individuals must pass an examination from one of the professional accounting
bodies abroad[4] or from their respective countries. The professional qualifications
from the United Kingdom are recognized in all the countries because of its
membership in the British Commonwealth. In fact, a professional accounting
qualification from a U.K. body such as the ACCA or CIMA is highly recognized
and preferred to those obtained locally, such as the Chartered Accountant (CA)
qualification from Ghana or Nigeria, and certification from local accounting
firms, commercial and industrial organizations and even the civil and public
services in ASSA countries. Recently, professional accounting qualifications
from any developed Anglophone country, such as the United States, Canada,
Australia and New Zealand, are also recognized. Accounting education and
training in ASSA countries is therefore highly influenced by the Anglo-
American system.

Pre-University Education

Pre-university accounting education and training in ASSA countries is primarily held in technical, vocational/commercial institutes and polytechnics. Most of these institutes prepare students to become bookkeepers, accounting technicians and/or professional accountants. Those who want to become bookkeepers or accounting technicians are prepared to write the U.K. Royal Society of Arts (RSA) examinations or obtain a diploma awarded by the local bodies, while those who want to become accountants are prepared to write either one of the U.K. professional examinations (especially, the ACCA or the CIMA) or their local professional examinations (Ghartey, 1978; Jagetia and Nwadike, 1983). Currently, only five accounting bodies in ASSA countries (those in Lesotho, Malawi, Swaziland, the United Republic of Tanzania and Zimbabwe) award an accounting technician's diploma.

Most of the polytechnics, technical and vocational/commercial institutes and the accounting bodies that award the accounting technician's diploma do not, however, provide adequate means of preparing students for the professional examinations due to lack of qualified teachers and absence of suitable correspondence materials, teaching aids and current foreign and locally produced textbooks. Furthermore, the contents of the curricula of these institutes are based purely on those of the U.K. bodies that produce professional accountants and accounting technicians, without any modifications and/or adaptations to suit the socioeconomic and cultural environments of ASSA countries. This has resulted in the production of poor quality bookkeepers and accounting technicians who lack the necessary HF required for effective recordkeeping, which is indispensable in keeping track of financial resources and for guarding against the misappropriation and embezzlement of funds and the inefficient use of economic resources in ASSA countries. Most of these graduates who are employed as accounting and/or audit clerks in government institutions, departments and other public organizations also perform duties that otherwise would have been performed by qualified accountants.

University-Level Education

At the university level, accounting programs are modeled after the Anglo-American system. This is because the accounting programs in ASSA countries were mostly designed by expatriate academics from the United Kingdom and the United States. The structure of the curricula of the first degree programs of the countries in West Africa and East Africa closely follows that of the United Kingdom while that of Southern Africa follows the U.S. system. The textbooks and teaching materials used in the programs are exclusively products of the Anglo-American system that emphasizes private sector enterprise accounting and auditing. There are neither locally produced textbooks nor teaching aids that make use of the unique socioeconomic and cultural environments in the region.

Accounting is, therefore, taught as if it were a universal subject, although it has been shown that the development of any accounting system is influenced by the cultural and socioeconomic environment (Gray, 1988; Samuels and Oliga, 1982). Moreover, the accounting curricula in ASSA countries emphasize a theoretical framework at the expense of the practical aspects of accounting. The contents of the accounting programs, therefore, fall short of the needs of ASSA economies.

Professional Accounting Education and Training

At the professional level, most students in ASSA countries are generally educated and trained toward obtaining one of the professional designations from the United Kingdom (i.e., the ACCA or the CIMA). This is because most of the professional accounting bodies in ASSA countries (e.g., the Zambia Institute of Certified Accountants (ZICA), the Botswana Institute of Accountants (BIA) and the Public Accountants' Examinations Council of Malawi (PAEC)) have examination arrangements with the ACCA. Registered students of these bodies write all the papers of the ACCA examinations with some papers (e.g., law and taxation) substituted for by local variants (Ndzinge, 1994). Students either study full time or work and study part time through nonformal methods such as correspondence courses in order to qualify for the U.K. designations. This method of qualifying as a professional accountant has resulted in high failure and dropout rates. For example, only about fifteen Malawians (Rowe et al., 1986), six Botswana nationals (Stokes, 1987) and six Swaziland nationals (SIA, 1989) qualified as professional accountants with a U.K. designation in 1986, 1987 and 1989 respectively.

It was therefore thought that the solution to producing more professional accountants is by establishing local training and examination programs. Most of the ASSA countries, therefore, established local professional bodies with examination programs that allow students to qualify as professional accountants in their home countries. Some of these countries include Nigeria, Ghana, Kenya, the United Republic of Tanzania, Zimbabwe and Lesotho. However, no change in the accounting curricula has taken place since the launching of these local programs. The structure of their curricula and examinations follow the Anglo-American pattern, which emphasizes private sector financial accounting and auditing, without due consideration to the financial information needs of ASSA countries that have large public sectors. For instance, the curricula of both the Institute of Chartered Accountants of Nigeria (ICAN) and the Institute of Chartered Accountants of Ghana (ICAG) are exactly the same as that of the ACCA. The failure and drop-out rates have therefore been extremely high, and the few who go through the system do not acquire the required HF that is crucial to the management of financial resources in these countries. Zimbabwe is the only ASSA country that has recognized the need for increased financial accountability and management in the public sector and has therefore created a professional accounting body exclusively for the public sector.

The concern that most professional accounting bodies have for educating and training accountants has been eclipsed by their commitment to credentialism and international recognition (i.e., "the diploma disease"),[5] which is irrelevant to the needs of ASSA countries. Moreover, "the desire amongst professional accountants to ensure the perpetuation of their privileged status and to safeguard the flow to them of high financial rewards accruing from the Western style of accounting bodies" (Ndzinge, 1994, p. 130) has made the professional bodies unable to make changes to the education and training of accountants, auditors and other accounting personnel to be more relevant to the social and economic needs of ASSA countries. It must be emphasized that there have been efforts in some ASSA countries to reform the accounting education and training programs; however, the recommendations have been prototypes of the traditional ways of educating and training accountants in Anglo-American countries, without modifications and/or adaptations to the local socioeconomic environments.[6]

The Need for Reform

Accounting systems are more than ways of organizing financial figures. They must be responsive to the financial and economic information needs of business managers, national development planners and administrators of a country. The goals of a nation state and the aspirations of a people influence the structure of a country's accounting system (Heely and Nersesian, 1993). For example, in Britain, the Companies Acts reinforce the managing of assets entrusted to stewards by shareholders; accounting responds to the needs of business and follows developments in commercial activities. The education and training of accounting and financial management personnel is therefore primarily geared towards meeting this goal.

The accounting education and training programs in ASSA countries, which follow the Anglo-American system, do not train accountants to work in economies that are dominated by the public sector and where the ownership of most business enterprises is in the hands of the same people or group of people. Furthermore, the programs fail to meet the needs of ASSA economies, since the contents of the curricula are based on completely different cultural and socioeconomic environments (particularly those of the United Kingdom and the United States). Although accounting practices should be dynamic and evolve to meet the changing needs of society, accounting education and training programs in ASSA countries are static and rigid. There is, therefore, the need to make the programs flexible enough to keep pace with the changing socioeconomic needs of ASSA countries.

Currently, there are few programs in the region that incorporate a course in business ethics, although almost all the professional accounting bodies in the region have ethical codes of conduct to which members (qualified and students) are expected to adhere. Abraham Briloff, a longstanding critic of the accounting profession, urges accounting educators to instill an "ethical compass" in their students so that they will enter the profession as committed to "the Principles of the Accountant . . . as [they] are [to] the Principles of Accounting" (1985, p. 35). The lack of attention accorded to the potential contribution of business ethics to the development of the HF has resulted in unethical behavior of many accountants, auditors, accounting technicians and bookkeepers, leading to continuing massive misappropriation and mismanagement of financial resources in ASSA countries. There is also lack of attention given to the development of leadership capabilities, people management and entrepreneurism in the accounting education and training programs. In fact, accounting programs that allow students to take social science courses such as ethics, psychology, philosophy, sociology, and so on, are a rare phenomenon in ASSA countries. The bookkeepers, accounting technicians and professional accountants are primarily trained to work in the public sector. Most of the accounting students have, therefore, developed unrealistic job expectations for the public sector, especially with government departments and other parastatal organizations, to the extent that creative ideas of establishing their own businesses and/or consultancies have dwindled completely. The need for reform is imminent. Pre-university, university and professional accounting education and training programs have to be made relevant to the cultural and socioeconomic needs of ASSA countries. This, however, cannot be achieved without astute leadership that possesses the relevant HF and knows how to achieve intended national goals through HF development.

A NEW STRUCTURE FOR ACCOUNTING EDUCATION AND TRAINING

Enthoven (1981) suggested that the right accounting education and training for developing countries is a combination of business enterprise accounting (i.e., financial, managerial, cost accounting and taxation), government accounting, national income accounting (i.e., accounting for national income, assets, debts, balance of payments, budgeting, etc.), and financial and operational auditing. Although this list is better than what is being offered by the professional accounting bodies and the educational institutions in the ASSA countries,[7] it will not facilitate the development of HF.

In a new global economy based on the acquisition of skills and knowledge and the ability and willingness to use this new knowledge, ASSA economies will fall hopelessly behind the rest of the world. They must establish policies and programs that support the education and training of accountants, auditors and other financial management personnel to acquire the HF, since they are the custodians and stewards of their financial and economic resources. The development of these human qualities in accountants, auditors and other financial man-

agement personnel through education and training will allow accounting to play
a useful and effective role in ASSA societies.

The Objectives of Accounting Education and Training

What should be the object of accounting education and training in ASSA
countries? One characteristic of a profession is that it is dependent on a specialized body of knowledge and skills acquired through both formal education
and practical training. The objectives of accounting education and training in
ASSA countries should therefore be geared towards (1) the development of
accountants with the knowledge, skills and attitudes that are necessary in sup-
plying useful, timely and reliable information for national economic planners
and other users of accounting information; (2) the development of accountants
who will be very effective and efficient in a public sector environment; and (3)
the development and inculcation of the relevant human qualities of accountability, dedication to duty, honesty, responsibility, integrity, and so on in accounts
so that they will be willing and ready to utilize their acquired knowledge and
skills for articulating and fostering the economic development process.

The accounting curricula in ASSA countries must therefore include not only
business enterprise accounting, government accounting, national income accounting and financial and operational auditing, but also subjects in business
ethics, leadership development, small business management and creativity. This
is because the accounting curriculum is one of the most important components
of the education and training of accountants. It is the primary medium through
which the objectives of accounting education and training in ASSA countries
can be implemented and achieved.

Operationalization

In order to make the accounting curricula effective in achieving the objectives
of educating and training accountants in ASSA countries, it must change with
the social and economic environment in which the accounting profession is
engaged. It must, therefore, be designed to reflect the financial and managerial
information needs of economic planners. This requires that the financial and
managerial information needs of the various ASSA countries be known before
the accounting education and training curricula can be designed to produce accountants and financial management personnel with the requisite knowledge and
skills.

Thus, the first step in the operationalization of the objectives of accounting
education and training is the determination of the requisite financial and managerial information needs of the various ASSA countries and the development
of accounting standards based on these information needs. Secondly, there
should be an introduction of new and relevant courses that emphasize the development of the HF relevant to the socioeconomic environment of ASSA coun-

tries. Courses such as business ethics, financial management of small business enterprises, public sector/government accounting and international accounting should be introduced. A course in business ethics will provide accounting, auditing and other financial management students with the tools and/or techniques and the conceptual framework for analyzing ethical issues. It will also increase their awareness to the actual and potential effects of unethical behavior to their communities and countries as a whole. The globalization of the world economy, through the proliferation of transnational corporations and the internationalization of capital markets, also requires the need for a reasonable level of understanding of the international dimensions of accounting.

Furthermore, to widen the educational base of accountants in ASSA countries, accounting students must extend their knowledge and skills to include a grasp of the social and economic environments in which they operate. They should therefore be provided with the opportunity to take courses in the social sciences such as psychology, philosophy and sociology. It must be emphasized that the introduction of these courses is not as important as the contents. The contents of the courses (except international accounting, which is supposed to provide accountants with a better understanding of the international dimension of accounting) must reflect the values, social norms, aspirations and the economic environments of the various ASSA countries. For example, the course in business ethics must be based on the traditional values, social norms, attitudes and policies relating to ethical considerations in decision-making in ASSA countries towards both private and public sector businesses, rather than on business ethics courses from Anglo-American countries. The ethical code of professional conduct of the local accounting bodies must be used in this process. There should also be the "case study" approach in the teaching of business ethics. This approach will offer students some experience in recognizing ethical problems and, therefore, a better chance of making ethical decisions after leaving school. Actual and potential cases of embezzlement of funds, corruption and misappropriation of funds in ASSA economies must also be used to develop the relevant HF in the accounting profession. Furthermore, apart from the business ethics course, ethics must also be integrated into all accounting curricula.

Thirdly, there must be a total revamping of existing course contents of the accounting programs (at the pre-university, university and professional levels) to emphasize the socioeconomic environments in the various ASSA countries. This means that there should be local production of suitable textbooks, professional journals and other relevant publications that use information about the various ASSA countries. There should be the discontinuation of books produced in the advanced countries that have no relevance to the economies of ASSA countries. The various ASSA governments can intervene in this matter by giving incentives to university professors and other professional accountants to produce textbooks and other teaching aids, which make use of information from the local environment. The ASSA governments can also arrange with the publishers of classic textbooks in the advanced countries to produce local editions that meet the needs and socioeconomic environments of ASSA countries. Government intervention should also take the form of the promulgation/enacting of laws requiring local professional bodies and other educational institutions to use the locally produced teaching materials in their programs. Government intervention is necessary to achieve the objectives of accounting education since a large proportion of the budgets of most local professional accountancy bodies and institutions of higher education in ASSA countries are government financed.

Fourthly, the various ASSA countries should introduce local bookkeeping certificates and accounting technician diplomas to produce bookkeepers and accounting clerks who are educated and trained in their socioeconomic environments. This can be done by individual ASSA countries or on a regional basis. The ideal situation is for individual ASSA countries to award their own bookkeeping certificates and accounting technician diplomas since "each country has its own political, social, economic, and cultural characteristics, and is highly probable that the goals and thus the information needs of the managers of the economy will differ from one country to another" (Briston, 1978, p. 120). However, due to the lack of technical and financial resources in all ASSA countries and the similarity in the socioeconomic conditions among them, it would probably be better to pool resources in the awarding of these certificates and diplomas. The governments of ASSA countries must also encourage their students to obtain these local certifications by giving them priority in the job market over those with foreign qualifications.

The professional bodies must also provide a means of enforcing their professional codes of ethical conduct to instill some confidence and credibility in the accounting profession. The primary role of the professional bodies is to provide leadership to their members by enhancing the quality of their professional performance, protecting the interest of the public and preserving and strengthening the accounting and auditing functions (Anderson, 1985). This can be done by a systematic monitoring and evaluation of the professional practice of their members with emphasis on the quality of their performance. There should also be a comprehensive examination of the relevance of the existing ethical codes of conduct to professionalism, integrity, accountability, responsibility and the commitment to quality service, so they are aligned to the interests of the various ASSA countries.

Furthermore, there should be a blend of theory and practice in the education and training of accountants. The universities should introduce a practical component in the accounting education curricula, while local professional bodies should increase the level of theoretical knowledge in their programs. It should be noted that most of the recommendations enumerated above are not easy to implement because of (1) financial and technical difficulties and (2) professional accountants who may not want their privileged positions jeopardized by the elimination of the status quo. As a result, they will not willingly support the reform process. But for ASSA countries to exercise effective control and management over their financial and economic resources, these changes in the accounting education and training programs are indispensable.

CONCLUSION

In this chapter, it has been shown that ASSA countries lack well-designed accounting information systems that are essential to the management of financial and economic resources in their economies. However, it has been argued that a well-designed accounting information system is a necessary but not sufficient condition for the effective management of financial and economic resources in an economy. This is because the operation of well-designed and effective accounting information systems depends on the availability of people trained to implement and maintain them. The accounting education and training programs at the pre-university, university and professional levels in ASSA countries have been modeled after the Anglo-American system. This phenomenon places emphasis on private sector financial accounting and auditing. The education and training of accountants, auditors and other financial management personnel in ASSA countries is, therefore, not geared toward satisfying the financial information needs of the social and economic environments of ASSA countries that are dominated by the public sector. Secondly, the education and training of accountants, auditors and other financial management personnel is not geared toward the development and inculcation of the relevant HF.

It has also been argued that it is not only the mere acquisition of knowledge and skills that is important in the education and training of accountants and other financial management personnel in ASSA countries, but also the ability and willingness of those trained to utilize acquired knowledge and skills to foster financial accountability and management in the economic development process. It is, therefore, concluded that unless the curricula of ASSA countries' accounting education and training programs are reformed to emphasize the development and the inculcation of the relevant HF in those who are, and would be, entrusted with the responsibility of managing their financial and economic resources, the massive misappropriation and embezzlement of funds and the mismanagement of financial and economic resources will continue.

NOTES

1. Most professional accountants in Anglophone sub-Saharan Africa received their qualifications from the developed world. Because of that, they are not familiar with the socioeconomic and legal environments in their own countries. They are therefore ineffective in using their expertise acquired overseas to solve and/or control the massive misappropriation of funds and mismanagement of financial and economic resources. They are therefore academically and/or professionally qualified but not in HF terms.

2. This is an independent Ghanaian newspaper.

3. See Abayo and Roberts (1992) for evidence from Tanzania; Parry and Groves (1990) for Bangladesh; and Rivera (1990) for Panama.

4. The professional bodies, which are mostly in the UK, are the Institute of Chartered Accountants of England and Wales (ICAEW), the Chartered Association of Certified Accountants (ACCA), and the Chartered Institute of Management Accountants (CIMA).

5. See Dore (1976).

6. See Ghartey (1978) for the case of Ghana.

7. Subjects offered by educational institutions and professional bodies in the region are mostly traditional ones such as economics, quantitative methods (business statistics), business management, law, financial accounting (introductory, intermediate and advanced), cost and managerial accounting, auditing and investigation, data processing/information systems, financial management and taxation.

REFERENCES

Abayo, J. A. and Roberts, C. 1992. "Does Training More Accountants Raise the Standards of Accounting in Third World Countries? Another Evidence from Tanzania." In R. S. O. Wallace, J. M. Samuels and R. J. Briston, eds., *Research in Third World Accounting, Vol. 2.* Greenwich, Conn.: JAI Press.

Adjibolosoo, S. 1993. "The Human Factor in Development." *The Scandinavian Journal of Development Alternatives* 12 (4): 139–149.

Adjibolosoo, S. 1994. "The Human Factor and the Failure of Economic Development and Policies in Africa." In F. Ezeala-Harrison and S. Adjibolosoo, eds., *Perspectives on Economic Development in Africa.* Westport, Conn.: Praeger.

American Accounting Association (AAA). 1986. *Future Accounting Education: Preparing for the Expanding Profession.* A Special Report by the Committee on the Future Structure, Content, and Scope of Accounting Education. Sarasota, FL.: American Accounting Association.

American Accounting Education Change Commission (AECC). 1990. "Objectives of Education for Accountants: Position Statement Number One." *Issues in Accounting Education* 5 (2): 307–312.

Anderson, G. 1985. "A Fresh Look at Standards of Professional Conduct." *Journal of Accountancy* (September): 91–106.

Briloff, A. J. 1985. "The Coming Storm in Ethics." *New Accountant* (September): 33–35.

Briston, R. J. 1978. "The Evolution of Accounting in Developing Countries." *The International Journal of Accounting Education and Research* (Fall): 105–120.

Briston, R. J. and Wallace, R. S. O. 1990. "Accounting Education and Corporate Financial Reporting in Tanzania." In R. S. O. Wallace, J. M. Samuels and R. J. Briston, eds., *Research in Third World Accounting, Vol. 1.* Greenwich, Conn.: JAI Press.

Chandler, J. S. and Hozler, H. (1981). "The Need for Systems Education in Developing Countries." In A. J. Enthoven, ed., *Accounting Education in Economic Development Management.* Amsterdam: North-Holland.

Dore, R. 1976. *The Diploma Disease: Education, Qualification and Development.* London: George Allen and Unwin Ltd.

Enthoven, A. J. 1973. *Accounting and Economic Development Policy.* New York: Elsevier.

Enthoven, A. J. 1977. *Accounting Systems in Third World Economies.* New York: North-Holland.

Enthoven, A. J. 1981. *Accounting Education in Economic Development Management.* Amsterdam: North-Holland.

Ghartey, A. 1978. "A New Perspective for Accountancy Education in Ghana." *The International Journal of Accounting Education and Research* (Fall): 121–132.

Ghartey, J. B. 1985. "Accountability, the Threshold of Political Instability, Underdevelopment, and Misery: The Case of Africa." *The International Journal of Accounting Education and Research* (Fall): 143–158.

Ghartey, J. B. A. 1994. "Action and Results Oriented Research and Consultancy Approach to Third World Accounting Education and Professional Development." In J. O. Burns and B. E. Needles, Jr., eds., *Accounting Education for the 21st Century: The Global Challenges.* Sarasota, Fla.: American Accounting Association.

Gray, S. J. 1988. "Towards a Theory of Cultural Influence on the Development of Accounting Systems Internationally." *Abacus* 24 (1): 1–15.

Heely, J. A. and Nersesian, R. L. (1993). *Global Management Accounting: A Guide for Executives of International Corporations.* Westport, Conn.: Quorum Books.

Jagetia, L. C. and Nwadike, E. C. 1983. "Accounting Systems in Developing Nations: The Nigerian Experience." *The International Journal of Accounting Education and Research* (Spring): 69–81.

Markell, W. 1985. "Development of Accounting Education and the Accounting Profession in Third World Countries: Botswana." *The International Journal of Accounting Education and Research* (Fall): 99–105.

Mirghani, M. A. 1982. "A Framework for a Linkage between Microaccounting and Macroaccounting for Purposes of Development Planning in Developing Countries." *The International Journal of Accounting Education and Research* (Fall): 57–68.

Ndzinge, S. 1994. "Aligning Accounting Education and Training to the Skills Needs of Developing Nations: The Case of SADCC." In J. O. Burns and B. E. Needles, Jr., eds., *Accounting Education for the 21st Century: The Global Challenges.* Sarasota, Fla.: American Accounting Association.

Ogundele, B. 1969. "The Accounting Profession in Nigeria: An International Perspective." *The International Journal of Accounting Education and Research* (Fall): 101–106.

Osiegbu, P. I. 1987. "The State of Accountancy Education in Nigeria." *The International Journal of Accounting Education and Research* (Spring): 57–68.

Parry, M. J. and Groves, R. E. 1990. "Does Training More Accountants Raise the Standards of Accounting in Third World Countries? A Study of Bangladesh." In R. S. O. Wallace, J. M. Samuels and R. J. Briston, eds., *Research in Third World Accounting, Vol. 1.* Greenwich, Conn.: JAI Press Ltd.

Perera, M. H. B. 1989. "Accounting in Developing Countries: A Case for Uniformity." *British Accounting Review* 21 (2): 141–157.

Porter, L. W. and L. E. McKibbin. 1988. *Management Education and Development: Drift or Thrust into the 21st Century.* New York: McGraw Hill.

Rivera, J. M. 1990. "The Accounting Profession and Accounting Education in Panama: A Survey." In B. E. Needles, Jr. and V. K. Zimmerman, eds., *Comparative*

International Accounting Educational Standards. Urbana-Champaign, Ill.: Center
for International Education and Research in Accounting, University of Illinois.

Rowe, D. N., Motshubi, L. J., Mundea, K. M., Sampio, J. and Hegarty, A. M. 1986.
Study of Accountancy Training in the SADCC Region (November). Cited in S.
Ndzinge, "Aligning Accounting Education and Training to the Skills Needs of
Developing Nations: The Case of SADCC." In J. O. Burns and B. E. Needles,
Jr., eds, *Accounting Education for the 21st Century: The Global Challenges.*
Seventh International Conference on Accounting Education, American Account-
ing Association, 1994.

Samuels, J. M. and Oliga, J. C. 1982. "Accounting Standards in Developing Countries."
The International Journal of Accounting Education and Research (Fall): 69–88.

"Scandals." 1994. *The Independent,* July 13, p. 209.

Stokes, K. C. 1987. *Proposals for the Development of the Accountancy Profession in
the Republic of Botswana.* Cited in S. Ndzinge, "Aligning Accounting Education
and Training to the Skills Needs of Developing Nations: The Case of SADCC."
In J. O. Burns and B. E. Needles, Jr., eds., *Accounting Education for the 21st
Century: The Global Challenges.* Seventh International Conference on Accounting Education, American Accounting Association, 1994.

Swaziland Institute of Accountants (SIA). 1989. *Membership Register.* Mbabane: Swaziland Institute of Accountants.

United Nations 1991. *Accountancy Development in Africa: Challenge of the 1990s.* New
York: United Nations Center on Transnational Corporations.

Wallace, R. S. O. and Briston, R. J. 1992. "Improving the Accounting Infrastructure in
Developing Countries." In R. S. O. Wallace, J. M. Samuels and R. J. Briston,
eds., *Research in Third World Accounting, Vol. 2.* Greenwich, Conn.: JAI Press.

Wallace, R. S. O. and Pendlebury, M. 1994. "Needs of Accounting Education in Developing Countries: An African Case Study." In J. O. Burns and B. E. Needles,
Jr., eds., *Accounting Education for the 21st Century: The Global Challenges.*
Seventh International Conference on Accounting Education, American Accounting Association.

10

The Human Factor in Marketing and Development in the LDCs

Samuel K. Bonsu

INTRODUCTION

Marketing and its role in socioeconomic development processes has been the focus of many scholarly endeavors (Wood and Vitell, 1986; Hosley and Wee, 1988; Savitt, 1988). Whatever the primary focus of their studies, academic researchers have often concluded that the discipline should not be ignored in development planning. In spite of overwhelming evidence in support of the benefits of marketing to development in advanced countries, lesser developed countries (LDCs) have often neglected marketing in their development plans (Abbott, 1968; Cateora, 1992). Where it has been accepted, marketing in LDCs has been treated with contempt and has failed to yield anticipated outcomes (Goldman, 1982; Samiee, 1990).

The failure and neglect of marketing in LDCs is partly attributable to the assumptions made by scholars in recommending marketing as a tool for LDC development (Joy and Ross, 1989). While marketing facilitates development, it may not be the agent of development ethos—the process that focuses all national energies on the task of development (Dholakia and Sherry, 1987). The absence of such an ethos may strongly inhibit the positive contributions of marketing to development. However, existing models of marketing in development ignore it. A more critical look at LDCs suggests a lack of the necessary indicators of a development ethos that is a probable explanation to the failure and neglect that marketing experiences in these countries.

The primary objective of this chapter is to propose an extended model for marketing in development. The proposed model is premised on the idea that development ethos is generated through an aggregate set of dimensions referred to as the human factor (HF). It is the level of HF development that determines the maginitude or depth of interaction among socioeconomic and political factors that yield the milieu in which marketing facilitates the achievement of development objectives. Attributes of a developed HF include a people's ability and willingness to apply their skills and knowledge through dedication and commitment to work for the benefit of society as a whole (Adjibolosoo, 1994a, 1995). The chapter argues that until LDCs develop their HF marketing will continue to have minimal effect on development efforts in these countries. The chapter also discusses how the relevant HF can be developed in LDCs.

MARKETING AND DEVELOPMENT: A REVIEW

Researchers differ sharply on their perspectives on the relationship between marketing and development. Two main themes pervade the literature and have guided discussions on this topic for the last three decades. These are the *determinist* and *activist* schools of thought (Bartels, 1977; Hilger, 1978; Cundiff and Hilger, 1979; Hosley and Wee, 1988; Savitt, 1988). A third view, the *interdependent* school, is emerging out of the criticisms leveled against the two dominant perspectives. In what follows, the views of each school are briefly discussed.

The Determinist School

The basic argument of the determinist school of thought is that marketing is a by-product of development and the extent of its role is dictated by the environment within which it operates. Bartels (1981) suggested a possible threshold level of development below which marketing in an economy does not constitute a formal activity and, therefore, may not be considered as a contributing factor to economic development. Moyer (1964, 1968) examined the relationship between the length and type of channels, on the one hand, and trade volume on the other. He reasoned that as a country develops, it pulls along its marketing organizations. If the positive trend in development persists, then the country will, at one point or another, have a shorter and more efficient distribution system.

Wadinambiaratchi (1965, 1972) argued that channel systems are responses to environmental variables that may not involve the marketing system. He concluded that since channel systems (and for that matter marketing) lag behind development, their analysis will indicate the level of development in the economies in which they are found. Douglas (1971) examined the relationship between channel complexities and per-capita income and capital formation across different countries. She observed patterns of consistency among countries at similar levels of development. Arndt (1972) also found consistent relationships between the sizes of retail establishments and the level of development in twelve developed countries. He identified retail performance as a function of various development indicators.

Figure 10.1
Determinist Model for Marketing in Development

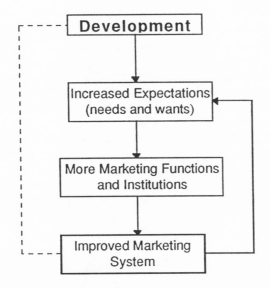

- - - - Relationship not
recognized in
determinist model

Development

Increased Expectations
(needs and wants)

More Marketing Functions
and Institutions

Improved Marketing
System

All of these studies show that marketing is dependent on the environments that create it. The determinist school model, summarized in Figure 10.1, suggests that with development comes increased demand for goods and services. Responding to this growing demand requires increased production and the identification and performance of a wider variety of marketing functions. Ensuing competition leads to marketing efficiency over time.

There appears to be two serious flaws in the determinist line of argument. The first is the failure to recognize the potential for the emerging marketing systems to impact development. Marketing is dynamic and changes with the times (Bartels, 1976). The changes that occur in the marketing system may alter values and belief systems of the society concerned, thereby influencing the next course of social, economic and cultural development (Darian, 1985; Dholakia and Sherry, 1987). Second, implicit in the deterministic line of thinking is the idea that once an economy is doing well, distribution channels will emerge and adapt to changes in the economy over time. Evidence from around the world shows that this is not always the case. Turkey, for example, made important development gains between the 1950s and 1980s but that country's development has not translated into changes in its distribution systems (Kumcu and Kumcu,

1987). A case study of Tunisia presents corroborating evidence (Miossec, 1990). It stands to reason, then, to effect advances in development in any society, marketers and other development planners should make conscious efforts to direct the attainment of expected outcomes. Herein lies the core of the activist argument.

The Activist School

The activist school of thought in marketing and development maintains that marketing is the most important stimulus to development. Marketing, according to this view, leads to changes in socioeconomic and cultural structures and institutions that contribute to the building of infra- and supra-structures that provide the basis for development (Drucker, 1958; Dholakia and Dholakia, 1982; Etemad, 1982; Etgar, 1983). Drucker (1958) contended that marketing is the single most effective contributor to economic development by way of optimizing active and latent resources, as well as the development of standards, entrepreneurs and managers. Entrepreneurial and managerial development among individuals and firms must be augmented by macro-marketing policies if they are to be effective in development efforts (Cundiff, 1982).

The bulk of activist research has focused on the need to modernize food distribution systems to make them more efficient (Hosley and Wee, 1988). Most of these studies decry the inefficient nature of food distribution systems in LDCs and recommend changes to rectify the situation. Proponents of this view maintain that improvements in channels of distribution lead to increased supply and demand, as well as a wider assortment of goods and services on the market (Layton, 1985a). Subsequent to this increase in supply and demand, competitors will emerge in all aspects of the economy, including the distribution sector.

Competition minimizes monopolistic tendencies, thus creating operational and cost efficiencies in marketing systems (Alderson, 1957; Anderson, 1970; Layton, 1985a). The incremental income resulting from the savings in distribution costs makes more money available in the economy, thereby leading to increased per-capita incomes through trickle-down effects (Galbraith and Holton, 1955). Increased competition and income may also lead to capital accumulation (Miracle, 1968), an essential requirement and propellant for further economic growth and development (Nurske, 1971; Todaro, 1992). This economic growth and development encourages further improvements in channels of distribution and all other aspects of marketing. The process is continuously repeated, thus establishing a predictable pattern of change (see Figure 10.2).

Recommendations for LDC development based on the activist model have sometimes been implemented at phenomenal costs, and yet have failed to be optimally beneficial to the recipient LDCs (Goldman, 1982; Wambi, 1988). This failure may be due to the many impediments to marketing in these countries, as well as the a priori assumptions of researchers on which the recommendations are based (Joy and Ross, 1989; Samiee, 1990).

Figure 10.2
Activist Model for Marketing in Development

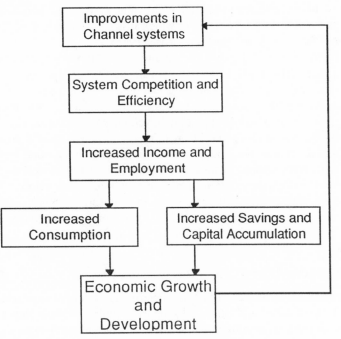

Most marketing ideas recommended for adoption in the LDCs have been transferred from regions whose social, cultural and philosophical values are different from those in LDCs. Myrdal (1972) argued that the consequences of using concepts designed to fit developed countries in LDCs can have disastrous implications. Several marketers have also warned against such action (Duhaime and Ross, 1988; Firat Kumcu and Karafakioglu, 1988). In spite of these warnings, LDC traditional marketing know-how, like other indigenous technologies, has often been ignored in the design and implementation of changes in the distribution sector because they are seen as obsolete, not adaptable to changing times and only suitable for rural communities (Brokensha, Warren and Werner, 1980; Emmanuel, 1982; Ofori-Amoah, 1988). The result of these actions is that local residents feel alienated. Being sidelined in the process of change, local market leaders feel threatened. They, therefore, design strategies to thwart the efforts of the champions of change. Marketing initiatives under these circumstances are unlikely to yield favorable results.

Second, the majority of activists presume an orderly and predictable manner of influence of marketing innovation on the socioeconomic and political development of LDCs. They presume that once an aspect of marketing is introduced into a system, it will be adopted in a predictable order among recipients and influence the environment in a fashion similar to that which was experienced in the region where the marketing innovation of concern was first applied (Moyer, 1968; Slater, 1968). Research, however, shows that the rate and level of adoption of any new idea is dependent on individual value systems, as well as the social, cultural and political environments in which it is presented (Rogers, 1962; Bartels, 1976; Duhaime, MacTavish and Ross, 1985).

The World Bank (1991, p. 45) points out that with the benefits of hindsight and advanced technology, LDCs are developing faster than their developed counterparts at a comparable stage of development. This goes to confirm that marketing environments in LDCs are essentially different from those of the developed world at a similar stage of development. Predicting the course of marketing adoption and its impact on LDC development should proceed only on recognition of the dynamic nature of the relevant marketing environment (Hosley and Wee, 1988). Inkeles and Smith (1974) report on how different levels of cultural exposure affect a person's willingness to change. People in LDC societies have very different levels of exposure to other cultures; it is perhaps better, then, to determine the level of conservatism in any of these societies prior to introducing marketing as a tool for development.

Interdependent School

The shortcomings of the activist and determinist schools of thought, coupled with the lack of substantial empirical support for either of these views, have led to a more recent line of thinking among students of marketing and development (Hilger, 1978). This emerging view supposes that marketing and development exert direct impact on each other and, therefore, chart each other's course. Since the *determinist* and *activist* perspectives have contributions to make to the role of marketing in development, their integration is the best way to minimize the impact of the shortcomings of each school of thought. Dholakia and Sherry (1987) proposed that marketing is not merely an indicator of cultural values in the economy in which it operates but also influences the nature of these values. Perhaps it is the milieu in which marketing operates that determines the type of approach that is most relevant.

In recognizing the unique nature of societies, it is best to suppose that in economies where managers and other innovators are aware of the power of marketing in development, it may be used to move a society toward a more desirable state; where marketing is not accepted, it may have to lag behind development (Duhaime, MacTavish and Ross, 1985, p. 4). In either case, the two phenomena continuously impact each other. Their interplay and subsequent sociopolitical and cultural implications chart the course of development and marketing systems in any economy (Darian, 1985). This relationship is illustrated in Figure 10.3.

A fundamental flaw inherent in all three models is that they all assume the existence of a knowledgeable, supportive and dedicated work force that is anxious to see changes in the system. This work force is also assumed to be willing

Figure 10.3
Mutual Relationship between Marketing and Development

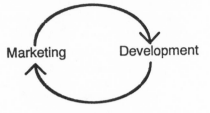

to use its skills in productive ventures for the benefit of society as a whole and to take business risks by adopting and investing in innovative ideas. Work ethics and development ethos of these kinds do not occur naturally; they are learned responses that can be hindered or facilitated by sociocultural and historical factors (Abudu, 1986; Ahiauzu, 1986a; Adu-Febiri, 1995). Effective utilization of marketing in LDCs thus requires that society continuously strive to attain and preserve such work ethics. Developing the HF may constitute a primordial means to achieving this objective.

THE HUMAN FACTOR IN MARKETING AND DEVELOPMENT

What is the Human Factor?

The HF is the "spectrum of personality characteristics and other dimensions of human performance that enable social, economic and political institutions to function and remain functional, over time" (Adjibolosoo, 1993, p. 142). The HF concept stresses the essence of the citizens' recognition of the need to move from one less desirable socioeconomic situation to a more desirable one. Its major role is to enlighten the populace on the relevance of their individual efforts to societal well-being and also to inculcate those values that are necessary to encourage these individuals to participate in concerted efforts necessary for the achievement of national goals. Dimensions of the HF include integrity, dedication, responsibility and accountability in the implementation of policies towards the attainment of development objectives. These dimensions sustain political harmony, the rule of law, a disciplined labor force and just legal systems, among other things (Adjibolosoo, 1993, 1994a).

In the presence of these positive human attributes, a development ethos would prevail. People would have a high level of trust in authority and in the social, economic and political systems. Hard work rather than bribery and corruption would serve as the means to acquiring material wealth and success. The experienced and educated would be more than willing to train newcomers. Intimidation in the workplace would be minimal due to the potential for legal reprisals to be meted out to aggressors (Hartstein and Wilde, 1994; Reynolds, 1994; Woods, 1994). Dedication and accountability would ensure adequate performance by each worker while, at the same time, holding certain corrupt practices in check. Social and economic deviants would be punished according to guidelines set by the legal establishment. Compensation structures would be organized effectively to require certain levels of performance from persons wishing to hold on to their jobs. Meritocratic systems would be the primary guide and determinant of job security. All of this would lead to the institutionalization of minimum standards of work performance—a situation that can shape societal attitudes towards work (Ahiauzu, 1986b).

The HF freely interacts with existing sociocultural, political and economic factors to yield a blend that has two primary potential outcomes. Figure 10.4 presents a simplified illustration of the process by which this may occur. The HF, being the most important element, mobilizes economic, social, cultural and political dimensions into a blend of factors that determine the presence or absence of appropriate development ethos in society. Where the HF is developed, the blend of factors is likely to be one that is conducive to development efforts and may lead to positive changes in all human dynamics and institutions (Adjibolosoo, 1994a, pp. 27–32). Under such circumstances, development ethos can emerge to allow marketing the opportunity to play its catalytic role in development.

Where the HF is poorly developed, the resulting factor mix generates situations that make it difficult for society as a whole to benefit. As shown in Figure 10.4, changes in social, cultural and political phenomena are negative. That is, they tend to promote deviant sociocultural norms that enhance individual well-being at the expense of society. The elite in society, who benefit the most from such biased individual gains, have no incentive to promote development awareness. Thus, the necessary development ethos is virtually non-existent, significantly stifling marketing's contribution to development.

Some researchers argue that social, cultural, political and economic factors should have certain enabling characteristics to be effective in facilitating change and development (Duhaime, MacTavish and Ross, 1985). It should be noted, however, that these enabling conditions have to be created since they do not occur naturally. The presence of the enabling characteristics and their interactions with other factors depend primarily on the extent of development of the prevailing HF, because it is the HF that guides the interrelationships among all the factors that contribute to the mix. In other words, regardless of the state of other factor endowments in a society, a developed HF can effectively and efficiently organize these factors to the optimal advantage of society. Japan and Singapore, with their limited raw material endowments and practically authoritarian political systems, would not have developed with factor endowments besides HF as the prime source of development.

With a developed HF, the factor mix will exert a favorable impact, generating development ethos and triggering marketing and other processes that may lead

Figure 10.4
Factor Mix for Development Ethos

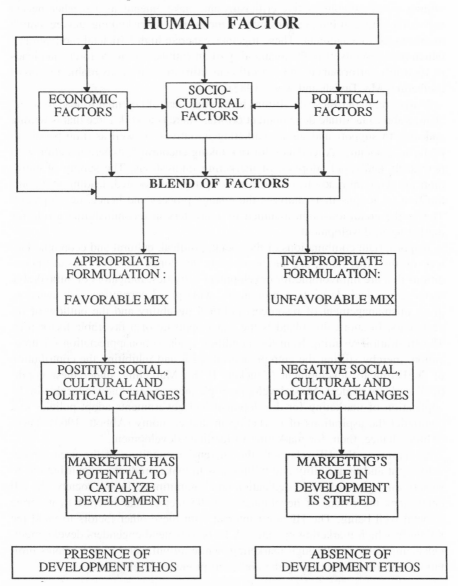

HUMAN FACTOR

| ECONOMIC FACTORS | SOCIO-CULTURAL FACTORS | POLITICAL FACTORS |

| BLEND OF FACTORS |

| APPROPRIATE FORMULATION : FAVORABLE MIX | INAPPROPRIATE FORMULATION: UNFAVORABLE MIX |

| POSITIVE SOCIAL, CULTURAL AND POLITICAL CHANGES | NEGATIVE SOCIAL, CULTURAL AND POLITICAL CHANGES |

| MARKETING HAS POTENTIAL TO CATALYZE DEVELOPMENT | MARKETING'S ROLE IN DEVELOPMENT IS STIFLED |

| PRESENCE OF DEVELOPMENT ETHOS | ABSENCE OF DEVELOPMENT ETHOS |

Source: Adapted from Adjibolosoo (1994), p. 28.

to human development (see Figure 10.4). The indicators of a favorable mix include people's willingness and ability to cooperate in efforts aimed at enhancing human development. Efficiency at work is preferred over sociocultural solidarity; respect for supervisory authority is at maximum and employees are willing to accept constructive criticisms and make amends as and when necessary. Other cultural implications may be the affinity for risktaking and preventive maintenance management. These together generate high "societal motivation," which manifests itself in the availability of an enthusiastic work force, and leads to high job performance and the efficient utilization of all available resources (Duhaime, MacTavish and Ross, 1985).

Marketing under these conditions has a great deal of potential to lead to social change and to facilitate development efforts. There is a work force that is willing and able to support and guide marketing initiatives, as well as train people to perform efficiently. A tendency for risk-taking encourages experimentation with new ideas and rapid adoption of marketing innovations. The supply of entrepreneurs who are ready to invest in new ventures is boosted, leading to a combination of actions that catalyzes the change process and hence, development. This is the condition often assumed by marketers in recommending a role for marketing in development.

Inappropriate combinations of the social, political, cultural and economic factors, on the other hand, are due to a poorly developed HF. They result in conditions that are unfavorable for development activities. Indicators of unfavorable factor mixes include acute conservatism, widespread corruption, risk aversion, gross mismanagement of resources, political instability and the outflow of investments. In short, this blend is the exact opposite of a favorable factor mix. The frustration resulting from this condition leads to nonappreciation for innovation, thereby stifling the entrepreneurial spirit and inhibiting the contribution of marketing to development (Drucker, 1958). Marketing, under these conditions, endures neglect. Most development planners are not knowledgeable in the application of marketing for development and governments adopt policies that contradict the aspirations of marketing in that economy (Abbott, 1968). There is little chance, then, for marketing to facilitate development.

In summary, the HF relates to the citizens' recognition of the need for development and their ability and willingness to make productive contributions to society through hard work, dedication and commitment. In any society, the HF determines the extent of development of the factors that interact to generate societal well-being. The HF must interact with these other factors to yield the milieu in which marketing operates. A favorable blend engenders development-enhancing activities through marketing, while an unfavorable one creates limitations and denies marketing the ability to promote development.

THE NATURE OF THE HF IN LDCs

A critical look at the LDCs will suggest that most of these countries are characterized by poorly developed HF and hence a factor mix that does not create a relevant development ethos. Although no comprehensive study has been conducted to determine the root of this problem in the LDCs, it can be argued that interaction between colonial domination and traditional cultures may have featured prominently in this development (Ahiauzu, 1986a; Adjibolosoo, 1995; Adu-Febiri, 1995). Corruption, political instability, gross mismanagement of resources, among other attributes are commonplace in these countries. Evidence to this effect is abundant in the popular media. For example, the November 14, 1994 *Newsweek* magazine article on corruption made numerous references to incidents in developing countries. Also, CBS devoted the bulk of its December 11, 1994 edition of *60 Minutes* to corruption in Nigeria. Newspapers in LDCs regularly report on embezzlement of funds by public officials. For the most part, the offenders in these cases get away with their crimes because they can bribe their way through the legal system. Corruption is not unique to the LDCs, as observed by Adjibolosoo (1994b). However, the mere fact that there are conspicuous and effective checks and balances (e.g., long jail terms for bribery, etc.) in advanced countries may deter this and other deviant behaviors.

In the LDCs, these deterrents have failed partly because state functionaries, who have the jobs to implement and enforce these laws, customarily lack the zeal and enthusiasm required for such responsibilities. This is, perhaps, a result of the perception that people have about government and its operations. For example, the general view among Ghanaians is that governments are entities independent of the individual and deserve no cooperation or sympathy from anyone. As a result, people working in and for government approach work with a lackadaisical attitude and usually seek to gain at the expense of government (Adu-Febiri, 1995). Given this, it is unlikely that they will be supportive of any government initiatives towards development unless they stand to make significant personal gains.

Similar observations have been made in other developing countries (Douglas, 1970; Ahiauzu, 1986b; Stewart and Nihei, 1987). Javanese culture, for example, stresses a basic cultural antipathy towards business and commercial enterprises and a reliance on government for marketing and other business initiatives. A worker will usually decide in favor of his or her own social group if there is a conflict between this group and the employer. Employees express discontent when a supervisor reprimands them for poor work performance. In fact, supervisors are often unwilling to exercise their leadership roles when it comes to disciplining employees who do not perform their tasks satisfactorily (Willner, 1969). Civil servants in Indonesia intermingle their private responsibilities with their public obligations and usually relegate the latter to the background. Promotion and pay differences are based more on seniority than on functional ability (Arndt and Sundrum, 1975; Jackson, 1978). This not only encourages low productivity in the public sector, but also eliminates the critical macro aspects of marketing required to promote development (Cundiff, 1982).

Political instability and gross mismanagement of resources are also dominant features of the LDCs. Political strife prevails in India and Pakistan because of religious and social differences. Ethnic differences have elicited violent political responses in Ethiopia, Sudan, Rwanda and other parts of Africa (*West Africa* 1994/1995). During times of political instability, people are more likely to be concerned with their basic safety and survival; efficient management of resources is not a priority (Maslow, 1970). The state of uncertainty discourages investors from supporting the local economy; foreign investors stay away while local investors look elsewhere to invest their wealth. Domestic capital formation is seriously hampered. This is the case in most LDCs (Todaro, 1992). Political instability also leads to the neglect of existing and planned infrastructures. Politicians are unwilling to sanction the maintenance of existing ones or the development of new ones for fear of being considered partisan to one side or another in the conflict. Besides, an infrastructure may be destroyed in the event of violent clashes, and there is no point investing in a project with no future.

The poor state of the HF in the LDCs is aggravated by the high levels of illiteracy (World Bank, 1991). Very few people living in these nations are educated well enough to appreciate the implications of these problems for their individual socioeconomic and political well-being. The majority of learned people from LDCs emigrate to other developed countries. They choose to do so either because of frustrations resulting from their inability to correct the vices they observe or for fear of being harmed by the political establishment, as was the case in Rwanda where intellectuals were the first target of massacres (*West Africa* 1994/1995). The educated few who stay behind are often the ones in positions of responsibility and authority, which give them relatively more access to state resources. They frequently abuse their authority by diverting state funds for private use. The lack of accountability in the LDCs and the apathy expressed by the citizens encourage such deviant behavior (Price, 1984).

These cases show that the HF, which is the major determinant of efficiency in any system, is poorly developed in most LDCs. The lack of the HF and the resulting impediments to development have serious implications for the potential of marketing as an agent of development. Marketing programs, like any other socioeconomic phenomena, have to be guided by a highly developed HF to be effective. In the absence of a properly channeled HF, marketing may be neglected, as has been the case in most LDCs (Drucker, 1958; Shapiro, 1965; Kaynak, 1982; Cateora, 1992). Even if marketing were accepted, a poorly developed HF will impede the attainment of marketing efficiencies, leading to failure in achieving anticipated objectives. Developing the appropriate HF in the LDCs, then, should be a top priority of marketers if marketing is to be accepted and recognized as a tool for development in these countries.

DEVELOPING THE APPROPRIATE HF IN DEVELOPING COUNTRIES[1]

Proponents of the HF concept argue that since it is not everyone who is inherently diligent, law abiding, dedicated, accountable, disciplined and willing to apply his or her skills and knowledge for the benefit of society as a whole, each individual has to be educated and trained to think and act in a manner consistent with the values and principles on which society is built. HF development in the LDCs amounts to sociocultural changes in these countries. It, therefore, presents major educational challenges to overcome. It is, however, a task that marketing can stand up to (Dholakia and Sherry, 1987).

Research shows that a person's exposure to other cultures can influence his or her perception of life and readiness for change (Inkeles and Smith, 1974). Studies in consumer behavior provide a number of cases from the LDCs where exposure to certain lifestyles increased both awareness in the products associated with these lifestyles and the desire to own them (Arnould and Wilk, 1984; Belk and Zhou, 1987; Belk, 1988, 1992). It appears that repeated exposure to other cultures may cause a person to consider alternatives to one's own culture and adjust if necessary. Marketing is well-suited to bring this about. Efforts to extend the application of marketing concepts have been made in domains previously considered to be outside the realm of marketing. For example, marketing approaches have promoted the implementation of family planning programs in India (Dholakia, 1984). Similar approaches can be adopted to develop the HF in the LDCs.

Although advertising has often been criticized for its negative impact (Pollay, 1986), it is a means of educating the developing world about the relevance of the HF to development efforts. In the late 1960s and early 1970s, Ghana embarked on an aggressive advertising campaign to minimize the incidence of bribery and corruption in the country. Radio and TV stations repeatedly featured advertisements for this purpose. Over time, the jingles for these advertisements became household tunes. Government offices also displayed posters, one that read, "Don't accept gifts, they corrupt." A comprehensive study of the impact of this campaign is yet to be conducted. However, one observable impact of this effort was that it brought the issue of work ethics to the Ghanaian populace. Bribery and corruption in Ghana and other LDCs persist up to this day in spite of all these efforts, suggesting the inability of advertising alone to contain the problem. Advertising should be combined with educational and promotional activities. For example, during radio and television campaigns, the champions of change must pay visits to local communities. Such visits must be aimed at educating the populace on the need for change and to seek their input on how this change can occur. Grassroots involvement through political marketing methods will increase the chances of success for Ghana's efforts (Mauser, 1983).

Marketing may also influence the development of the HF in the LDCs through cultural and religious institutional approaches. Technology and religion have been the basis for HF development in developed countries (Weber, 1958; Palancha, 1985). In many cases, these two factors transformed attitudes and values into ones that encourage hard work, honesty and frugality. Similarly in the LDCs, religion and other cultural institutions have significant roles to play in changing attitudes that will lead to the transformation of the HF in favor of hard work and development-mindedness (Darian, 1985). Religious movements in Africa are preaching hard work and honesty (Turner, 1985). Marketing can facilitate such efforts by promoting cultural awareness. This will involve an aggressive effort to educate people (formally and informally) on their cultural history, which provides evidence of the presence of effective checks and balances and a strong work ethic among African societies (Davidson, 1964).

Once developed, the HF will organize all the other factors (e.g., social, political, cultural and economic) in a manner that will allow their interaction to be most favorable to development and pave the way for marketing to play its development enhancing role. With a developed HF, attributes like dedication to work and society, discipline, honesty, the rule of law and accountability will prevail. These attributes interact with existing social, political, cultural and economic dynamics. The resulting situation encourages innovation and entrepreneurial development that will be guided by the rule of law and guarded by a dedicated and accountable work force (see Figure 10.5).

Marketing innovations should be examined for compatibility with the recipient countries' social, economic, political and cultural environments (Ricks, 1993). Innovations should also be tested for relative advantage over the marketing system they are intended to replace and for ease of communicability (Rogers, 1962; Rogers and Shoemaker, 1971). If innovations possess these features, they are most likely to be more efficient than existing marketing systems. Guided by the developed HF, marketing innovations may result in efficiency and may force competition in the marketing system, with traditional systems adjusting to meet the competition (Layton, 1985; Miossec, 1990). The net effect will be enhanced efficiency and increased economic output.

The increase in output will only indicate economic growth. Economic development occurs when the incremental output is equitably distributed among all in society and there are declines in unemployment, income disparities and poverty rates (Seers, 1969; Nafzinger, 1984). Distribution of the incremental output is a function of individual actions (hard work deserves bigger shares) and sociopolitical dynamics (governments ensure access to minimum share through social welfare programs) through marketing and other processes (Fisk, 1987). When a society can barely meet its food, clothing and shelter needs, it is unlikely to focus on anything but means of survival. With successful economic development plans, policies and programs, basic level needs will be satisfied and higher level needs get some attention (Maslow, 1970). The HF will guide and empower people through educational and promotional activities. The majority of people in society will be fully equipped to question inequalities that may exist in their society and ask for rectification where necessary. An ultimate effect of this process would be positive changes in sociocultural and other human dynamics (see Figure 10.5). The HF should be frequently reorganized in response to changes in society to ensure that these changes continue to meet the needs of society and that improvements in systems and institutions are sustained (Duhaime, MacTavish and Ross, 1985).

Figure 10.5
The Human Factor, Marketing and Development

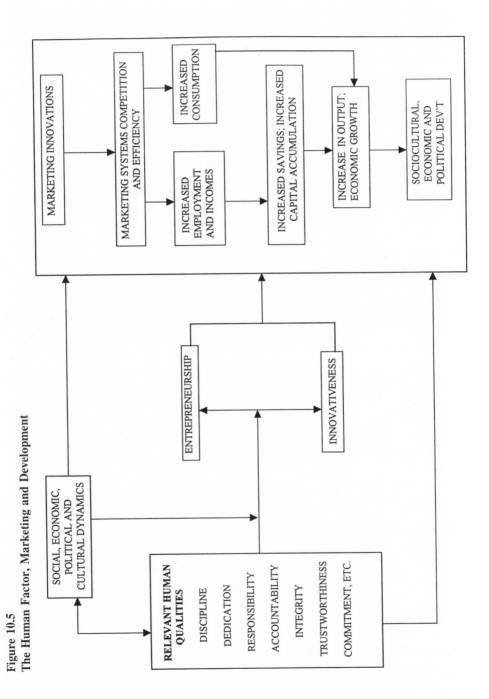

CONCLUSION

Existing models of marketing and development assume the presence of a highly developed set of dimensions referred to as the HF in all societies. Evidence from the LDCs reveals that this assumption is unfounded. This chapter shows the need for marketers to focus attention on developing the appropriate HF in the LDCs. The success or failure of marketing as an agent of development is a function of the extent to which a society's HF is developed. In its absence, marketing will not achieve its full potential as a viable contributor to development. Implementing marketing programs in the LDCs to enhance development efforts will, therefore, be irrelevant if the HF is not fully developed. It is necessary, therefore, to determine the extent of HF development in any LDC prior to introducing marketing in the hope of influencing the course of development.

Being a relatively intangible variable, the HF has often been ignored in favor of its more tangible and measurable economic counterparts. Social scientists have only recently recognized the HF as perhaps more important than any other factors in generating development (Higgins, 1968; Palanca, 1985). A challenge to marketers and other development researchers is to engage in a search for a systematic measure of the HF to ensure its enhanced application in marketing and LDC development. An objective measure is likely to make it easier to recognize what dimensions of the HF need attention in any specific country. In this effort, a reexamination of some proposed measures in sociology, economics and business present interesting prospects (Inkeles and Smith, 1974; Hofstede, 1984; Ragin, 1987; Estes, 1988; UNDP, 1990)

NOTE

1. This section recognizes the fact that marketing and other development processes continually exert significant impact on one another for their mutual benefit. The section implicitly endorses the interdependent school of thought.

REFERENCES

Abbott, J. C. 1968. "Marketing Issues in Agricultural Development Planning." In R. Moyer and S. Hollander, eds., *Markets and Marketing in Developing Economies.* Homewood, Ill.: Irwin.

Abudu, F. 1986. "Work Attitudes of Africans, with Special References to Nigeria." *International Studies of Management and Organization* 16 (2): 17–36.

Adjibolosoo, S. 1993. "The Human Factor in Development." *The Scandinavian Journal of Development Alternatives* 12 (4): 139–149.

Adjibolosoo, S. 1994a. "The Human Factor and the Failure of Economic Development and Policies in Africa." In F. Ezeala-Harrison and S. Adjibolosoo, eds., *Perspectives on Economic Development in Africa.* Westport, Conn.: Praeger.

Adjibolosoo, S. 1994b. "Corruption and Economic Development in Africa: A Comparative Analysis." In F. Ezeala-Harrison and S. Adjibolosoo, eds., *Perspectives on Economic Development in Africa.* Westport, Conn.: Praeger.

Adjibolosoo, S. 1995. *The Human Factor in Developing Africa.* Westport, Conn.: Praeger.

Adu-Febiri, F. 1995. "Culture as the Epitome of the Human Factor in Development: The Case of Ghana's Collectivistic Ethic." In S. Adjibolosoo, ed., *The Significance of the Human Factor in African Economic Development.* Westport, Conn.: Praeger.

Ahiauzu, A.I. 1986a. "The African Thought-System and the Work Behavior of the African Industrial Man." *International Studies of Management and Organization* 16 (2): 37–58.

Ahiauzu, A. 1986b. "Management and Organization in Africą." *International Studies of Management and Organization* 16 (2): 3–95.

Alderson, W. 1957. *Marketing Behavior and Executive Action: A Functionalist Approach to Marketing Theory.* Homewood, Ill.: Irwin.

Anderson, D. A. 1970. *Marketing and Development, the Thailand Experience.* East Lansing: Michigan State University.

Arndt, H. W. and Sundrum, R. M. 1975. "Wage Problems and Policies in Indonesia." *International Labor Review* (November): 360–387.

Arndt, J. 1972. "Temporal Lags in Comparative Retailing." *Journal of Marketing* 35 (October): 40–45.

Arnould, E. J. and Wilk, R. R. 1984. "Why Do the Natives Wear Adidas?" In T. Kinnear, ed., *Advances in Consumer Research, Vol 11.* Provo, Utah: Association for Consumer Research, pp. 748–752.

Bartels, R. 1976. *The History of Marketing Thought.* Columbus, Ohio: Grid Publishing.

Bartels, R. 1977. "Marketing and Economic Development." In P. D. White and C. C. Slater, eds., *Macromarketing: Distributive Processes from a Societal Perspective.* Boulder, Colo: Business Research Division, University of Colorado.

Bartels, R. 1981. *Global Development and Marketing.* Columbus, Ohio: Grid Publishing.

Belk, R. W. 1992. "Third World Tourism: Panacea or Poison? The case of Nepal." *Journal of International Consumer Marketing* 5 (1): 27–68.

Belk, R. W. 1988. "Third World Consumer Culture." In E. Kumcu and A. F. Firat, eds., *Marketing and Development: Toward Broader Dimensions.* Greenwich, Conn.: JAI Press.

Belk, R. W. and Zhou, N. 1987. "Learning to Want Things." *Advances in Consumer Behavior* 14: 478–481.

Brokensha, D., Warren, D. M. and Werner, O. 1980. *Indigenous Knowledge Systems and Development.* Washington, D.C.: University Press of America.

Cateora, P. R. 1992. *International Marketing.* Boston: Irwin.

Cundiff, E. W. 1982. "A Macromarketing Approach to Economic Development." *Journal of Macromarketing* 2 (Spring): 14–19.

Cundiff, E. W. and Hilger, M. 1979. "Marketing and the Product Consumption Thesis in Economic Development." In G. Fisk, R. Nason and P. D. White, eds., *Macromarketing: Evolution of Thought.* Boulder, Colo.: University of Colorado.

Darian, J. C. 1985. "Marketing and Economic Development: A Case Study from Classical India." *Journal of Macromarketing* 5 (Spring): 14–26.

Davidson, B. 1964. *The African Past—Chronicles from Antiquity to Modern Times.* Boston: Little, Brown.

Dholakia, N. N. and Sherry, J. F. 1987. "Marketing and Development; A Resynthesis of Knowledge." In J. Sheth, ed., *Research in Marketing, Series No. 9.* Greenwich, Conn.: JAI Press.

Dholakia, R. R. 1984. "A Macromarketing Perspective on Social Marketing: The Case of Family Planning in India." *Journal of Macromarketing* 5 (Spring): 53–60.

Dholakia, R. R. and Dholakia, N. 1982. "Marketing and the Newer Theories of Development." In G. S. Kindra, ed., *Marketing in Developing Countries.* London: Croom Helm.

Douglas, S. 1970. "Science and Technology and the Political Culture." In Howard Beers, ed., *Indonesia: Resources and their Technological Development.* Lexington: University of Kentucky Press.

Douglas, S. P. 1971. "Patterns and Parallels of Marketing Structures in Several Countries." MSU *Business Topics* 19 (Spring): 38–48.

Drucker, P. 1958. "Marketing and Economic Development." *Journal of Marketing* 22 (January): 252–259.

Duhaime, C. P. and Ross, C. 1988. "Management Technology Transfer to Developing Countries: Problems and Possible Solutions." Proceedings of Workshop on Transfer of Western Management Expertise to Developing Nations. Montreal: McGill University Centre for Developing Area Studies.

Duhaime, C. P., MacTavish, R. and Ross, C. 1985. "Social Marketing: An Approach to Third World Development." *Journal of Macromarketing* 5 (Spring): 3–13.

Elliot, M. 1994. "Corruption: How Bribes, Payoffs and Crooked Officials Are Blocking Economic Growth." *Newsweek,* November 14, p. 40.

Emmanuel, A. 1982. *Appropriate or Underdeveloped Technology?* New York: John Wiley and Sons.

Estes, R. J. 1988. *Trends in World Social Development: The Social Progress of Nations, 1970–1987.* New York: Praeger.

Etemad, H. 1982. "Is Marketing the Catalyst to the Economic Development Process?" In G. S. Kindra, ed., *Marketing in Developing Countries.* London: Croom Helm.

Etgar, M. 1983. "A Failure in Marketing Technology Transfer: The Case of Rice Distribution in the Ivory Coast." *Journal of Macromarketing* 3 (Spring): 59–68.

Firat, A. F., Kumcu, E. and Karafakioglu, M. 1988. "The Interface between Marketing and Development." In E. Kumcu and A. F. Firat, eds., *Marketing and Development: Toward Broader Dimensions.* Greenwich, Conn.: JAI Press.

Fisk, G. 1987. "Macromarketing and the Quality of Life." In A. C. Samli, ed., *Marketing and the Quality-of-Life Interface.* New York: Quorum Books.

Galbraith, J. K. and Holton, R. H. 1955. *Marketing Efficiency in Puerto Rico.* Cambridge, Mass.: Harvard University Press.

Goldman, A. 1982. "Adoption of Supermarket Shopping in a Developing Country: A Selective Adoption Phenomenon." *European Journal of Marketing* 16 (1):17–26.

Hartstein, B. and Wilde, T. 1994. "The Broadening Scope of Harassment in the Workplace." *Employee Relations Law Journal* 19 (4): 639–653.

Higgins, B. 1968. *Economic Development: Problems, Principles and Policies.* New York: W.W. Norton and Company.

Hilger, M. T. 1978. "Theories of the Relationship between Marketing and Economic Development." In P. D. White and C. C. Slater, eds., *Macromarketing: Distributive Processes from a Societal Perspective.* Boulder, Colo.: Business Research Division, University of Colorado.

Hofstede, G. 1984. *Culture's Consequences: International Differences in Work-Related Values.* Beverly Hills, Calif.: Sage Publications.

Hosley, S. and Wee, C. H. 1988. "Marketing and Economic Development: Focusing on Less Developed Countries." *Journal of Macromarketing* 1 (Spring): 43–53.

Inkeles, A. and Smith, D. H. 1974. *On Becoming Modern.* London: Heinemann.

Jackson, K. D. 1978. "Bureaucratic Policy: A Theoretical Framework for the Analysis of Power and Communication in Indonesia." In K. D. Jackson and L. Pye, eds., *Political Power and Communication in Indonesia.* Berkeley: University of California Press.

Joy, A. and Ross, C. 1989. "Marketing and Development in Third World Contexts: An Evaluation and Future Directions." *Journal of Macromarketing* 9 (Fall): 17–31.

Kaynak, E. 1982. *Marketing in the Third World.* New York: Praeger.

Kaynak, E. 1986. *Marketing and Economic Development.* New York: Praeger.

Kumcu, E. and Kumcu, E. M. 1987. "Determinants of Food Retailing in Developing Economies." *Journal of Macromarketing* 7 (Fall): 26–40.

Kumcu, E., Firat, A. F. and Karafakioglu, M. 1988. "The Interface between Marketing and Development." In E. Kumcu and A. F. Firat, eds., *Marketing and Development: Toward Broader Dimension.* Greenwich, Conn.: JAI Press.

Layton, R. 1985a. "Trade Flows in Macromarketing Systems: Part I-A Macromodel of Trade Flows." *Journal of Macromarketing* 5 (1): 35–48.

Layton, R. 1985b. "Marketing Systems in Regional Economic Development." *Journal of Macromarketing* (Spring): 42–55.

Maslow, A. 1970. *Motivation and Personality.* New York: Harper and Row.

Mauser, G. A. 1983. *Political Marketing.* New York: Praeger.

Mentzer J. T. and Samli, A. C. 1981. "A Model for Marketing in Economic Development." *Columbia Journal of World Business* 16 (Fall): 91–101.

Miossec, J. 1990. "From Suq to Supermarket in Tunis." In A.M. Findlay, R. Paddison and J. Dawson, eds., *Retailing Environments in Developing Countries.* London: Routledge.

Miracle, M. P. 1968. "Market Structure in Commodity Trade and Capital Formation." In R. Moyer and S. Hollander, eds., *Markets and Marketing in Developing Economies.* Homewood, Ill.: Irwin.

Moyer, R. 1964. "The Structure of Markets in Developing Economies." *MSU Business Topics* 12 (Fall): 43–60.

Moyer, R. 1968. "International Market Analysis." *Journal of Marketing Research* 5 (November): 353–360.

Myrdal, G. 1972. *Asian Drama: An Inquiry into the Poverty of Nations.* New York: Vintage Books.

Nafzinger, W. E. 1984. *The Economics of Developing Countries.* Belmont, Calif.: Wadsworth.

Nurske, R. 1971. "The Theory of Development and the Idea of Balanced Growth." In A. B. Mountjoy, ed., *Developing the Underdeveloped Countries.* New York: John Wiley and Sons.

Ofori-Amoah, B. 1988. "Ghana's Informal Aluminum Pottery: Another Grassroots Industrial Revolution." *Appropriate Technology* 14 (4): 17–19.

Palanca, E. H. 1985. "Religion and Economic Development." In F. Ferre and R. Mataragnon, eds., *God and Global Justice.* New York: Paragon.

Pollay, R. W. 1986. "The Distorted Mirror: Reflections on the Unintended Consequences of Advertising." *Journal of Marketing* 2 (April): 18–36.

Price, R. M. 1984. "Neo-colonialism and Ghana's Economic Decline: A Critical Assessment." *Canadian Journal of African Studies* 8 (1): 163–193.

Ragin, C. C. 1987. *The Comparative Method: Moving Beyond Qualitative and Quantitative Strategies.* Berkeley: University of California Press.

Reynolds, L. 1994. "Court Rulings and Proposed Regs will Guide Harassment Policies." *HR Focus* 71 (4): 1, 8.

Ricks, D. 1993. *Blunders in International Business.* Cambridge, Mass.: Blackwell.

Rogers, E. 1962. *Diffusion of Innovation.* New York: The Free Press.

Rogers, E. M. and Shoemaker, F. F. 1971. *Communication of Innovations: A Cross-Cultural Approach.* New York: Free Press.

Samiee, S. 1990. "Impediments to Progress in Retailing in Developing Nations." In A. Findlay, R. Paddison and J. Dawson, eds., *Retailing Environments in Developing Countries.* London: Routledge.

Savitt, R. 1988. "The State of the Art of Marketing and Economic Development." In E. Kumcu and A. F. Firat, eds., *Marketing and Development: Toward Broader Dimensions.* Greenwich, Conn.: JAI Press.

Seers, D. 1969. "The Meaning of Development." *International Development Review* 11 (4): 2–6.

Shapiro, S. J. 1965. "Comparative Marketing and Economic Development." In George Schwartz, ed., *Science in Marketing.* New York: John Wiley and Sons.

Slater, C. C. 1968. "Marketing Processes in Developing Latin American Societies." *Journal of Marketing* 32 (July): 50–55.

Stewart, C. T. and Nihei, Y. 1987. *Technology Transfers and Human Factors.* Toronto: Lexington Books.

Todaro, M. 1992. *Economics for a Developing World.* London: Longmann.

Turner, H. W. 1985. "The Relationship Between Development and the New Religious Movements in the Tribal Societies of the Third World." In F. Ferre and R. Mataragnon, eds., *God and Global Justice.* New York: Paragon.

United Nations Development Program (UNDP). 1990. *Human Development Report.* New York: Oxford University Press.

Wadinambiaratchi, G. 1965. "Channels of Distribution in Developing Economies." *Business Quarterly* 33 (Winter): 74–82.

Wadinambiaratchi, G. 1972. "Theories of Retail Development." *Social and Economic Studies* 4 (December): 391–403.

Wambi, B. 1988. "Western Technology Transfers Have Hurt the Third World: An Indigenous Development Model Is Needed." *IDRC Report* 17 (1): 24–25.

Weber, M. 1958. *Protestant Ethic and the Spirit of Capitalism.* New York: Scribner.

West Africa Magazine. 1994/1995. December 26/January 8.

Wood, V. R. and Vitell, S. J. 1986. "Marketing and Economic Development: Review, Synthesis, and Evaluation." *Journal of Macromarketing* 6 (Spring): 28–48.

Woods, R. H. 1994. "The Supreme Court on Gender Discrimination: No More 'Hostile' or 'Abusive' Work Environments." *Cornell Hotel and Restaurant Administration Quarterly* 35(1): 20.

World Bank. 1991. *World Development Report.* New York: Oxford University Press.

11

Staying Educated and Maintaining Professional Competency

Senyo B-S. K. Adjibolosoo

INTRODUCTION

To keep and maintain something in a sound state implies that one has previously acquired the item/object or has achieved some standard that needed to be kept, protected and/or maintained. As such, staying educated, as is suggested by the title of this chapter, implies remaining or continuing to be educated over a considerable length of time, if not for one's whole lifetime. The title suggests that those who have acquired some education and training must keep the level of acquired education and do everything necessary to keep their acquired knowledge active. It does not mean that one remains in the same position or level of knowledge long after one has completed formal schooling. One has to keep up with new knowledge and new developments in one's area of expertise. One has to support and/or strengthen one's acquired training and education.

Similarly, to maintain professional competency is to preserve one's expertise in one's profession. In a world that is always changing, this implies that one continues to preserve and also update previously acquired knowledge and/or skills. Every scholar, academician and professional throughout Africa needs to keep his or her acquired knowledge and skills in excellent condition.[1] Failure to do so will imply future depreciation in skills, talents, abilities, knowledge and so on.

In view of these observations, the primary objective of this chapter is to discuss certain procedures and programs that have been used successfully elsewhere to keep people continuously educated. The hope is that the discussion in this chapter will pave the way for further research and analysis regarding how African scholars, academicians and professionals can always stay educated and also maintain their professional effectiveness.

EDUCATION AND PROFESSIONAL COMPETENCY IN
AFRICA

To many people in the years past, to be educated usually implied learning to read and write. Even today, many people still have this lopsided view of what education actually means. As such, in many developing countries—especially African countries—the emphasis is usually placed on the "three Rs." To many people in Africa, therefore, formal education has been viewed either as a meal ticket (*gye ko didi*) or a certificate to prestige and/or honor. As such, Africans seem to be hit by an educational nausea, which Dore (1976) has labeled *the diploma disease*. Yet in recent years, many African scholars, academicians and professionals are gradually realizing that the mere acquisition of diplomas, certificates and degrees does not help them find jobs and be employed in these jobs for as many years as they desire. Dore (1976, p. 3) observed:

[I]n the ex-colonies the patterns of the modern sector were set by the colonial administration; the style of life which they established—and the income levels that sustain them—have tended to persist beyond independence. In the late sixties, the Ugandan graduate just entering the civil service could expect his income to be fifty times the average income per head in Uganda. Even in India, after a much longer period of independence under governments with a much more explicitly egalitarian philosophy, the ratio was twelve to one. Who would not want a visa into the bridge-head zone? What parent, if he could afford it and felt his son had a chance, would not want to send his child to primary school to get him into the visa queue? What politician could resist the demands of parents for more secondary schools, for a bigger queueing area? Even if the number of visas eventually to be issued is fixed and already vastly oversubscribed for, no one likes his child to be told already at the end of primary school that he has been ruled out of consideration, that he cannot even stay in the queue.

It is clear that in Africa, the race is for diploma, certificate and/or degree acquisition. This is viewed as a necessary visa for gaining entry into prestigious employment in the modern sector. Moreover, it accords prestige to both parents and their "educated" children. Busia (1964, p. 80) observed that "everywhere in Africa, even illiterate adults eagerly seek schooling for their children, and are prepared to make big personal sacrifices to secure it for them. Formal schooling has now come to be regarded as essential not only for equipping the individual to earn a living but also for equipping Africa's peoples for nationhood." The belief in education as the sole vehicle whereby one's children can attain better employment and higher incomes has misled many African parents and their children to focus on mere knowledge acquisition and credentialization. To them, the most important issue relates to how to obtain the diploma, regardless of whether any learning has transpired or not.

In the same way, once an individual obtains his or her educational visa and is ushered into gainful employment, it is no longer necessary for him or her to continue learning and/or updating knowledge in an area of expertise. The idea of being continuously educated, therefore, seems to be a foreign concept to many Africans who have acquired their meal tickets. It is commonplace all over Africa that many individuals and civil servants do not keep themselves updated in new knowledge. Certain professors hang on to their old and outdated lecture notes and use them over, and over and over again. They care less about updating these notes that they have used to teach for the last ten, twenty or thirty years! They are usually far, far behind the development of new ideas, theories and principles in their own areas of expertise. This also keeps their students in the dark about new developments in the field. Of course, in the view of such professors, education is nothing more than a mere program aimed at helping students to acquire meal tickets by passing stipulated examinations. This being the case, it is not very necessary to keep the knowledge base revised and updated on a continuing fashion.

Since mediocrity births more mediocrity, students who have been trained in this fashion also leave school with their meal tickets and do exactly as their professors did. For example, in the civil service, many of these graduates who have successfully acquired jobs fail to continue to educate themselves. The best some of them do is to read local newspapers during their official work hours. Outside the reading of newspapers, there is very little reading and/or study accomplished. Their acquired knowledge, therefore, turns stale over time. As such, they fail to undertake viable research and also write meaningful scholarly papers. While I was on research tour to Africa in June 1994, I met a university professor and engaged him in conversation regarding research and publications. After having discussed research-related issues with him, his response was:

[I]t is nice that most scholars in the developed countries are able to continue with research and publication. Over here, many of us cannot do so because we are very much concerned about our daily bread. When we wake up everyday, our primary concern is about how to acquire some food for the family. We spend most of the day trying to find sustenance for the whole family. By the time we settle back in our offices, we are so exhausted that we cannot even think about doing meaningful research. Worst of all, even to update our own knowledge for teaching purposes is not easy. At best, we try as much as possible to keep our jobs by doing whatever we can to help our students. The types of research some of us are involved in are those designed and engineered by the World Bank, the International Monetary Fund (IMF), the United Nations Development Program (UNDP), the Food and Agricultural Organization (FAO), International Labor Organization (ILO), United Nations Educational, Scientific and Cultural Organization (UNESCO) and many others. Although many of us are aware that the research programs being pursued by these organizations do not necessarily address the real problems of our society, we cannot refuse to work with them because we need the foreign exchange with which to achieve a better living standard for ourselves. To this, let me also add that many professors and lecturers are more interested in receiving funding (i.e., in foreign currencies) to attend overseas conferences than to receive funds to do research at home.

This professor acknowledged, however, that there are a few scholars who have been very successful in their continued research and ability to provide for their families. The African educational problem is much more complicated than many people usually think. Yet people gloss over these shortcomings and continue to pursue programs that fail even before their scheduled implementation dates. If African countries are to make any progress, their educational system needs to be revised and its goals reformulated to help bring about changes in thinking regarding how education can be used to develop the HF in Africa. In view of this, the following quotes from Campbell (1956, p. 46) are relevant here:

1. A man [or woman] who in any station of life is an upright man [or woman], fair and just in his [or her] dealing, kindly and considerate to his [or her] neighbors, is a living example of the good. We come to know the good less by any process rational thinking than by acquaintance with the good. The moral progress of any people depends partly upon the vision and vigor of its prophets, but more upon the example of those men and women who by reason of consistent and faithful lives are judged worthy by their fellows.

2. The exercise of character involves the ability to see the variety of action that is possible in a given concrete situation, the moral sensitivity to assess the nature of the consequences of each line of action, and the will to choose that which will best serve the good. . . . Training of character is no easy business that can be accomplished in one step. . . . It must not stop at the establishment of rules, or sooner or later a man [or woman] will fail to do right either because he [or she] finds himself [or herself] in a situation not covered by the rules or because the sanction of the rules has gone weak.

3. Two important elements in the exercise of character are discernent and judgment, and these are gifts which can be developed only by taking the achieved circumstances of life in a given situation.

4. Education will fail in its object if it does not inculcate a respect for truth. Whenever the old and new are as intermixed as they are in Africa it is particularly difficult to distinguish the true from the false. There is always the temptation to assume that the new is necessarily true and the old false, or the reverse. The development of this ability to distinguish the true from the false must be a fundamental aim of education.

These statements call for a more intensive discussion and analysis of the African educational system in order to discover what has gone wrong and how it can be fixed (see details in Chapter 1). In a sense, it is critical to find out what scholars and/or professionals must be doing in order to keep their acquired knowledge up to date and relevant to finding solutions to current problems. By so doing, Africans may be better positioned to deal effectively with day-to-day problems. Campbell (1956, p. 43) suggested, therefore, that education must be successful in inspiring societies to pursue and achieve the best for themselves. They must be able to provide the best amenities for people and also furnish them with the viable environment in which they can develop their aptitudes, talents and skills. To Campbell (1956, p. 43), education must prepare everyone to live and enjoy the most complete life. People who are trained and educated in this manner must acquire and possess a sense of social purpose, maintain professional conduct, pursue professional competency in terms of effectiveness and efficiency, and maintain high levels of integrity, accountability, responsibility and commitment.

In the information age, many things are often in a continuing state of flux. Knowledge itself is not only changing very fast—at a speed probably greater than that of lightning—but is also continually increasing in volume. As such, today's ideas, principles, theories and philosophies will not necessarily be relevant to the search for solutions to tomorrow's problems and difficulties to be faced by all humanity. It is quite likely that techniques used to solve society's problems yesterday and today may not be appropriate for those of tomorrow. This observation, therefore, requires that every scholar, academician and/or professional must continuously update his or her stock of knowledge. Those who fail to do so will wake up one day and realize that the whole world has left them too far behind to catch up. In this way, they will not only lose their jobs and/or businesses, but also be left with no other opportunities for employment. These people will not be able to solve any problems because their existing stock of knowledge and/or information will be outdated.

When this misfortune happens to an individual, the impacts on society might not be that grave. However, if it becomes a society-wide phenomenon, the whole society will be launched into severe and permanent problems. This society will find it too difficult to decipher its problems, carefully articulate solutions to them and solve them successfully. It will also experience either stagnation or continuing decline in its ability to deal with the more complex problems of modern society and therefore suffer an ongoing decline in input productivity. Because relevant knowledge in areas such as medicine, technology, engineering, organization, planning and management will be lacking, this society will be placed on a trajectory of decay. It will be infested with disease, hunger, extreme difficulties and other types of discomfort that do not promote the good life. All this will lead to further deterioration in the knowledge base. In the end, just like certain mining towns and/or cities die because the minerals in the mine have been exhausted, these societies will also finally die. To prevent this from happening in Africa, African scholars have to stay educated and also maintain competence in their chosen professions.

STAYING EDUCATED

One of the easiest things to do is to acquire academic knowledge in the field one has chosen. Education, however, is more difficult and complicated to acquire. When the process of knowledge acquisition through schooling is completed, one is faced with the issue of remaining knowledgeable and acquiring education throughout one's lifetime. As is always the case, some professionals can continually coast on knowledge and skills gained while at school. Others, however, cannot because the production of knowledge and the emergence of new developments in certain areas of human endeavor are changing so fast that only people who are able to update their education will be of service to humanity. In view of this, two critical questions arise: "Why is it necessary for a professional to stay continually knowledgeable and educated? How can a person always stay knowledgeable and educated in a particular field, vocation and/or profession?" In what follows, I will discuss briefly some proposed answers to these questions.

Service to humanity is one of the greatest accomplishments an individual can make in life. John Comenius (1592–1670) once said, "Let us have but one end in view, the welfare of humanity; and let us put aside all selfishness in consideration of language, nationality, or religion."[2] Those who desire to advance the general welfare of all humanity cannot afford to remain ignorant about what is happening in their chosen areas of study and expertise. True, effective and efficient service to all humanity requires the ability of the professional to determine pertinent problems and also the skills to successfully articulate relevant solutions to them. Professionals who stay educated and continuously knowledgeable in their fields are people who possess the potential to work assiduously for the welfare of humanity, assuming that they also possess the human factor (HF). In a world where change is happening rapidly, every professional needs to keep himself or herself abreast of the changing times. Continuing knowledge production leads to the discovery and development of new ideas, procedures and technology. Some of these new developments are usually more effective and efficient in accomplishing tasks than traditionally known ones. It is an asset, therefore, for every professional to be aware of what is happening in his or her own profession and also in other relevant areas.

Staying well-informed and educated is critical for enhanced practice and productivity in one's profession. It refreshes and rejuvenates the individual in the sense that one gains continuing insight into how to perform relevant tasks more efficiently and successfully. This brings to mind the circumstances surrounding the pregnancy and birth of a couple's two children:

When the woman was pregnant with their first child, she had to be transfused almost every other week throughout her whole pregnancy. This was necessary for her to carry the pregnancy successfully to its term of maturity. Two years later, when she was pregnant with a second child, her hematologist told the couple that he had come across a new body of literature that explains how pregnant sickle-cell anemic women can carry their pregnancies to their full term without being frequently transfused. Truly, the woman successfully carried the pregnancy to its full term with few blood transfusions. Had the hematologist not kept himself continually informed and educated, he would have done things the same way as he did in the case of the first pregnancy. Instead, he discovered a more efficient procedure for accomplishing the task with little risk to the woman.

Similarly, the magnitude of any risk can be minimized or erased completely by reducing the level of uncertainties surrounding a task or a project. One of the most effective ways of dealing with these continuing uncertainties is through knowledge acquisition. Although it may not necessarily imply that more knowledge, data and/or information is preferred to less, it is, however, the case that the level of one's professional confidence increases with the acquisition of greater know-how. It is in view of this that I am convinced that it is crucial for every professional to always stay knowledgeable and educated.

In terms of self-interest, professionals who continuously remain informed and educated may always maximize the net value of their lifetime wealth, because they will always attract more clients, customers or patients. People do not only look for just any service, but for one they believe will be to their best interest. They will, therefore, look for professionals who have developed a good reputation. For example, people will always look for the most well-known professionals such as lawyers, doctors, psychiatrists and engineers. In the area of academics, parents prefer to send their children to educational institutions that are known to have professionally competent teachers, who are not only good at teaching but also keep themselves informed and educated in their academic disciplines. These teachers are usually better prepared to facilitate and encourage learning. They possess the ability to lead students to develop great insights in relevant subject areas.

As noted earlier, staying knowledgeable and educated is a *sine qua non* to problem-solving and professional competency. There is a great deal of knowledge that is still hidden from the present domain of human knowledge and comprehension. For example, humanity has been unsuccessful in dealing with certain ailments like cancer and AIDS, because it lacks the true knowledge that is necessary for overcoming such problems. If professionals remain stagnant in terms of knowledge, they will find it extremely difficult to develop solutions to these problems. However, by staying educated and always learning new things, the chances of finding solutions will increase significantly. Those who stay educated will, through their devotion and dedication to knowledge acquisition, use and dissemination, help humanity to discover what it needs to achieve and maintain progress.

Furthermore, continuing knowledge acquisition and education enhances human performance and thus reduces the risk of too many mistakes and the resulting lawsuits, as is common in the United States. In recent years, businesses, government officials and professionals have been subjected to a countless number of lawsuits. These lawsuits, given their level of success, threaten the survival of private professional practice in society. Their magnitude can be reduced through continuing knowledge acquisition and education. As professionals increase their knowledge and sharpen their skills, their efficiency will also increase, *ceteris paribus*. Once the fear of failure and the chances of being sued are minimized, professionals become more competent and increase their desire to pursue lifetime learning. Acquired skills may yield to the goddess of atrophy when they remain unused over a considerable length of time (Harbison, 1973, p. 81). Similarly, knowledge gained but left unused may also become either dormant or sterile. However, by engaging in continuing education, skills and knowledge will be regularly updated.

RELEVANT ACTIVITIES FOR STAYING EDUCATED

It is a must that every professional stay informed and educated after having obtained his or her degree and/or diploma. This does not necessarily mean going back to college to take additional courses. Although this can be done when required in some cases, there are many other formal and informal programs that can facilitate continuing professional education. In what follows, I present and discuss a few of the programs that can be of value to professionals in Africa. The effectiveness of many of these activities has been proven in the developed countries. With slight modifications, they can be used successfully by Africans to stay knowledgeable and educated.

Departmental Professional Development Meetings

This is one of the easiest and cheapest ways of staying educated and keeping one's knowledge and expertise updated all through the years. These meetings are usually organized internally for all individuals who work in the same department in facilities such as universities, colleges, hospitals and government offices. During such meetings, one of the members of the department is given the opportunity to present ideas, views, theories, principles and conclusions from a research paper. When the paper is presented, it is then discussed among all the participants. During the discussion period, questions are asked and relevant answers provided. Where there are any doubts, the participants engage in lengthy debates regarding the views presented by the author of the paper.

When properly conducted, these departmental professional development meetings help others learn about new developments in their disciplines. Attendees may also gain additional insights regarding related research projects in which they can become involved. Others are challenged to read additional relevant literature to update their own stock of knowledge in the area being discussed. Those who regularly attend these meetings are usually well informed about what is happening around them in their individual disciplines. They may not necessarily be knowledgeable in everything but at least will be aware of what is happening. They get to know what problems need to be solved and what related issues need to be researched. Cross-fertilization ensues and ideas and views are exchanged. Individual presenters receive relevant comments and other useful suggestions from their colleagues, which can be used to improve the research in progress.

This environment is usually a friendly one where younger scholars can receive a great deal of help from the more mature professionals. The nonthreatening environment serves as a powerful incubator in which future scholars are trained and educated in an informal way. Above all, this environment nurtures young students who are learning to become productive scholars. As they attend these meetings, they learn from all other professors—some whom they never learned from before. The practice will also help these students realize how important it is to keep informed in one's own area of expertise. When graduating and finding employment elsewhere, they will continue to participate in such programs because they might already understand their true value.

Further Studies and Staff Training Programs

Training programs are another way for scholars to stay educated and maintain professional competency. Programs involving further studies provide the individual with meaningful opportunities where he or she can either explore and acquire more knowledge and information or just update what has already been learned. In other circumstances, individuals use these opportunities for further studies to engage in higher degree programs in their own areas of expertise. For example, a bachelor's degree holder may engage in either a master's or Ph.D. program. During the course of the program, the individual gains further advanced knowledge in a field. It also provides the resources to explore new developments and advancements in the field.

Training programs help leaders and professionals, such as engineers, technicians, doctors, lawyers, managers and administrators, become more refreshed and up-to-date about new knowledge in their areas of specialty. Above all, while engaged in such training programs, individuals come into contact with their counterparts from other parts of their own or other countries. They make friends, compare notes and share views about how they go about their own businesses and/or duties. These informal moments of sharing also serve as excellent fora for every participant in the training programs to learn and acquire new insights into what is happening in his or her field and area of expertise. People from the more remote areas are able to hear and learn from scholars of high reputation in their specialized areas.

Those who attend these training programs sometimes engage in group projects and solve problems with others. They do not only learn theories, but also put them into practice through teamwork. Training programs that have been successfully carried out act as inspirations for all attendees. Most of these participants go back to their jobs well refreshed, having developed new zeal for their jobs and ready and willing to do their best in their employment. They realize their own potentialities and limitations and learn to deal successfully with them. At the end of these programs, successful individuals will become more knowledgeable and resourceful in their vocations. The insights gained become sources of academic and professional strength. These people act and work with more confidence than they would have done without having attended the training programs or gone away for further studies.

Regional/International Seminars and Conferences

Like departmental professional development programs, regional and/or inter-national seminars and conferences also serve as effective measures for keeping updated and highly informed about what is happening in one's field. In order to receive the maximum benefits from such conferences, though, one must attend with the desire to learn from others. To achieve the maximum gain from atten-dance at these conferences, people must not treat them as mere family holidays as some scholars do. It is also important to present scholarly papers. Knowing that you will be facing renowned experts in your field, you will prepare yourself thoroughly so as not to make a fool of yourself in the presence of colleagues. Time spent to prepare effectively prior to the conference date and presentation will help you learn many more things than you probably would have learned in your regular routine and schedule.

Even long before the conference, while making your preparations for your presentation, you should consult other colleagues to share your insights, views and conclusions. This will furnish them with the opportunity to provide you with meaningful feedback. It will also help you to revise and/or reformulate some of your own propositions and conclusions.

Every scholar, academician and professional should attend at least one inter-national conference and/or seminar per annum. Those who fail to do so in their own areas of expertise will sooner or later become dinosaurs in their fields. They will not only be left behind by their colleagues, but also will have no influence on the development of their field. They would be better off to change careers, an extremely difficult task to accomplish in certain cases.

Scholarly Exchanges

Scholarly exchanges also serve as effective ways through which scholars, academicians and professionals can keep abreast of new knowledge and ongoing developments in their own areas of expertise. These exchanges provide the par-ticipants with new environments and resources in which they can practice their acquired skills. Such programs also provide opportunities to undertake additional research in one's area of expertise or other related areas of interest. Moreover, these exchange programs furnish scholars with the opportunity to write and present scholarly papers and/or essays.

Those who engage in exchange programs and their family members can learn new things and also become more familiar with certain cultures they might have only read or heard about. The new experiences gained will go a long way to enhance the scholar's own knowledge and professional abilities. Truly, one will be kept continuously educated. As is also the case for other related programs, scholarly exchanges open a whole new world to participating scholars. They meet their colleagues, make new friends and also engage in collaborative re-search. Through the process of collaboration, they gain newer insights into their fields and also learn to work in teams and/or groups. The advantages to these exchanges are so great that those who have the opportunity should grab them.

Reading Professional Literature

Any scholar, academician and professional who fails to develop and keep up with the habit of reading and gleaning information from relevant books, journals and magazines will soon be uneducated in his or her own area of expertise. Scholars who are truly interested in seeking and finding solutions to the problems of humanity need to keep abreast of changes. One of the cheapest ways of doing so is to develop a continuing personal reading program. In developing this program for yourself, try as much as possible to venture outside your own area of expertise. Widen your horizon and increase the diversity of your knowledge base.

Reading local newspapers, magazines, journals and letters will not only keep one informed about what is happening, but will also keep him or her updated about recurrent problems of society. It is always the case that by reading what others have written, we all gain useful insights about issues around which our lives revolve. Scholars who engage in these reading activities are always full of ideas for dealing with the pertinent difficulties that prevail in society.

Pleasure reading is also extremely productive. It not only relaxes and increases one's thinking faculties, it is also an effective source of personal entertainment.[3] In some cultures, many people especially enjoy reading materials when they go on long journeys—they read in the car, train, buses, airplanes, etc. This is a great habit to form. It makes effective use of one's time that is otherwise wasted. It can hardly be denied that those who pursue programs of voracious reading and thinking are individuals who gain a great deal of knowledge, insight, understanding and wisdom. African intellectuals need to engage themselves in these activities. Reading activities must not cease as soon as one obtains his or her meal tickets (i.e., degrees, diplomas, certificates, etc.).

If African countries want to make education more meaningful and relevant, it is important that the value of reading be inculcated in students before their graduation. Otherwise, the graduates will stop reading as soon as they are engaged in the employment of their own choice and/or dream. When this happens, African societies will be faced with a leadership that is extremely ignorant of the times and pertinent problems of their societies. I dare say that this is actually the case in Africa today. Many individuals in leadership positions are not properly informed about what is happening in their own countries. As such, how can they act as agents of change and problem solvers? This cannot happen without staying educated and maintaining professional competency.

Attendance at Public Lectures

Public lectures offer a more casual program whereby an intellectual can keep abreast with what is happening in his or her field. These lectures are usually diverse, wide and/or general in scope, and can cover almost all subject areas, running from archaeology to zoology. Although an individual does not have to attend every public lecture, the habit can be formed to attend a few in a year. Since these lectures usually deal with existing problems and suggested solutions, intellectuals will find them to be academically stimulating.

Attendance at these public lectures can also create the forum for extensive and productive discussions on social, economic, political, intellectual and cultural issues of interest to society. At these lectures, it is likely that one will make friends and later engage in relevant individual and collaborative research projects.

Akin to public lectures are town meetings. In recent years in the United States, these meetings allow people to engage in conversations and discussions based on current issues. Every person has the chance and freedom to speak his or her mind on pressing social issues. Even by just attending these meetings, one is able to learn a great deal regarding people's views, insights and beliefs and how they stand on pertinent social issues. Such fora also create opportunities for scholars and nonscholars alike to express their ideas. They surely do produce food for thought. Thus, academicians, scholars and professionals should not shun these meetings. Rather, those who are interested in keeping informed about burning society issues should take advantage of them, if available. Where they are currently not available, they can be created by those who are interested in organizing and running them. In Africa, these meetings will be extremely useful in the villages and towns. They will be of help to many, including teachers, civil servants, traders and farmers.

Continuing Debates, Dialogues and/or Discussions

Debates, dialogues and discussions are also very productive and effective when properly planned. In some societies, debating clubs/societies are common and are used effectively as means for addressing social, economic, political and cultural issues. Many scholars will find them extremely stimulating. Again, they will listen to experts debate about issues of critical importance in society. In other cases, techniques and procedures can be debated in order to further knowledge in these areas. Many issues such as the role of religion in economic growth and development, euthanasia (i.e., mercy killing—doctor-assisted suicide) and public funding of certain programs and activities can be debated. These programs also create the opportunities for scholars to keep abreast with the development of new ideas and knowledge.

Correspondence and/or Distance Education

Correspondence and/or distance educational programs have been used effectively in the developed countries. These programs provide opportunities for individuals who do not have required educational facilities in their own areas of expertise. Through correspondence and/or distance educational programs, scholars are able to learn under the tutorship of excellent professors and other knowledgeable scholars from a distance.

These programs are usually challenging and stimulating. Students are furnished with course materials and questions through which they learn and complete their program of studies. In the modern era in the advanced countries, multimedia techniques are being designed to help improve upon the effectiveness of correspondence and/or distance education. Lessons are mailed out to students in either visual or hearing modes. Students who receive these lessons follow instructions to complete their assignments over a period of time to complete their degrees, certificates and diplomas. These techniques have also been used successfully to carry out education and training programs in prisons in the developed countries.

Although African countries may not possess all the modern multimedia tools, correspondence and/or distance educational programs can be used in one form or another to help scholars, academicians and professionals improve themselves. Mobile libraries can be developed and used to assist those who work in the remote villages and towns. This program will furnish these employees with reading materials throughout the years to keep them abreast with new developments in their own areas of expertise.

Films and Movies

Films and movies, especially documentary films, are extremely useful in helping people learn, comprehend and gain further insights into related issues and/or problems in society. They provide the opportunity for people to sit down and learn from the views expressed by others in the film. Most documentary films are about real-life circumstances in society. They present documentations on social, economic, political, intellectual and cultural problems in society. They also highlight the various ongoing clashes among different ethnicities. In most cases, they are very thought-provoking. Many of these films do not provide the viewers with any definitive answers and/or solutions to problems, but are provocative enough to get men and women searching for answers.

These films become more rewarding when they are shown and then discussed in a group forum. Fresh in people's minds, almost everyone picks up an issue of personal interest. As such, individual participants have the opportunity to learn from other people's insights. Such meetings can lead to the creation of permanent discussion group meetings and ongoing scholarly research activities. Documentary films and other movies that are properly used have the potential to enhance the knowledge and understanding of scholars, academicians and professionals. Through them, many will learn about new problems and what others are doing to look for possible solutions. In view of these observations, it is important that anyone who desires to keep oneself updated about societal or professional issues should view documentary films and/or other relevant movies.

Although there is a financial aspect to each of these educational programs, the focus must not be on cost. The real concern must be on how to improve people's abilities and performance on the job. Otherwise, those who are obsessed with gaining salary increases will attend these programs and yet come back to their offices having learned virtually nothing. These people are only happy about the income raises they receive for having participated in the programs in question. Sad to say that existing programs are carried out with the sole motive of personal financial gain. To some scholars, these programs are nothing more than mere academic exercises.

Although what has been discussed so far in this chapter is not exhaustive, it is, however, aimed at continuing HF development. As such, when any of these scholarly and/or professional programs fails to achieve significant HF development, it will have been a useless exercise.

MAINTAINING PROFESSIONAL COMPETENCY

Although every professional needs to maintain professional competency through most of the programs described earlier, it is likely that not every one of them will want to. In view of this observation, it is important to develop and institute relevant programs to encourage every professional to maintain competency in his or her field of expertise and/or practice. This can be accomplished at four different levels: (1) individual self-interest, (2) mandatory membership in professional organizations, (3) private activism and (4) government regulation and/or direct action. Each of these is discussed in detail in the following paragraphs.

Individual Self-Interest

In a liberal society, the pursuit of self-interest is expected to make people function at their best, if not inhibited in any way. By so doing, as they strive to promote their own self-interest, they unconsciously end up promoting the interests of society (Smith, 1985). If this were always true, one would expect that all scholars, academicians and professionals would always engage themselves in scholarly activities to promote their businesses. In this way, they would also pass on some of their gains to the whole society.

Therefore, it might be extremely important for African governments to create vital environments where all intellectuals are willing to engage continuously in knowledge acquisition and the educational programs discussed earlier in this chapter. In a sense, the environment must make scholars, academicians and professionals perceive that they will surely receive and enjoy the gains of their continuing training and educational programs.

Since it is quite possible that an uncontrollable behavior of self-interest may lead to many difficult problems for society, institutions must be properly equipped to deal successfully with those who abuse the freedom and rights of others in order to promote their own goals. I must also add that in cases where the HF is properly developed, one would expect that self-interest will yield the best results for individuals in particular and society in general. As such, to create the enabling environment, government plans, policies, programs and projects must focus on continuing HF development. These programs must always encourage scholars to proceed with self-improvement programs. Once these programs become effectively operational, everyone in society will surely want to be on top of things in his or her area of service and/or expertise.

Mandatory Membership in Professional Organizations

One relevant way of keeping self-interest in check is the development of regulations[4] that will encourage and urge scholars, academicians and professionals to take membership in relevant professional bodies and/or organizations. These organizations must develop their own codes of ethics and professional behavior. Procedures must be put in place to address any observed infringements. Members who act unseemly must be brought before an ethical review board, staffed by men and women of high integrity, accountability, responsibility and commitment. They must be people who are prepared to make sure that the image of their professional organization is not tarnished in any way.

Continuing practice in a field, business or profession must be contingent on one's continuous maintenance of membership. This must also involve ongoing participation in professional programs such as seminars, conferences, debates and discussion group meetings. Members who continuously fail to keep themselves up-to-date with new knowledge must be stripped of the privilege of practicing in their profession. That is, if necessary, their professional licenses and/or certificates should be revoked. When this policy is effectively enforced, individuals who know that professional misconduct would lead to the permanent loss of their certificates and/or licences to practice will do their best to maintain their professional competency. Organizations that fail to do so would be weak and ineffective in their performances. They may not please the public. Too much liberalism can also be extremely destructive.

Private Activism

The existence of a private citizens' action group (PCAG) might also be very effective in encouraging scholars, academicians and professionals to maintain their integrity, accountability, responsibility and commitment to their society and clients. This activists' group must keep in check the behavior and activities of all professionals and follow closely their professional practices and activities. Like Greenpeace, an organization concerned about the environment and nuclear testing and that also makes sure that businesses that are destroying the environment have their products boycotted, the activists' group must also be in the position to know how members of professional bodies go about their general everyday businesses.

In cases where individuals bring complaints against some professionals, the PCAG must carry out a thorough independent investigation. Any fraudulent behavior need not be condoned. It must be dealt with appropriately. Complaints that are found to be true must be brought to light and the perpetrators be given the most appropriate punishment. Members of this group must not act as a witch-hunting panel. If they do so, they will defeat the whole purpose of their existence. Their programs and activities must serve as both a deterrent against bad behavior and encouragement to scholars, academicians and professionals who strive to offer their best to society. This group must also work hand-in-hand with the various professional organizations. Based upon their findings and observations, the PCAG could make recommendations to the appropriate professional organization regarding the behavior and conduct of its members who are under investigation or have already been investigated. Then the professional body will take over the case and act accordingly. Where the professional body is seen as being weak, the activists' group may appeal to the government to take up the case and have it dealt with as the law may require.

Again, when properly done, this group's activities and performances will truly keep all scholars, academicians and professionals on their toes. They will do their best to be informed and well-educated in their areas of expertise.

Government Regulation and/or Direct Action

Government action must be a measure of last resort, only to be used in the presence of excessive HF decay and/or underdevelopment. It is, however, important that there exist national rules and regulations regarding professional conduct. Professional bodies must be encouraged to keep their members aware of government's rules and regulations. However, when these bodies fail to accomplish their tasks, the government must come in to make sure everything is done as required by the law. As such, government regulations and/or direct action must be aimed at encouraging scholars, academicians and professionals to continuously keep themselves informed and educated. All of this will help further the desire to always be informed and educated in one's field of expertise.

IMPLICATIONS FOR POSITIVE CHANGE

Each program discussed above requires the willingness of individuals to make the required and necessary changes in the way they do things. Yet change does not only happen in terms of staying educated and maintaining professional competency. What is critical is the presence of relevant factors that can bring about a long-lasting attitudinal change. Fox, Mazmanian and Putman (1993) noted that changes in professional performance are brought about by one's desire to excel, the existence of continuing innovation and one's unhappiness with existing procedures (see also Bennet and Fox, 1993, p. 269). As is usually the case, by interacting through scholarly programs, scholars, academicians and professionals alike will learn a great deal from each other. These programs will provide them with the relevant opportunities through which they can learn to understand and also work hand-in-hand with others.

Scholars who realize that they are being left behind by colleagues may have to change immediately or risk losing their professional practice. This can be a positive stimulant in creating a healthy competition among scholars, academicians and professionals. The competitive process will in itself lead to the development and acquisition of new knowledge in many fields of study and practice. Above all, it will not only weed out the mediocre and inefficient practitioners, but also enhance the efficiency and continuing performance of all individuals who desire to be on top of what they do in their professions. The successful individuals will continue to look for real solutions to existing problems in their areas of expertise. In this way, scholars, academicians and professionals will continuously stay educated and also maintain their professional competency. This kind of process is what Africa needs right now.

CONCLUSION

In Africa, once many people complete their formal education, little effort is made thereafter to stay continually informed and educated and also maintain professional competency. This behavior on the part of many high school, college, and university graduates has been costly to Africa in terms of social problems, economic decline and political instability. To overcome problems of economic stagnation and underdevelopment in Africa, scholars and professionals need to keep abreast of change. This requires continuing education for every person both inside and outside the classroom. As discussed in this chapter, various groups need to establish relevant incentive structures to facilitate individual desire to engage in continuing education and also to maintain professional competency. Many of Africa's problems can be solved if African intellectuals and professionals will get into the habit of engaging in programs that will lead to the development of insights into pertinent problems and hindrances to progress. Without this engagement, it will be impossible to overcome the continuing complex problems prevalent on the continent.

NOTES

1. As is usually the case, when a nation's capital stock is not maintained regularly, it depreciates continuously. In the final analysis, the whole capital stock collapses and becomes unuseable. As such, people who have acquired human capital have to both maintain and update it on a continuing basis. In the modern world, where information is changing every moment, new knowledge and developments (i.e., inventions and innovations) quickly render certain forms of human capital obsolete. For this reason, those

who wish to either maintain, preserve or update their existing human capital stock have either to stay educated, maintain professional competency, or both.

2. See Peter (1977), p. 250.

3. Here, I am not talking about literature that will usually lead to deviant behavior. It must be literature that has the capability to tease one's thinking faculties and, at the same time, serve as a clean source of meaningful entertainment: Lots of issues to think about, laugh at and/or cry about. Novels from other cultures can be very useful in this regard. Africans are really blessed with what has become known as *African Writers Series*. Books in these series are written by African scholars who use a great deal of local proverbs, adages, etc. Their stories are set in Africa and usually deal with pertinent problems in typical societies. African scholars, academicians and professionals, who engage in reading this literature, will truly be informed about African communities. They may also be moved to seek solutions to some of the problems described in the stories. The role and importance of this literature to HF development and the attainment of progress in Africa are discussed in Chapter 3 of this book.

4. Recall that the mere development and implementation of rules and regulations will not guarantee that people will do what is expected of them all the time. As such, one of the best ways of achieving this goal is through successful HF development programs. For a detailed analysis of this issue, read Adjibolosoo (1995).

REFERENCES

Adjibolosoo, S. 1995. "A Human Factor Perspective on Failing Social Institutions and Systems." Unpublished discussion paper, Trinity Western University, Langley, B.C., Canada.

Bennett, N. L. and Fox, R. D. 1993. "Challenges for Continuing Professional Education." In L. Curry, J. F. Wergin and Associates, eds., *Educating Professionals: Responding to New Expectations for Competence and Accountability.* San Francisco: Jossey-Bass Publishers.

Busia, K. A. 1964. *The Challenge of Africa.* New York: Praeger.

Campbell, J. M. 1956. *African History in the Making.* London: Edinburg House Press.

Dore, R. 1976. *The Diploma Disease: Education, Qualification and Development.* London: George Allen and Unwin Ltd.

Fox, R. D., Mazmanian, P. E. and Putman, R. W. 1993. *Changing and Learning in the Lives of Physicians.* Westport, Conn.: Praeger.

Harbison, F. H. 1973. *Human Resources as the Wealth of Nations.* New York: Oxford University Press.

Peter, L. J. 1977. *Peter's Quotations: Ideas for Our Time.* New York: Bantam Books.

Smith, A. 1985. *The Wealth of Nations* (edited by Andrew Skinner). New York: Penguin Books.

Selected Bibliography

Achebe, C. 1966. *A Man of the People.* Nairobi, Kenya: Heinemann Kenya.

Achebe, C. 1988 [1963]. *No Longer at Ease.* Nairobi, Kenya: Heinemann Kenya.

Adjibolosoo, S. 1993. "The Human Factor in Development." *The Scandinavian Journal of Development Alternatives* 12 (4): 139–149.

Adjibolosoo, S. 1994a. "The Human Factor and the Failure of Economic Development and Policies in Africa." In F. Ezeala-Harrison and S. Adjibolosoo, eds., *Perspectives on Economic Development in Africa.* Westport, Conn.: Praeger, pp. 25–37.

Adjibolosoo, S. 1994b. "Corruption and Economic Development in Africa: A Comparative Analysis." In F. Ezeala-Harrison and S. Adjibolosoo, eds., *Perspectives on Economic Development in Africa.* Westport, Conn.: Praeger.

Adjibolosoo, S. 1995a. *The Human Factor in Developing Africa.* Westport, Conn.: Praeger.

Adjibolosoo, S. 1995b. "The Genesis of Entrepreneurial and Commercial Decline in Africa." Unpublished discussion paper, Trinity Western University.

Adu-Febiri, F. 1995a. "Culture as the Epitome of the Human Factor in Development: The Case of Ghana's Collectivistic Ethic." In S. Adjibolosoo, ed., *The Significance of the Human Factor in African Economic Development.* Westport, Conn.: Praeger.

Adu-Febiri, F. 1995b. "Is Africa's Development a Basket Case?" *Review of Human Factor Studies* 1 (1): 45–60.

Bowles, S. and Gintis, H. 1976. *Schools in Capitalist America: Educational Reform and the Contradictions of Economic Life.* New York: Basic Books.

Busia, K. A. 1964. *The Challenge of Africa.* New York: Praeger.

Campbell, J. M. 1956. *African History in the Making.* London: Edinburg House Press.

Dahl, R. A., ed. 1966. *Political Opposition in Western Democracies.* New Haven, Conn.: Yale University Press.

Dolphyne, F. 1991. *The Emancipation of Women.* Accra: Universities Press.

Dore, R. 1976. *The Diploma Disease: Education, Qualification and Development.* London: George Allen and Unwin Ltd.

Fox, R. D., Mazmanian, P. E. and Putman, R. W. 1993. *Changing and Learning in the Lives of Physicians.* Westport, Conn.: Praeger.

Harbison, F. H. 1973. *Human Resources as the Wealth of Nations.* New York: Oxford University Press.

Harder, H. J. 1995a. "Not Just a Good Idea—Marketing Bangladesh's Rower Pump." *Waterlines* 13 (3): 28–30.

Harder, H. J. 1995b. "Human Context, a Critical Factor in Technology Transfer for Development." In S. Adjibolosoo, ed., *The Significance of the Human Factor in African Economic Development.* Westport, Conn.: Praeger.

Kaynak, E. 1982. *Marketing in the Third World.* New York: Praeger.

Kaynak, E. 1986. *Marketing and Economic Development.* New York: Praeger.

Katz, M. B. 1971. *Class, Bureaucracy, and Schools: The Illusion of Educational Changes in America.* New York: Praeger.

Kimble, G. H. T. 1960. *Tropical Africa. Vol. I.* New York: Twentieth Century Fund.

Laski, H. J. 1917. *Studies in the Problem of Sovereignty.* New Haven, Conn.: Yale University Press.

Lively, J. 1975. *Democracy.* London: Oxford University Press.

Locke, J. 1924. *Two Treatises of Civil Government.* London: Dent.

Machiavelli, N. 1970. *The Prince.* London: Hammondsworth Books.

Mansfield, E. 1968. *The Economics of Technical Change.* London: Longman.

McClelland, D. 1971a. "The Achievement Motive in Economic Growth." In P. Kilby, ed., *Entrepreneurship and Economic Development.* New York: Free Press.

McClelland, D. 1971b. *Motivational Trends in Society.* Morristown, N.J.: General Learning Press.

Ofori-Amoah, B. 1988a. "Ghana's Informal Aluminium Pottery: Another Grass-Roots Industrial Revolution?" *Appropriate Technology* 14 (4): 17–19.

Ofori-Amoah, B. 1988b. "Improving Existing Indigenous Technologies as a Strategy for the Appropriate Technology Concept in Ghana." *Industry and Development* 23: 57–79.

Ofori-Amoah, B. 1990. "Technology Choice in a Global Industry: The Case of the Twin-Wire in Canada." Unpublished Ph.D. Thesis. Burnaby, B.C.: Simon Fraser University, Department of Geography.

Ofori-Amoah, B. 1993. "Technology Choice and Diffusion in the Manufacturing Sector: The Case of the Twin-Wire in the Canadian Pulp and Paper Industry." *Geoforum* 24 (3): 315–326.

Ofori-Amoah, B. 1994. "Technological Change Strategy for Economic Development in Africa." In F. Ezeala-Harrison and S. Adjibolosoo, eds., *Perspectives on Economic Development in Africa.* Westport, Conn.: Praeger.

Ofori-Amoah, B. and Adjibolosoo, S. 1995. "Crises as Windows of Opportunity: Prospects for Africa's Economic Development in the Twenty-First Century." Paper presented at Africa 2000 Conference, Hofstra University, Hempstead, N.Y., October 12–14.

Onimode, B. 1988. *A Political Economy of the African Crisis.* London: Zed Books Ltd.

Palmer, E. 1979. "Ngugi's *Petals of Blood.*" *African Literature Today* 10: 153–166.

Peter, L. J. 1977. *Peter's Quotations: Ideas for Our Time.* New York: Bantam Books.

Petini, R. L. 1976. *Hill of Fools.* London: Heinemann Kenya.

Pye, L. 1962. *Politics, Personality and Nation-Building.* New Haven, Conn.: Yale University Press.

Sharma, K. L. 1980. *Entrepreneurial Growth and Development Programs in Northern India: A Sociological Analysis.* New Delhi: Abhinav Publications.

Smith, A. 1985. *The Wealth of Nations* (edited by Andrew Skinner). New York: Penguin Books.

Thiong'o, N. wa. 1977. *Petals of Blood.* Nairobi, Kenya: Heinemann.

Trivedi, M. 1991. *Entrepreneurship Among Tribals.* Jaipur, India: Printwell.

Zack, A. M. 1966. ''Developing Human Resources: A New Approach to Educational Assistance in Africa.'' In W. Y. Elliott, ed., *Education and Training in Developing Countries: The Role of U.S. Foreign Aid.* New York: Praeger.

Index

Achebe, Chinua, 39–44. *Works: Arrow of God*, 38; *A Man of the People*, 39, 40, 42, 43, 46, 49; *No Longer At Ease*, 39, 40, 41, 42, 46, 49; *Things Fall Apart*, 39, 40

Accounting education and training in Anglophone sub-Saharan Africa: background literature, 128–129; current state of, 129–133; need for reform, 132–133; new structure for, 133–137; and operationalization, 134–137; pre-university education, 130; professional accounting education and training, 131–132; university-level education, 130–131

African countries (ACs): civil society in, 63–64; colonial legacy, 10–11; education during colonial era, 2; focus of educational programs, 14–15; goals of education and training, 13–14; and multiparty politics, 53–54; past and present attempts at human resource development, 2–4; shortcomings of existing educational and training programs, 4–11

African writers: function and responsibilities (of effectual writers), 37–38; importance of in nation-building, 37

Agricultural sector in Africa: advanced education, 105–106; and development, 102; need for new perspective, 102–104; need to increase food production, 99–101; present-day solutions, 101–102; suggestions for Africa, 106–107; training farmers, 104–105

Aristotle, 1, 56

Conference on Continuing Education and Universities of the Asia and Pacific Region, 65–66

Co-op education, 94

Democracy and education, 55–57

Denial and projection syndrome, 26

Developing countries (DCs), financial difficulties in educational sector, 29

Entrepreneurship development in Africa: anatomy of, 73–74; entrepreneurs and underdevelopment, 74–77; lack of community spirit, 76–77; strategies for preparing entrepreneurs for industrial development, 77–79; theoretical background, 72–73

Gye ko didi, 7, 162

Human factor: and agencies of education and training, 28–32; defined, 21; and development of the whole person, 26–28; nature of in LDCs, 150–152

Human factor engineering programs, 12–13

Human rights and social justice, 61–64

Humpty Dumpty, as symbol of the plight of humanity, 24–25

International Conference of Free Trade Unions (ICFTU), 4

International Development Association (IDA), 3

International Labour Office, 10

Japan, and successful leadership development, 93

Kalabule system, 75

Leadership development in Africa: enhancing effectiveness of, 90–92; grooming and managing people, 86–87; model for grooming and managing the workforce, 87–90; observed quality of leadership and workforce, 84–86; producing effective managers and leaders, 92–95

Leisure-time Instruction Act, 66

Less developed countries (LDCs), financial difficulties in educational sector, 29

Makola, 10

Marketing and development in LDCs: Activist School, 144–146; Determinist School, 142–144; human factor in, 147–152; Independent School, 146–147

Petini, R. L., 39, 44–46; Hill of Fools, 39, 44–46, 49

Political culture, development of, 57–61

Professional competency in Africa, 162–165; implications for positive change, 176–177; maintaining, 174–176; staying educated and relevant activities for, 165–174

Systems fallacy syndrome, 26

Technical innovation in Africa: as a human factor process, 116–119; developing an appropriate human factor for, 119–121; sources of, 113; strategies for, 113–114; theories of, 112–116

Tocqueville, Alexis de, 25, 59

United Nations: Expanded Program of Technical Assistance (EPTA), 2–3; Operational and Executive Personnel Program, 3; Special Fund, 3; World Public Campaign for Human Rights, 61

United States International and Educational Exchange Acts, 3

University mission statements, 31

Unscrupulous entrepreneurs, 74–75; and misuse of acquired profits, 75–76

Thiong'o, Ngugi wa, 38, 46–49. Works: A Grain of Wheat, 38; Petals of Blood, 40, 46–49, 50; The River Between, 38; Secret Lives, 38

Whole person, defined, 20

World Federation of Trade Unions (WFTU), 3

About the Editor and Contributors

MOSES ACQUAAH is a doctoral student in organizations and strategic management at the University of Wisconsin-Milwaukee and a research associate with the International Institute for Human Factor Development (IIHFD). Mr. Acquaah has a B.A. in social science from the University of Science and Technology (U.S.T.), Kumasi, Ghana and a post-graduate diploma in development studies from the University of Cambridge, United Kingdom. He also has an M.A. in economics and an M.B.A. in accounting, both from Simon Fraser University, Burnaby, British Columbia, Canada. Prior to pursuing graduate studies, he worked as an assistant research officer with the Bureau of Integrated Rural Development (BIRD), U.S.T., Ghana, where he was involved in the planning, implementation, monitoring, and evaluation of rural development projects sponsored by international agencies such as the United Nations Development Program (UNDP), the European Community (EC) and the Ghana government. Mr. Acquaah was a recipient of the British Government Overseas Development Administration Scholarship (ODASS) in 1987–1988. His research interests include the human factor and accounting education, corporate strategy to enhance productivity, international accounting and business, and fisheries management.

SENYO B-S. K. ADJIBOLOSOO is currently an associate professor of business and economics at Trinity Western University. He graduated with a Ph.D. in economics from Simon Fraser University, Burnaby, British Columbia, Canada in 1988. Since his graduation, he has been a full-time faculty member at Trinity Western University, where his research interests include heteroskedasticity pretesting in regression analysis, human factor development, development education, history of economic thought and international business and trade. He has published numerous articles in econometrics and economic development and has written and edited several books on the significance of the human factor in economic development. He is currently the director of the International Institute for Human Factor Development (IIHFD) (an institute solely devoted to researching the human factor and its role in economic development). He is also the editor of the *Review of Human Factor Studies*.

FRANCIS ADU-FEBIRI holds a Ph.D. in sociology from the University of British Columbia, Vancouver, British Columbia, Canada. His research focuses on tourism and culture, the environment, the sociology of development, race and/ or ethnic relations, dynamics of African societies and human factor engineering. He has published scholarly papers on tourism and Third World development, the state of racism in contemporary capitalist societies, social inequalities in contemporary African societies and the human factor. He is a full-time faculty member at the department of social science, Camosun College, Victoria, Canada. He is writing a book on Ghana tourism. Dr. Febiri is a research associate with the International Institute for Human Factor Development (IIHFD).

JOHN A. ANONBY took his M. A. at the University of British Columbia and his Ph.D. at the University of Alberta, in the area of renaissance and seventeenth-century literature, facilitated by several Canada Council Doctoral Fellowship awards. He has published in a variety of areas, including Canadian and African literature. He is currently professor of English at Trinity Western University and is a frequent visiting professor at the University of British Columbia.

SAMUEL K. BONSU is a graduate student in marketing and development at Simon Fraser University, Burnaby, British Columbia, Canada. His research interests include traditional marketing systems in the developing countries and alternative approaches to development in the developing countries. Mr. Bonsu is a research associate with the International Institute for Human Factor Development (IIHFD).

HAROLD J. HARDER is an associate professor of business and economics at Trinity Western University. Dr. Harder obtained his Ph.D. degree from Iowa State University in agricultural climatology. He served as director of a relief and development program in Bangladesh. The program included agricultural development activities, small industry development and dissemination of technologies appropriate to the needs and resources of small-farm operators and small entrepreneurs. He now teaches courses in Third World development and in business statistics. He has published on agriculture-related topics and on topics dealing with Third World development issues. Current research interests include leadership training, especially across cultural boundaries, the role of expatriates in Third World development and the effectiveness of various approaches to economic development. Dr. Harold Harder is a research associate with the International Institute for Human Factor Development (IIHFD).

BENJAMIN OFORI-AMOAH obtained his Ph.D. degree in geography from Simon Fraser University. He is an assistant professor of geography at the University of Wisconsin-Stevens Point, Stevens Point, Wisconsin. He is the director of the Africa Specialty Group of the Association of American Geographers. Dr. Ofori-Amoah is an economics geographer with research and teaching interests in regional economic development. He has published numerous articles in this area of interest with reference to both developed and developing countries. His current research projects include the relevance of conventional development theories to Africa and development education. Dr. Ofori-Amoah is a research associate with the International Institute for Human Factor Development (IIHFD).

MIKE OQUAYE obtained his Ph.D. from the University of Ghana. He is currently teaching at the department of political science, University of Ghana. He is a member of the distinguished Ghana Bar Association and the Honorable Society of Lincoln's Inn in London. Dr. Oquaye is a barrister of the Supreme Court of England and Wales and of the Superior Court of Ghana. Dr. Oquaye has written and published many articles and books. He has received several prestigious awards including the Ghana Book Development Council Award in 1981, the Ghana Association of Writers Award for the best work in politics and philosophy in 1987 and the CORDESRIA award for Economic and Social Research in Africa in 1987. His current research interests include government and politics in Ghana, the history of political thought and social political theory.

ISBN 0-275-95491-9

EAN

9 780275 954918

90000>

HARDCOVER BAR CODE